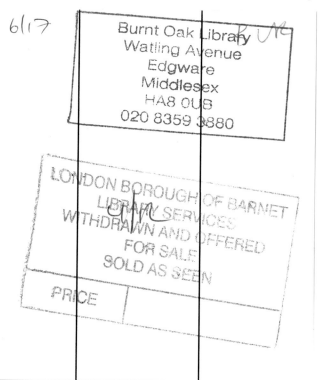
Please return/renew this item by the
last date shown to avoid a charge.
Books may also be renewed by phone
and Internet. May not be renewed if
required by another reader.

www.libraries.barnet.gov.uk

BARNET
LONDON BOROUGH

D1334342

AFTER THE
BERLIN WALL

AFTER THE
BERLIN WALL

PUTTING TWO GERMANYS
BACK TOGETHER AGAIN

CHRISTOPHER HILTON

London Borough of Barnet	
Askews	Oct-2009
943.155	£18.99

First published 2009

The History Press
The Mill, Brimscombe Port
Stroud, Gloucestershire, GL5 2QG
www.thehistorypress.co.uk

British Library Cataloguing in Publication Data.
A catalogue record for this book is available from the British Library.

ISBN 978 0 7509 5075 6

Printed in India by Nutech Print Services

Can Germans still claim a common identity after forty
years of partition or are there now two different ways of
thinking and living?
Peter Daniel, *The German Comedy*, 1991

Carlo says he does not regard himself as East or West;
he has no prejudice. Is that the future?
Yes. European. I believe his is the generation which will just
grow up thinking of themselves as Germans or Europeans. Even
among the three children there is a difference. For instance, the
little one – Elisa – goes to a school where the children learn Spanish
and part of the lessons are in Spanish. For Elisa, Honecker, the
GDR and The Wall have no meaning but Hitler somehow does. He
is always there. He is in the newspapers every day.
Heike Herrmann, interview, 2008

CONTENTS

FOREWORD

The first part of Adolf Hitler's war ended with a single shot one April afternoon in 1945.

In the concrete Berlin catacomb he had had built so deep underground that he'd be safe from everyone – except, as it turned out, himself – he fired the shot into his temple while he bit on a vial of poison. The Third Reich he created to last 1,000 years limped on for another seven days, morally bankrupt and directionless, but the real end came with the shot.

In the aftermath, Germany would be divided and Germans forced to live in different countries, East and West, with a wall and shoot-to-kill guards between them. The catacomb was dynamited years later and, by chance, The Wall ran directly across the ground above it, then looped round the Brandenburg Gate – symbol of the city and now symbol of its division – a short walk away.

The second part of Adolf Hitler's war ended with an explosion of champagne corks one November night in 1989 and people dancing on that loop of The Wall at the Brandenburg Gate.

The German Democratic Republic (GDR), a self-proclaimed sovereign state whose leader, Erich Honecker, had insisted The Wall would last for a hundred years,[1] could not withstand this dance of death. It limped on for another five months, morally bankrupt and directionless, but the real end came with the champagne corks.

After that, Easterners had a real election and used it to vote themselves out of existence. As far as I am aware, no other country except Austria in 1938 has ever done this, and whether Austria – under extreme Nazi pressure to join the German Reich – actually did remains problematical. The Nazis gave them an 'election' and 99.73 per cent of the population said yes, a highly suspicious total made even more suspicious because of its familiarity to so many totalitarian regimes.[2]

From the outside, the GDR had a look of immovability and permanence, every aspect of life tightly controlled by the ruling Party and monitored by the security service, a monstrous, malign octopus. Strategically it was a key Soviet ally, the guarantee that these Germans at least would never again attack the Russian Motherland and were consequently locked into the Communist trading bloc (COMECON) and military alliance (the Warsaw pact). The Soviet Union had 350,000 troops stationed there.

Four weeks after Honecker said what he said, The Wall had gone and with it the GDR, gone without a shot fired or even a sprained ankle. The decision to open The Wall was announced by Günter Schabowski, a member of the Politbüro with responsibilities for East Berlin, at a press conference in the early evening of 9 November 1989. He was speaking in answer to a question (initiated by an Italian journalist) and had been given papers covering new orders but not actually read them. He read them now and they said the border was to open. He was asked when; he consulted the papers and said 'immediately, without delay'. This was a defining moment for millions of people all over the Germanys, even though Schabowski's replies were reticent because he hadn't read the papers, creating a sense of ambiguity. His jowled face and sonorous voice became a defining image, too.

In this book many people will refer to it quite naturally as something central to their memories and their lives.

The third part of Adolf Hitler's war began one October day in 1990 when East and West reunited, although everybody knew the truth. The FRG – with three times the population and the third largest economy on earth – was about to ingest the GDR whole, a python and a piglet.[3] Wolfgang Schäuble, the FRG's chief negotiator, wrote:

> In my talk to them I kept saying: Dear folks, this is about the GDR's affilia-
> tion with the Federal Republic, not the other way around … This is not the
> unification of two identical states. We do not start from the very beginning
> with equal starting positions. There is the Basic Law and there is the Federal
> Republic of Germany. Let us proceed on the assumption that you have
> been excluded from both for forty years.[4]

This new Germany would be run from the Reichstag, a very short walk from the Brandenburg Gate, as politicians put East and West back together for the first time since 1945. That involved marrying totalitarian communism with democratic capitalism, both of which had been constructed with characteristic German thoroughness, heightening every difference between the two.

Nobody had ever done this, either.

The takeover touched everything in the East: government, law, the judiciary, the police, whatever the East German government owned, including all the farmland, property and industry. It involved teachers and education, the whole medical profession and hospitals, crèches and kindergartens, foreign policy and the military, because one week two armies had been prepared to kill each other, the next they were in the same army. It involved bringing together two phone systems and the two postal services, two railways, all the roads and different speed limits. It involved women's rights, abortion, every aspect of welfare, pensions, the rights of trade unions, arts and food subsidies, rents, housing, the price of milk and what you could buy in the corner shop. It involved one currency replacing the other, dismantling the East's vast internal intelligence network with all the nightmarish revelations that would have to bring, fundamental alterations to newspapers, magazines and television. And then there was the shoot-to-kill policy at the wall, something else with nightmarish consequences.

More than all this, the takeover touched everything people thought: how life worked and why it worked like that, what was normal and what abnormal, what society was and was not, what you knew and what you didn't know, what you could do and what you couldn't. All these were subject to questioning in the East as the GDR began to break up, the economy floundered and significant proportions of the population – bemused, disorientated, disenchanted and prey to every neon sign beckoning from the West – were ripe for the ingestion.

I repeat: nothing like this had ever been tried before, and anyway, the divisions had seemed too deep and too permanent. Two distinct normalities had matured down the years, fostering two distinct personalities, and they had very few points of contact, physical or intellectual. Ordinary Easterners watched Western TV, which was and wasn't a point of contact but – except pensioners, being sometimes allowed to attend significant family events or officially sanctioned trips – they couldn't visit the West. Moreover, Westerners found the GDR unattractive and chose more exotic destinations except when they visited relatives bearing gifts, making even that point of contact problematical in terms of Eastern resentment. There were no plans for the reunification and as the people danced on The Wall nobody knew what was going to happen next.

While it stood, The Wall confirmed every stereotype about itself because, mute and brutal, it could do nothing else.

When Hitler pulled the trigger Germany was a devastated corpse which the victorious Allies dissected into their own zones: the Soviet Union took the east; the British, Americans and French took the west. Berlin, 120 miles inside the Soviet Zone, was cut into four sectors in the same way.

By 1949 the Cold War had chilled to the point where the western parts became the Federal Republic of Germany (FRG) and the eastern part the GDR, each created in the image of its conquerors. (The FRG, incidentally, was sometimes known as West Germany and the GDR as East Germany. I have used the initials throughout although when interviewees spoke of West and East I left that alone. You know exactly what they mean. I have also used a capital W when people mean the West in general, and the same for the East.)

The chill deepened and geography became central. To prevent the GDR disintegrating by mass emigration its government erected what became known as the Iron Curtain from the Baltic to the Czech border, although Berlin remained an anomaly because it was inside the GDR but under four-power control and therefore open.

The Soviet Sector became the capital of GDR, despite the fact that the other three powers did not recognise this. The Western sectors became West Berlin; part of the FRG but with a special status. The post-war settlement would be expressed in geography and geometry.

The flight from the East, easy in Berlin where all you had to do was walk across the street to the West or board an underground train, ceased in August 1961 when the GDR built The Wall through the middle of the city and continued it into the countryside, round West Berlin in a tight embrace. From then on, the real divergence began and by 1989 people in their late twenties on either side had lived their whole lives with it. This is important. In the FRG, from the 1960s, only small majorities thought unification a real possibility and by 1987 this had fallen to 3 per cent. Evidently the situation was the same in the GDR. The Germans on both sides, confronted with a realpolitik hardened by the passage of time, accepted the division and lived with it. In a 1984 survey, 83 per cent of the FRG's citizens accepted the existence of two German states, although 73 per cent said Germans were one people.[5]

Rudolf Bahro, a perceptive GDR Party member whose free thinking led him into exile in 1979, said in 1980:

> You find that workers will grouse and swear about conditions when they are in their factory, but when some well-heeled uncle arrives on a visit from West Germany, they stand up for the GDR and point out all the good things about it, all the disadvantages they had to overcome after 1945, and so on. Although the state's demands for loyalty are widely resented, I would say that in normal, crisis-free times there is a sufficiently high degree of loyalty to assure the country's viability.

Bahro said in 1983: 'The Soviet Union has specific reasons for wanting to hold on to East Germany and, in view of the proximity of NATO and West Germany, would never allow any experiment in the GDR unless it were an absolutely safe manoeuvre. So an opposition there has no possibility of crystallizing.'[6]

Bahro, of course, was speaking before Mikhail Gorbachev's liberalisation. His words reflect – accurately, I am sure – the position when he spoke them. They are valuable for that reason, and valuable also because they show the extent of the change to come.

Another perceptive German, Peter Schneider, set out (in 1990) the position from the West. 'No one wanted to admit it, but we saw and treated East Germans as foreigners; in fact, according to polls, a majority of young people defined East Germany as a foreign country.' He broadened that, asking rhetorically how a Pole from Warsaw could communicate with a cousin in Chicago after decades of enforced separation in different systems. He pointed out that other politically divided countries – China, Vietnam, Korea – provoked the same question: a Chinese man from Hong Kong meeting his uncle from Beijing; a Cuban boxer meeting someone who had fled in a Miami bar.[7] They spoke the same language but could they communicate, which is not the same thing at all? Could the Germans?[8]

The depth of the divergence between the GDR and the FRG remained, for all this, an academic question; unquantifiable, uncharted, problematic and distantly intriguing until 1989. Then, very suddenly, and from almost nowhere, it arrived with irresistible momentum. There were clues about the depth, visible clues. West Berlin, fattened by subsidies from the FRG, exuded prosperity. It had been extensively rebuilt after the war and its widest avenue, Kurfürstendamm, contained shops to rival any in London, Paris, New York or Tokyo. West Berlin was lively, cosmopolitan, edgy, happening – spiced by student vitality, bohemians, military drop-outs and artists as well as a lot of solid businessmen making money. It had, too, a frisson of danger because the Red Army was just over there.

Far from being fattened by subsidies the GDR was starved because the Soviet Union demanded, and took, enormous reparations after the war. Marxist historian Eric Hobsbawn has written that the country had

> a monstrous all-embracing bureaucracy which did not terrorise but rather constantly chivvied, rewarded and punished its subjects. The new society they were building was not a bad society: work and careers for all, universal education open at all levels, health, social security and pensions, holidays in a firmly structured community of good people doing an honest day's work, the best of high culture accessible to the people, open-air leisure and sports, no class distinctions.

Hobsbawn goes on to point out that the 'drawback, apart from the fact, unconcealable from its citizens, that it was far worse off than West Germany, was that it was imposed on its citizens by a system of superior authority … [People] had no control over their lives. They were not free.'[9]

Another historian, Mary Fulbrook, has written that when The Wall fell 'Westerners were aghast at the state of East Germany: the crumbling housing; the pot-holed, cobbled roads; the brown coal dust and the chemical pollution in the industrial centres of the south; the miserable offerings in the shops, the relative paucity and poor quality of consumer goods …'[10]

It seemed clear from the West: communism had failed and Easterners would quickly satisfy their subterranean desires by becoming Westerners themselves.

It seemed clear from the East: nothing was clear any more.

Regardless, the third and final part of Hitler's war – putting Germany back together again – had begun. This is the story of what happened to people in the midst of that over the ensuing twenty years, as the first generation who had known nothing but unification reached adulthood. It does not pretend to be a text book, teeming with statistics, pie charts, graphs and the rest. It's about people chosen to illustrate as many experiences as possible and from both sides of the long-vanished Wall: a sequence of insights from the ordinary players caught up in a unique drama. Their experiences may or may not be typical and in these circumstances perhaps no experiences could be. There is, I hope, enough solid information to give the interviews their true contexts. The chapters cover a lot of territory, too – in order: The Wall, religion, the artists, the property nightmare, health, teaching history, the police, the army, the unemployed and Dresden, a unique city bearing the full weight of Germany's past, present and future.

Hitler remained a presence, a darkened background spectre, even as Germany was being put back together and, moving towards twenty years since the fall of The Wall, he suddenly emerged in the foreground. An affiliate of Madame Tussauds was established in Berlin and included a wax dummy of him in his last days. It was inevitably a very controversial matter because it invited Germans, as they shuffled by, to face – literally as well as figuratively – the demons of their own past.[11]

Madame Tussauds opened and the second visitor in vaulted the rope cordon, seized Hitler and wrenched his head off (the body was fibreglass, the head beeswax). As the man, described as a forty-one-year-old former policeman, was wrestled by security staff he shouted 'never again war'. He added he was delighted it had happened in the presence of the waxwork of Willy Brandt, who fought the Nazis, was mayor of West Berlin when The Wall went up and became FGR Chancellor.

This is the story of many, many other people wrestling their demons.

Notes

1. 'Die Mauer wird in fünfzig und auch in hundert Jahren noch bestehen bleiben, wenn die dazu vorhandenen Gründe noch nicht beseitigt sind.' (The Wall will remain fifty and even a hundred years if the reasons that led to it are not removed by then.)

2. The GDR held local elections on 7 May and these were subsequently discovered to have been fraudulent, provoking simmering rage within the country

for all the obvious reasons. Ordinary people had had enough of the 98.85 per cent approval, a percentage unthinkable in any properly democratic country.
3. The mechanism of unification was to use Article 23 of the FRG's Basic Law, which could be implemented quickly – Chancellor Helmut Kohl evidently feared circumstances might change, thwarting the whole thing. This did mean, however, that the GDR was absorbed into the FRG model. The alternative would have been to use Article 146.

Ms Kubisch explains: The basic law for the FRG (in its old version) offered two possibilities for reunification: by the accession of other parts of Germany to the territory of the FRG according to Article 23 or through a new constitution according to article 146, which would have to be decided by the German people.

> **Article 23**: 'Dieses Grundgesetz gilt zunächst im Gebiet der Länder Baden, Bayern, Bremen, Groß-Berlin, Hamburg, Hessen, Niedersachsen, Nordrhein-Westfalen, Rheinland-Pfalz, Schleswig-Holstein, Württemberg-Baden und Württemberg-Hohenzollern. In anderen Teilen Deutschlands ist es nach deren Beitritt in Kraft zu setzen.'
> [This basic law applies in the first instance to the area of the Länder of Baden, Bayern, Bremen, Groß-Berlin, Hamburg, Hessen, Niedersachsen, Nordrhein-Westfalen, Rheinland-Pfalz, Schleswig-Holstein, Württemberg-Baden und Württemberg-Hohenzollern. It is to be brought into effect in other parts of Germany after their accession.']

The decision for an accession rather than a new state constitution was actually made during the first free elections in the GDR on 18 March 1990. The majority of GDR citizens voted for those parties that were in favour of accession according to Article 23. Correspondingly, the People's Chamber decided on 23 August 1990 for GDR accession to the territory of the Basic Law effective from 3 October 1990.

> **Article 146**
> **(Duration of validity of the Basic Law)**
> This Basic Law, which since the achievement of the unity and freedom of Germany applies to the entire German people, shall cease to apply on the day on which a constitution freely adopted by the German people takes effect.

4. *Der Vertrag: Wie ich über die deutsche Einheit verhandelte*, Schäuble.
5. Figures in *Rewriting The German Past*.
6. *From Red To Green*, three interviews with Rudolf Bahro.

7. *The German Comedy* by Peter Schneider. Capitalist Hong Kong and communist China were reunited in 1997, although this was not comparable to the two Germanys because Hong Kong was a British colony, not an independent country recognised by the United Nations. A more apt comparison would be uniting communist China and capitalist Taiwan – which has not happened. Korea, of course, remains separated and more bitterly so than the Germanys ever were. North and South Vietnam were essentially peasant countries, the North finally overrunning the South in 1975. The South did not vote itself out of existence.

8. An example of this is the simple word *freedom*. To a GDR citizen it might mean freedom from unemployment, freedom from the tyranny of rents you couldn't afford, freedom from inflation, freedom from anxiety over medical bills. To an FRG citizen it might mean freedom to vote for different parties, freedom to travel, freedom to read, write and say whatever you wanted. I can't resist a little joke built upon this: capitalism is the exploitation of man by man, communism just the opposite.

9. *Interesting Times*, Hobsbawm.

10. *The People's State*, Fulbrook.

11. Birgit Kubisch points to a much more mundane consideration: Germany has no history of waxwork museums and depicting people, any people, like that would be controversial.

ACKNOWLEDGEMENTS

Thanks primarily to Birgit Kubisch, without whom this book wouldn't have happened; she took the photographs. She was instrumental in finding many of the subjects for interview, organised everything in Berlin, handled a great deal of research, translated background and interpreted. She also read the manuscript pointing out errors along the way, as did John Woodcock, an old friend, Berlinophile (if I can invent a word) and professional journalist. He contributed questions to several interviews and wrote a perceptive description of the GDR Museum (see Afterword).

The following were kind enough to give interviews: Hagen Koch; the late Dr Johannes Althausen; Pastor Christian Müller; Father Gregor Hohberg; Thomas Motter; Peter Unsicker; Claudia Croon; Heike Herrmann; Fulvio Pinna; Dr Ellen Händler (Press Officer, BVD); Dr Wolfgang and Inge Bringmann; Dr Ulrich and Anne Bartel; Kerstin Paust-Loch and Rudolf Loch; Richard Piesk; Dr Falk Pingel, deputy director of the Georg-Eckert Institute for International Textbook Research, Braunschweig; Dr Alan Russell, co-founder of The Dresden Trust; Dresden resident Cornelia Triems-Thiel; Christoph Münch, *Dresden Marketing GmbH i.G.*; Marion Drögsler, chairman, *Arbeitslosenverband Deutschland e.V*; Detective Police Commander Bernd Finger, Criminal Investigation Department, LKA 4; Dr Rüdiger Wenzke MGFA, Potsdam; Manuela Damianakis, Head of Press Office, Senate Department for Urban Development; policemen Frank Thomas and Raymond the border guard; Birgit Hartigs of the *Undine Wohnprojekt*; Angelika Engel; Regina S. and Friedrich E. of *Sozialwers des dfb*, Berlin; Brigitte Triems; Yvonne Triems; Marcel Franke; Constanze Paust; Dagmar Althausen who helped find interviewees, and to Axel Hillebrand.

Professor Dr Norbert Walter, Chief Economist with the Deutsche Bank Group, has kindly allowed me to quote from a penetrating and authoritative article he wrote in the *American Institute for Contemporary German Affairs*. Dr Dorothea Wiktorin (Department of Geography, Cologne University) has written a notable study on the property problems and has kindly allowed me to quote extensively from it. Gregory Pedlow, Chief, Historical Office, Command Group, SHAPE, gave an invaluable insight into the united German army within NATO. Professor Norman Blackburn kindly granted permission to quote from his essay on Dresden in the book *Why Dresden?* An article in *Contemporary Review* 12/1/2000 by Dr Solange Wydmusch was extremely helpful in providing background for Chapter Two. Many other sources have been quoted, covering the important aspects of unification, and these are fully acknowledged in the footnotes and Bibliography, but two in-depth studies were particularly invaluable, *Education in Germany since Unification* (edited by David Phillips) and *Divided in Unity* by Andreas Glaeser. I have leant heavily on them and I am extremely grateful to Associate Professor Glaeser, of the Social Sciences Department at the University of Chicago, for permission to quote. Thanks to *Dresden-Werbung und Tourismus GmbH* (Praktikant Marketing) for a map of the city, and especially Cornelia Sanden for visitor statistics. Kristina Tschenett, Press Officer, *Senatsverwaltung für Finanzen* provided information on the land at the Wall. Miriam Tauchmamnn, Press Officer, Police President was an invaluable conduit to Commander Bernd Finger.

All unsourced direct quotations in the text are from interviews with the author.

AUTHOR'S NOTE

For those who are not German experts:

The GDR had effectively three leaders (general secretaries of the all-powerful Socialist Unity Party): Walter Ulbricht (1950–71), Erich Honecker (1971–October 1989) and Egon Krenz (October–December 1989). I don't include Hans Modrow (1989–90) or Lothar de Maizière (1990) – who were Chairmen of the Council of Ministers – because in their time the country was disintegrating. They inherited the endgame.

The GDR state security organ was called the *Ministerium für Staatssicherheit* (Ministry for State Security), usually abbreviated to the Stasi.

The period when the GDR collapsed is sometimes known as the *Wende*, the turn.

West Germans are sometimes called *Wessis* and East Germans *Ossis*, giving a wonderful play on words, *Ostalgie* – Easterners' nostalgia for the GDR.

The FRG was organised into ten *Länder* (or states) and on unification the GDR was divided into five (Mecklenburg-Vorpommern, Brandenburg, Sachsen-Anhalt, Sachsen [Saxony] and Thüringen). The two halves of Berlin formed a sixteenth.

The main shopping thoroughfare in West Berlin was the Kurfürstendamm, often abbreviated to the Ku'damm.

TIMELINE

1945
7 May   Germany surrenders
3 July   Allied troops take over their four sectors in Berlin
16 July   Potsdam Conference begins
2 August   Potsdam Conference ends

1946
21 April   Communist Party and Social Democrats form the SED
                 (Socialist Unity Party) to rule East Germany

1947
5 June   Marshall Plan launched

1948
21 June   Deutsche Mark introduced in the West
24 June   Berlin blockade and airlift begins
24 July   East German Mark introduced

1949
4 April   NATO formed
11 May   Berlin blockade and airlift ends
24 May   FRG (Federal Republic of Germany) founded in the West,
                 merging the American, British and French Zones
7 October   GDR (German Democratic Republic) founded in the East
                 from the Soviet Zone, with East Berlin as its capital

1953
16 June   GDR workers uprising over increasing work norms

1955
9 May   FRG accepted into NATO
14 May   Communist states, including the GDR, sign the Warsaw Pact

1958
27 October   Walter Ulbricht, GDR leader, threatens West Berlin
10 November   Soviet leader Nikita Khruschev says it is time to cancel
                    Berlin's four-power status

1961
4 June   At a summit in Vienna, Khruschev tries to pressure US
                    President John Kennedy to demilitarise Berlin
1–12 August   21,828 refugees arrive in West Berlin
13 August   Berlin Wall built

1963
26 June   Kennedy visits Berlin and makes his 'Ich Bin Ein Berliner'
                    speech

1968
21 August   Warsaw Pact countries crush Prague Spring

1970
19 March   Willy Brandt visits GDR city Erfurt as part of his Ostpolitik
                    policy

1971
3 May   Ulbricht forced to resign, succeeded by Erich Honecker

1972
October   Traffic Agreement signed, giving FRG citizens access to
                    the GDR
21 December   Basic Treaty signed, the FRG in effect recognising the GDR

1973
18 September   The GDR and the FRG admitted to the United Nations

1985

11 March   Mikhail Gorbachev elected General Secretary of the
                    Soviet Communist Party

1987

12 June   Ronald Reagan speaks at the Brandenburg Gate: 'Mr
                    Gorbachev, tear down this wall.'

7–11 September Honecker visits FRG

1989

2 May   Hungary opens its border with Austria, allowing GDR
                    holidaymakers to cross

7 May   GDR elections with 98.85 per cent for the government
                    and widespread allegations of fraud

4 September   Leipzig demonstrations begin

30 September   GDR citizens in FRG Prague Embassy told they can
                    travel to the West

6 October   GDR fortieth anniversary

18 October   Honecker forced to resign, succeeded by Egon Krenz

4 November   A million people demonstrate in East Berlin

9 November   The Wall opens

29 November   Chancellor Helmut Kohl issues plan for a 'confederation
                    leading to a federation in Germany'

7 December   Krenz resigns. GDR government meets opposition parties

8 December   SED Congress elects a new generation of leaders

19 December   Kohl visits Dresden, crowds chant 'we are one people'.

1990

18 March   Free GDR election, Christian Democratic Union gain
                    40 per cent of the vote

1 July   Currency union

3 October   Germany reunited

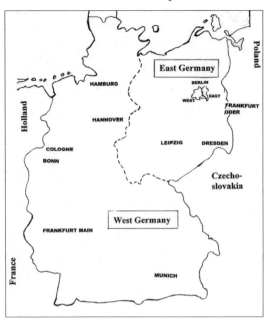

Map 1. The postwar division of Germany with Berlin isolated deep in East Germany (the GDR). Poland was given German territory up to the Oder.

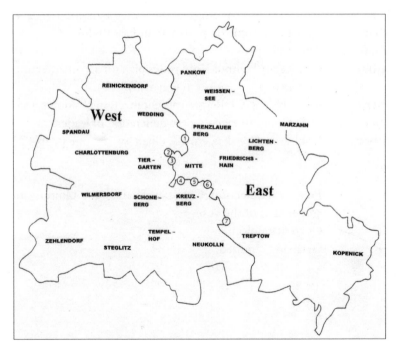

Map 2. The postwar division of Berlin: the East – the Soviet Sector – becoming the capital of the GDR; the three Western sectors surrounded by the GDR. The French were in the north, the British in the centre and the Americans in the south. The numbers show where the checkpoints through The Wall were: 1 – Bornholmer Strasse; 2 – Chausseestrasse; 3 – Invalidenstrasse; 4 – Friedrichstrasse (Checkpoint Charlie); 5 – Heinrich-Heine-Strasse; 6 – Oberbaumbrücke; 7 – Sonnenallee.

1

HISTORY LESSONS FROM THE WALL MAN

You don't know it, and most Berliners don't either, even as a name. Leuschnerdamm is an ordinary street bearing no obvious resonance.

Occasional pedestrians – reflecting, inevitably, the colours and dress codes of a modern international city – walk by just as they walk by everywhere else. This day an African woman with two heavy shopping bags plods forward on her eternal journey. A couple hold hands and giggle, a limitless future in front of them. Cyclists, invariably young women and some towing two-wheel kiddiekarts, pedal by, slender legs pumping evenly. The traffic is light.

On one side of the street, cars are parked flank-to-flank in the white boundary bays painted across cobblestones, an ordinary arrangement for parking. A terrace of tall buildings, all apartments except a couple of entrances to businesses, looms behind them. Each house has a small garden and some tall trees give privacy as well as a certain charm. On the other side of the street, a low brick wall masks sunken gardens immediately behind it. They are immaculately maintained and offer an arbour of calm: benches where people sit and eat their sandwiches, doze or chat, pathways where joggers grunt and pant. Further away the breeze ruffles a surprisingly large artificial lake but the brick wall masks that, too, because it is sunken to the same level as the gardens.

Leuschnerdamm rests, like a thousand others, in the great web of Berlin streets and if you walk it, which will take four or five easy minutes, you'll probably have forgotten it when you reach the far end. It's so slight – a curve straightening towards a bridge – that you have to strain to see it on maps, and anyway, maps are devoid of meaning now except in terms of orthodox cartography. The maps have become mute but once they screamed.

Leuschnerdamm has had four distinct locations although it's always been exactly where it is. That's a very Berlin situation created by commerce, war, defeat, chance and geometry; the sort of situation which in any other city anywhere would make it resonate as a freak, a tourist attraction, a former potential battleground, a site of genuine historical importance and, in the sane world, an impossibility. That it has become ordinary *is* Berlin.

There are three resonances but you have to deduce two of them and deliberately pause to see the third. The first is the pavement in front of the apartments. It comprises old, uneven slabs with a patchwork of running repairs which form a slightly unkempt mosaic. This is the sort of thing which offends the German sense of order and propriety, and you'd have expected it to be completely re-laid years before. What can it mean that it hasn't been?

The second is a sequence of holes bored into the cobblestones and filled with black tarmacadam. They are a little way from the lip of the pavement, are equidistant and in a row. They follow the curve, follow the straightening towards the bridge but, just in front of it, cross to the side of the brick wall. What can that mean?

The third will tell you. A black and white photographic display has been arranged in the window of one of the businesses. It is easy to walk past it and most do. The cyclists and motorists never see it at all. You have to stand, peer and concentrate because one photograph, a panoramic view, gives you everything all at once. It is so stark it does not require a caption and, like emerging from sunlight, your eyes need time to adjust. At first it seems to be a lunarscape with houses – the apartments – but as your eyes adjust it transforms itself into the Leuschnerdamm which was somewhere else altogether: depending on which side chance had placed you, a frontier community confronting Ronald Reagan's evil empire or a frontier community confronting the imperialist-fascist-capitalist running dogs.

The Wall ran where the dark tarmac holes are – they were supports for an earlier version of it – so the terraced houses and the unkempt pavement were in the West, the cobbled road in the East. The pavement became a gully; the 12ft Wall to one side of it, the apartments and their little gardens to the other. The pavement was wide enough for pedestrians but not for delivery vehicles and access had to be from the rear of the apartments. There's no doubt why the pavement was neglected. Re-laying it would have been logistically diffi-cult and few people used it anyway – the residents, mostly. It might have been a private, forgotten fragment of West Berlin, darkened by the trees.

In the photograph, the little brick wall, the sunken gardens and the lake appear as a broad area of perfectly level, raw, raked earth forming the death strip. Apart from a couple of mushroom-shaped watch towers there is nothing on the Eastern side of the Wall but emptiness. Nothing.

The fall in November 1989 altered all that. The lake has been excavated (it was filled with rubble from the bombed buildings after the war, hence the chance to create the level ground) and now offers a wooden platform like an inland jetty – decking – with tables and chairs, and a mini-restaurant. Pretty waitresses flit to and fro. It's popular with people who take lunch, like a glass of wine, a beer or a coffee. Stones, arranged like a rockery, butt up against the jetty's lip and some turtles live down there. Their shells are the same colour and shape as the stones so that, astonishingly, even when you are close to them you can't always pick them out. Sometimes they lower themselves deftly into the water and chug off, their little dark heads bobbing to the surface, going under, bobbing up again.

Emboldened sparrows scour for crumbs. A lawnmower moans from the sunken gardens.

Opposite Leuschnerdamm, ringing the other side of the lake, another terrace of apartments has been built where The Wall ran. This street, Legiendamm, is a parallel shape to Leuschnerdamm and thus its twin. The buildings, pleasantly pastel-shaded, radiate a modern style and confidence.

Jochen Baumann moved from the Western town of Freiburg to Leuschnerdamm in November 1989, when The Wall still stood, because 'I wanted an alternative lifestyle' and Kreuzberg offered that. The fact that The Wall was there kept rents low. Now, autumn 2008, 'this is still the poorest area … in the whole of Germany so you have here a clear confrontation between the poorest and the new rich ones. The new rich ones are looking across from the East to the poor ones in the West …'

Legiendamm is clearly a desirable location: central, affording a most charming vista of the sunken gardens and the lake. You can imagine estate agents feasting on it, emphasising how wholesome the area is, how nice. The estate agents probably won't be mentioning maps because it gets complicated. For logical reasons Leuschnerdamm used to be called Elisabethufer and Legiendamm used to be called Luisenufer. *Ufer* means shore: the roads ran along either flank of a waterway which linked the distant River Spree to the distant Landwehr Canal, passing through the lake along the way. Barges plied their trade along it quite normally, from river to canal and back again.

Think Amsterdam and you get the idea.

In 1926 the waterway was filled and made into gardens so the shores no longer existed, and the street name changed in parallel, because *damm* means something built up – in this case, filling the waterway. The lake, however, remained; isolated now.

You can trace the story of most European cities through what streets and squares are called, ranging from original purpose (Middle Way, Flower Street) through place associations (Dresden Street, Frankfurt Alley) to notable figures (Alexander Square, Friedrich Street). Then there are the politicians, who may or may not be notable. The names usually act as a kind of record, a continuum, from the mists of the past to the near-present. One Berlin problem remains that all too often they don't. In 1947 both names changed.

Luisenufer became Legiendamm after Carl Legien, a trade unionist. The East Germans rarely resisted the chance to impose old left-wing heroes on the street names and, in the end, did it in profusion. After reunification, this meant trouble. The point, however, is that very rarely have streets in European cities carried an ancient name from the mists, been suddenly renamed something completely different and then just as suddenly reverted to the original. After 1989 it would happen all over East Berlin, the streets and squares becoming a record of history reversed.

Elisabethufer became Leuschnerdamm after Wilhelm Leuschner, a trade unionist, demonstrating that West Berlin was not averse to imposing old left (but never, of course, right) wing heroes on the street names, although it usually resisted the temptation.[1]

If you saw The Wall on any day between Sunday 13 August 1961, when it went up, and Thursday 9 November 1989, when it came down[2], Leuschnerdamm and its twin will be readily intelligible to you.

Berlin had always been isolated on the Brandenburg plain towards the Baltic, much nearer Poland than Western Europe. That made it awkward when the Allies came to divide Germany into their own zones – American, British, French and Soviet – at the war's end. Berlin would lie deep inside the Soviet Zone and it, too, was to be divided, but into sectors – again American, British, French and Soviet – using the city's twenty ancient districts. The Soviets took the eight in the east and centre, the French the two in the northwest, the British the four opposite the centre and the Americans the six in the south-west.[3] The fact that the boundaries were ancient became awkward in itself because the city had naturally functioned as a whole, the boundary lines between the districts signifying nothing physical. Down the centuries the city grew over them like any other city. The terraced apartments in Leuschnerdamm happened to be in the Kreuzberg district (under American control), the cobbled road in Mitte (under Soviet control).

The arteries keeping West Berlin alive would become the autobahns and railway lines crossing the Soviet Zone from the West. They were, of course, vulnerable to the shifting climates of the Cold War because they could be blocked so easily and quickly, but that wasn't foreseen in 1945, not with the Soviets as gallant comrades in arms; not with Uncle Joe Stalin beaming benevolence.

In 1949 the three Western zones became the Federal Republic of Germany (FRG) and in response Stalin formed his zone into the German Democratic Republic (GDR). There were legal niceties here. As the whole of Berlin was under Allied control, the city ought to have remained separate from the two new Germanys, and the American, British and French Sectors did, forming West Berlin. The Soviets ignored this and made their eight districts into the capital of the GDR – something the West did not accept. They retained the right of free access to East Berlin and, from 1961 to 1989, sent daily patrols across in jeeps to protect and perpetuate that right.

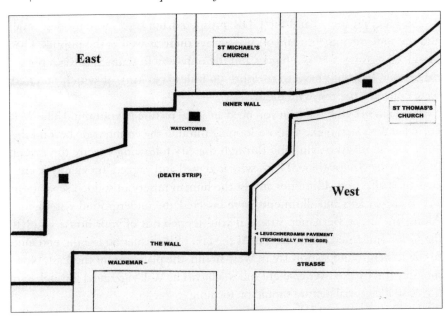

Map 3. The Wall at Leuschnerdamm, showing how the death strip was created by levelling gardens, a lake and a road. Note how The Wall ran between the two churches, bisecting their communities.

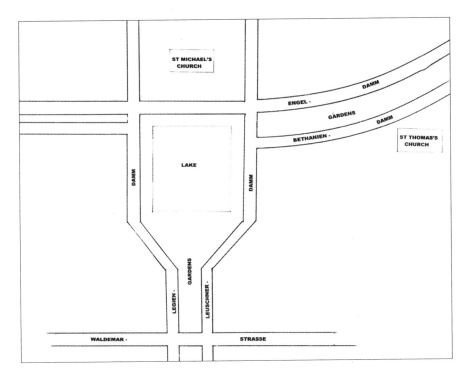

Map 4. Leuschnerdamm after The Wall and even imagining it has become extremely difficult.

The FRG prospered and the GDR prospered, but on a more modest scale, and the unflattering comparison was always there as well as the politics. That produced a rising tide of refugees and the only way to staunch it was a physical barrier. It would have to measure 99 miles (156 km), of which 66 (107) were concrete, the rest wire mesh.

If you haven't visited Berlin you need an aerial picture in your mind: The Wall encircled West Berlin like a noose, looping through the countryside beyond the Western suburbs then running through the city following exactly the extent of the Soviet Sector there. That's why it zigged and zagged. Inevitably it created anomalies and absurdities amidst the human misery of sudden separation: 192 roads, gardens and allotments were bisected, the underground system, too. Along one street, Bernauer Strasse, if you stepped out of your house you left the GDR and entered West Berlin. At the end of Bernauer Strasse the entrance to the underground station lay in West Berlin, the platforms in the East. Now multiply this by the twenty-eight miles which The Wall zigzagged through and a very strange aerial picture should be forming.

The Wall is convenient shorthand for what it really was: a fortification of medieval character and mindset. The outer Wall, the one in all the photographs – 12ft high (3.6m) and of interlocking slabs with the curved pelmet on top to hamper grip – faced West Berlin. The death strip stretched behind it, every yard covered by watchtowers. The inner Wall uncoiled at the far side of the death strip so anyone fleeing had to climb this, sprint across the strip and get over the 12ft Wall. There were refinements in the death strip, like patrol jeeps, attack dogs, tank traps, scatter guns with tripwires and, according to rumour, concealed mines. There were obstructions, like the Church of Reconciliation in Bernauer Strasse, which was isolated within the death strip and eventually blown up. Part of its cemetery fell within the death strip too, and soldiers exhumed graves and moved them. From north to south, and for the twenty-eight miles, the death strip was the level, raked, raw earth or sand affording no cover to a running man – or woman.

The width of the death strip was governed by the space available, itself dependent on the ancient boundaries. In some places, for example where the lake had been beside Leuschnerdamm, it extended over a considerable area; in others it was as narrow as the road between two rows of houses. And that's the way it was from 1961 to 1989, by which time a whole generation had been born and grown up in the GDR who had known nothing else and virtually none of whom had seen West Berlin, never mind set foot in it.[4] They have now been able to set foot in it for going on two decades, and nothing could look more normal than Leuschnerdamm or those who sit on the jetty and sip a pleasantly chilled glass of white wine delivered to the table by a pretty waitress.

There's a repetitive saying about *The Wall in the Head*, meaning virtually all the twenty-eight miles of it have gone yet it remains in people's minds – an insidious mental barrier and maybe even harder to cross than the physical one. You still find East Berliners who feel West Berlin is somewhere else, and West Berliners who feel the same about the East. On one and the same day, Birgit Kubisch and I spoke to a man in the West who said 'our taxes are financing the East, that's where all the development is' and a man in the East who insisted 'the West is keeping all the money, look at all the new buildings there'. New buildings are going up everywhere and the city will continue to resemble an industrial site for a generation, but both men had persuaded themselves this wasn't really happening. They couldn't get their minds round The Wall in their minds.

It is true the physical Wall has gone except for what you might call extended fragments: a section at Bernauer Strasse and a longer section called the East Side Gallery bordering the River Spree. Once upon a time, after the fall, artists apportioned their own parts of this, using the vertical slabs as canvas, and created witty, perceptive murals: Honecker kissing Brezhnev, a Trabant bursting through, invocations to peace and love, that sort of thing. Then the graffiti raiders came with their childlike slogans and kindergarten shapes, and now it's a dreary procession of nihilism, more sad than evocative; a wall in a slum.

The sightseers are drawn, or taken, to Checkpoint Charlie, known throughout the world between 1961 and 1989 as the microcosm of ultimate confrontation. Here the two dominant power blocs of the twentieth century came face to face every hour of every day at what had been a resolutely ordinary intersection between a side street and an avenue. A plain white line across the avenue delineated the exact place of division. No other city on earth had so many of its basic functions dictated by geometry.

Remember, the West did not recognise the GDR or East Berlin as its capital, and under the post-war settlement Berlin remained one city, at least in theory. The Western side of Checkpoint Charlie reflected this because, in the middle of the road, a modest military hut operated no control over anyone going to the East or coming back. Beside the hut a tall sign announced in English, French and Russian that you were leaving the American Sector. That was all.

The Eastern side reflected the reality with an entrance through The Wall covered by watchtowers, a sprawling control system under an awning like an aircraft hangar with lanes for vehicles and pedestrians, then low buildings where you handed your passport through an aperture to be inspected, verified and stamped by hands you couldn't see, then a wave of a border guard and you could proceed into East Berlin.

Checkpoint Charlie did resonate as a freak place, a tourist attraction, a potential battleground – in 1962 Soviet and American tanks did come literally face to face here – a site of genuinely historical importance and, in the sane world, an impossibility. That it never became ordinary *is* Berlin, too.

It has gone now, replaced by a skyscraper, an office block or some such building; big, new, glistening and anonymous.

There are other fragments: a hut remains in the middle of the road, a hoarding with pictures on it tells the tale, the famous museum dedicated to Wall escapes still overlooks where the checkpoint was. Ironically, the fall of The Wall – to select just one example – restored Leuschnerdamm's death strip to life but brought an emptiness to Checkpoint Charlie. The sightseers mill and wander, guides in a dozen languages give their commentaries, and everybody looks completely lost. Who can imagine today that at this intersection, with ordinary traffic ebbing across like at every other intersection, an armed encampment was just *here*, watchtowers manned by guards who would shoot to kill were just *there, there* and *there*, that The Wall ran just *that way down there* and *this way down here*? – that *just over there* a young East German, Peter Fechter, was shot and left to bleed to death?

There's a souvenir-cum-bookshop incorporated into the museum and the pleasant young assistant explains that the sightseers always ask the same questions: 'Are the little chunks of The Wall on sale here real?' and 'where can I see it?' You can't, unless you go to Bernauer Strasse or the East Side Gallery and even there you won't be getting the old impact. For the full experience you'd need the real thing and that's as dead as the cemetery in Bernauer Strasse – or it would need to be in your head, and for that you'd have to be a Berliner.

At the intersection a kiosk rents out taped commentaries so you can follow the course of The Wall, and there's an artefact to aid you, a twin row of cobblestones which charts its course *exactly*, re-enacting the geometry. The cobblestones are set into roads and pavements, which produces a particular irony because now cars can drive over them and pedestrians can walk over them quite normally, even though they mark something so tall people couldn't see over it and couldn't cross without risking their lives.

You might imagine that the cobblestones would faithfully follow the entire Wall, so you could start in the north of Berlin and finish in the south retracing every foot of it, but you can't. Sometimes new buildings straddle it and sometimes it's just not there. Leuschnerdamm has its original cobblestones, the ones with the black tarmac holes in them, but no twin row.

It spawns a joke: *we're in Kreuzberg* – home of the Turkish community, the avant garde, the bohemian and the dubious – *and who ever remembers us?*

The route from Kreuzberg to Checkpoint Charlie is tortuous, with and without the cobblestones marking the way. If you turn right at the top of Leuschnerdamm and cross the bridge you're in Waldemarstrasse; the buildings to the left in the West, Legiendamm and the wide, cleared death strip to the right. Nature had reclaimed it so completely that it resembles a jungle, an astonishing sight in the middle of a modern city where every square metre is precious, finite and worth a fortune – until the inevitable diggers come, and work on foundations for another high-rise to begin.

The death strip still cuts its great zigzagging swathe, an equally astonishing sight in a city of today. Because the inner and outer walls have gone the strip is a mysterious place, meaningless in a modern context and, until the developers get their hands on it – as they are beginning to do – useless to all except wildlife and dog walkers. At the end of Waldemarstrasse, where new buildings are coming up like mushrooms, the death strip crosses the road into more jungle, so overgrown that you have to stoop and duck if you follow the ribbon of patrol road the military jeeps used. If you are intrepid enough you'll reach Heinrich-Heine-Strasse where a checkpoint used to be and where, one distant day, President Richard Nixon came for his feel of The Wall. Like Checkpoint Charlie the buildings have all gone but its tall, curving arc lamps remain, illuminating a car park.

Before the GDR, the avenue was called Prinzenstrasse, innocuous enough and ideal for renaming. The GDR did not exclusively reach for communist and anti-fascist figures and figurines for its thoroughfares. Heinrich Heine (1797–1856), a German Jew from Düsseldorf of impeccable middle-class credentials – father a merchant, mother sophisticated, and money in the family – became a lyrical romantic poet. Cumulatively, Heine was a long, long way from the GDR but it had several goals which it pursued implacably, and culture was one of them.

After reunification, when the reverse-history began to rename the renamed streets in the East, trouble in many guises and nuances did arrive very quickly. We'll be coming to that. It would, however, be bad news for many great German heroes of the revolution, and Ho-Chi-Minh-Strasse had no chance (it was named that in 1976, reverted to Weißenseer Weg in 1992).

Heinrich-Heine-Strasse survived, Prinzenstrasse presumably gone forever (in the east; the western part remained and remains Prinzenstrasse) this second time round, and there the avenue remains: long, ramrod straight and with everyday traffic flowing along it, as resolutely ordinary in its way as Leuschnerdamm or the junction which became Checkpoint Charlie. Of course, to call an avenue after a lyrical poet where border guards had orders to shoot to kill might be regarded as deliberately provocative, but it wasn't. It was just Berlin, abnormality co-existing with normality in an adaptive way.

On the other side of Heinrich-Heine-Strasse the death strip stretches past modern apartment blocks in the West. There are twin roads here, equidistant and with only a hedge of small bushes between them; one road built specifically to give access to the apartments because the other, the original road, which would have done that was just behind The Wall. Both are called Sebastianstrasse.

At the end of Western Sebastianstrasse, which is halfway up Eastern Sebastianstrasse, you turn left, the death strip a jungle again, past a school and on, turning left and right: this is the ancient boundary between bohemian Kreuzberg and the Mitte district, the pride of the East and the historic centre of old Berlin. You're in amongst tall buildings which have consumed the death strip and you're walking towards Checkpoint Charlie. It's a lot of layers and they're everywhere you look, even if you need a tutored eye to see them.

Many perceptive words have been written about The Wall, and a single sentence by Peter Schneider in his study *The Germany Comedy: Scenes of Life After The Wall* (1991 – that's important) has a haunting quality. He broods if 'it was The Wall alone that prevented the illusion that The Wall was the only thing separating the Germans'. He was introducing the concept that the two Germanys had grown far apart, but as long as The Wall stood a pretension could be maintained that they hadn't. People could say it was the only thing dividing them.

The truth of it is not in doubt and this book addresses two questions: amid all this bewildering geography and geometry, all these cobblestones and street corners, how far apart were they and, these twenty years later, how close?

One man knows about The Wall and knows about the layers. He painted the original white line at Checkpoint Charlie in 1961 and, one way or another, has devoted the rest of his life to working The Wall then preserving the memory of it. To find him you have to go into the East, to a broad, straight artery called Alt-Friedrichsfelde which still looks like the East – the width of the road dictated by Socialist planning, the great throng of Plan 1 workers' apartment blocks lining it like sentries guarding the past. Hagen Koch lives in one and although there is ample parking – East Berlin had space – and a few trees for decoration, no real attempt has been made to landscape the grassy area. Socialist planning contented itself with the functional (which was all it could afford anyway). The hall leading to the lift has been repainted, however. It looks fresh and eternally new in the Western way.

There is a resonance on one of the lift's walls: a montage of small advertisements behind a glass frame. You're reminded of the classic film *Goodbye Lenin* where a devoted member of The Party goes into a coma after a heart attack, misses the fall of The Wall and, to prevent the shock of another heart attack killing her when she comes out of the coma, the family maintain a pretence that the East still exists. She's bedridden and that helps but eventually she notices a Coca Cola[5] pennant unfurled down the wall of the building opposite. The idea of having something so totemically Western there revealed everything.[6] The montage on the lift wall revealed everything, too. The capitalists with their market economy have reached everywhere, even here, and the residents seeing it every day can hardly avoid it cementing into normality.

Hagen Koch is a jolly, voluble, passionate man of great theatrical gestures with his hands. He's had heart bypasses which haven't slowed him. He has to stand when he talks because he needs room for the gestures, needs movement because he is constantly hunting out material to reinforce what he is saying. He doesn't speak. He declaims.

His apartment divides into strictly private – which is bedroom, lounge and kitchenette – and public – which is his small study and two ordinary corridors. Here in this confined space he has amassed more documentation and memorabilia on The Wall than exists anywhere else. He has ranks of hard-backed folders teeming with original papers, photocopies, maps and photographs. In 1988 a unique sequence of black-and-white pictures were taken inside the death strip for official East German use. He has these, of course, and despite many offers won't sell. They belong to important history, he says, and they must be available to everybody. He has newspaper cuttings from the four corners of the earth properly filed. He has a row of videos and, now, DVDs and CDs. He can show you Walter Ulbricht's order to build The Wall in 1961. He has that, of course. Shelves teem with models, badges, statuettes and pennants which are definitely *not* Coca Cola. The very last visa stamping machine used at Checkpoint Charlie for passports is here, of course.

The story of the Archive has its own layers. A month after the fall,

the Brandenburg Gate opened, so I can go there, I can touch it, I can go through. That was when I had the idea, because I at the time was responsible for the protection of cultural materials and buildings in the GDR. Since they were removing The Wall I was thinking *what will be left when that's happened?* I was responsible for it as an historical monument. I took one of the stamps from a border guard (who wouldn't need it any more) and that was the way I got into the history of The Wall. It was 1700 hours, 22 December 1989.

The GDR government said everything must go, the victims of The Wall said everything must go but in the spring of 1990 the government changed and I was made the Prime Minister's special envoy for the preservation of the documentation about the demolition of The Wall. I started with documenting what they did and got the government's permission to collect documents as well.

At a party at Checkpoint Charlie in June 1990, attended by the last border guards and Rainer Hildebrandt[7],

somebody said I was *Stasi*. There – the Brandenburg Gate – I started to deal with The Wall and there – at Checkpoint Charlie – I started to deal with my own past. That was when I started to collect all the documents. I was allowed to take copies, although I didn't want the documents for myself. Four weeks after reunification the West German government came and threw everything out. They took all the documents and put them in a skip because they were meant to be destroyed. I went there in a van, took it all out of the skip and brought it home.

(Layers? The legal status of the Archive is pure Leuschnerdamm. Koch was hauled before a court in 1994 because he had broken GDR law by not destroying the Archive when the GDR said everything must go, but the GDR no longer existed. Possession, as the saying goes, is nine-tenths of the law but who legally does the Archive material belong to? Koch? Some obscure ministry? Who can know? 'The Archive is still in the same position: nobody really wants it among the decision making bodies.' You bet. The important aspect is that it exists, and, courtesy of Koch, it's available.)

The fact that the Archive is so popular, and used so much, must prove people are still fascinated by The Wall even twenty years later.
   'It is getting even more.'
   Should not more of The Wall have been preserved?
   'It's not about quantity.'
   But people come to Berlin and they can't see it and they can't visualise it.
   'It's more a question of what-was-it and not where-was-it?'
   All right, let's go directly to one of the big questions. Is Germany able to deal with its past?
   'No. In today's[8] newspaper, the *Berliner Zeitung*, there is an article which says 11 per cent want The Wall back.'

That sentiment cuts across both sides because the GDR physically vanished as a country leaving citizens who had known only centralised certainties adrift, then marooned, bemused, abandoned, lost and – mostly – full of trepidation if not outright fear; but West Berlin also vanished. It ceased to be a prosperous island subsidised by the Federal Republic, cosy, insulated, offering itself not quite as toy town, but not as a capital either. Aside from historical connotations and a few buildings, West Berlin was provincial and deeply content to be that. The 11 per cent split both ways.

   Koch is an important figure because his life reflects so many of the layers, and does it brutally. Once upon a time he was a believer and member of the *Stasi*, an organisation for which hatred is only exceeded by that for the Gestapo and SS. The *Stasi* (as we have seen in the Foreword, an abbreviation of *Ministerium für Staatssicherheit* – Ministry for State Security) was Orwellian in that it consciously tried to set up a bureaucracy which would know and record just about everything, about just about every East German citizen. They became, under their gnome-like leader Erich Mielke – a man bereft of taste or vision – a state within a state. The GDR was paranoid about many facets of life and the *Stasi* enacted the paranoia.

   Once, the CIA, exploring ways to assassinate Fidel Castro, considered slipping him an exploding cigar. The *Stasi*, and arguably only the *Stasi*, could compete with that in the realm of the ridiculous: storing a collection of underwear so dogs could sniff and track down whoever owned them, timing how long ice skater Katarina Witt took to make love, and expending enormous quantities of man-hours surveying people. Hundreds of files bulged and choked with useless information, like what time they went out to buy milk and what time they came back with it.

The *Stasi* was sinister in a spider's web way, too, and was unaccountable. Mielke allegedly held incriminating documents about the GDR Politburo in his safe, including something on leader Erich Honecker, but, more than that, by definition a secret organisation run on this scale could only be accountable to itself because only it knew what it was doing. It was everywhere, watching everything. To protect the purity of the GDR revolution it was prepared to abandon decency, the rule of law and ultimately common sense. They tapped so many phone conversations that they were months, perhaps years behind in transcribing them: an object lesson in futility.

Their headquarters in Normannenstrasse, just outside the city centre, resembled a fortress and, significantly, was the only Berlin building stormed when The Wall came down. There are conflicting reports about who did the storming but no doubts that they wanted to get their hands on what was in there, and did. The extent of what they found was a moment of genuine shock and, when the individual *Stasi* files were subsequently opened, the sense of shock deepened because families sometimes discovered they had been informing on each other, and friends discovered it, and colleagues, and lovers, and dissidents.

The fact that Koch went from believer to wanting to leave the *Stasi* in 1985 has not enabled him to escape the stigma of being *Stasi*, so that more than three decades after he did leave, and two decades after the fall, it is still used as a stick to punish him. He describes having a *Stasi* past as a 'hot problem'. This is even more poignant because, understandably, former *Stasi* personnel (they're all former now, of course) have spent the past two decades saying little and staying out of sight, while Koch has cultivated a certain gregarious visibility: frequently he's on television and appears in documentaries; he gives interviews and lectures; he writes books. He has his own website. He *wants* to talk about it, not in order to exculpate himself – that couldn't be done even if he tried – but because The Wall, the *Stasi* and the whole situation are matters of historical importance and thus as open to discussion as anything else.

Koch says:

You have to tell history the way it was. After the Second World War, Germany was divided by the Allies. We in the East were taught about how bad imperialism was, warmongering and so on, and the West was taught that communism was aggression, warmongering and so on. There was a goal: that the West Germans and the East Germans get into a fight with each other in the sense of representing the two opposing world powers, the Soviet Union and America. Now both sides don't want to admit that they were wrong: no Germans will admit they fought for *their* world power against the other Germans.

I have a good friend, Oliver North.[9] We were in a film together for Fox News in the USA about the role of Kennedy in the building of The Wall. Oliver North brought American documents and I had my archive with Russian documents. It was a good film about the cold war and it was very successful in the USA because between us we had a lot of information.

Thereby hangs a challenge to the accepted version of the The Wall going up, which is that to staunch the flow of refugees from East to West duplicitous Walter Ulbricht schemed, lied and carefully plotted to build it.

'Every film that you can see about The Wall starts with Ulbricht's words "nobody has the intention of building a wall", but Ulbricht wanted a ring round the whole of Berlin from 1953 on, not a wall. This was his plan and his goal.'

Ulbricht (with Soviet leader Nikita Khruschev as his master) needed simultaneously to avoid creating a confrontation, which in a nuclear age was outright insanity, but still prevent the refugees, who were travelling from all over the GDR, getting into East Berlin. Once there they used the overground or underground train systems, caught a bus or simply walked into the West, where they could settle or be flown to West Germany. Dividing the city with a wall violated the post-war Allied settlement and risked the confrontation, but setting up a ring outside the city didn't because it would be in the Soviet Zone, not a violation of the Allies' Berlin agreement. The ring would stop the refugees before they got through to the city.

By 1961 the refugee tide was rising so fast it threatening to empty the GDR. Ulbricht would have to do something, but what?

In early June, Khruschev and the new American president, John Kennedy, met in Vienna. Khruschev, sensing Kennedy's inexperience, bellowed, bullied and laid down a six-month ultimatum over Berlin. Koch recounts:

> On 15 June 1961 Ulbricht gave a Press Conference, and from a female jour-nalist on the newspaper *Frankfurter Rundschau* came a question. 'Are you of the opinion that the workers at the Brandenburg Gate should erect a border installation?' [The Gate was the city's symbol and a crossing point between East and West.] Ulbricht had the ring around Berlin in his head but she asked specifically about the Brandenburg Gate. He said 'nobody has the intention to build a wall' – he used the expression wall although nobody has asked anything about a wall – meaning to seal off the Brandenburg Gate.

Ulbricht's words, never shown within the context of the question he'd been asked, were portrayed as a deliberate lie in the West because the received wisdom decreed that he knew he was going to build a wall[10], or may even have been publicly introducing the idea of one to panic Easterners into flight in ever greater numbers, forcing Khrushchev to give permission to build it.

In the doublespeak of the East, if Ulbricht solemnly assured an international press conference he wasn't going to build one, it obviously meant he was.

What Koch has said directly contradicts that.

Kennedy reported on his meeting with Khruschev to the American Congress. Kennedy only talked about West Berlin and he formulated three essentials: access to West Berlin, freedom for West Berlin and no threatening of West Berlin. Only after this speech did Khruschev and Ulbricht start thinking about putting a wall through the city without causing a confrontation.

In other words, they deduced that Kennedy had given them tacit permission by default – by only mentioning West Berlin.

On Monday 7 August there was a special meeting of the Politburo. On 8 August, Khruschev gave a Berlin Press Conference and on Wednesday 9 August it is decided that the border should go through the town. It is only then that they really decided it. Until that time the plan had been the ring around Berlin because one of Kennedy's essential demands was no threatening West Berlin.

It happened that the GDR Politburo, who before were in the Pankow district of Berlin at the end of 1960 and the beginning of 1961, went to Wandlitz [a pretty, rural place some 25km north of the city]. They went there because it was outside the ring.

The Wall went up on the night of the 12th and day of 13 August. No material had been stockpiled except barbed wire. 'If, as has been said, erecting it was the concerted action of all the Warsaw Pact countries then there must have been plans, and this is why I get into trouble – because I tell the story as it really was. I can prove Ulbricht didn't really lie because he didn't *have* any maps or plans.' The Wall was initially the barbed wire stretched between posts, which had to be hastily erected – you can see the drilling of the holes, the jack-hammers battering cobblestones, in virtually any film about The Wall, just as you'll hear Ulbricht's words.

The implications of Koch's claims are that if Ulbricht had had the ring instead, Berlin might have been given a completely different history: the GDR would have remained an obedient Soviet satellite and East Berlin under four-power control. That would have had international consequences, removing some of the coldness from the cold war. The Wall would never have fallen because it would never have been built and the neighbourly residents of Elisabethufer and Luisenufer would have remained residents of Elisabethufer and Luisenufer, sitting on the jetty by the lake sipping white wine or perhaps a cappuccino.

It is a simple truth: Berlin is the most fascinating, maddening and complex city in the world.

Koch is defensive about the GDR.

> We had to pay the reparations whereas in the West you had the Marshall Plan and the economic miracle. The East had to pay for it all. The few things that were left here were taken by the Soviet Union as reparations. We had no Marshall Plan. And after reunification along comes the West with the big cars and says: 'you in the East are stupid and you are lazy because you are not so well off.' Public opinion is that the government of the GDR had driven the country down, but there was nothing left after the War so you cannot drive something down which you don't have. We worked more than the people in the West – until, finally, there was a kind of resignation. Today's evaluation is very unreal.

The Wall in the Head? You decide.

Koch gives evidence of it in Western heads. He's made a film about The Wall which, he says,

> is forbidden in Germany. There is no written document that says it must be forbidden but nobody wants to have the film because, as they say, I am taking part in it as a guide and you can't have a former *Stasi* member doing that. They say that, if I do it, all the other *Stasi* officers will think they can too. I've taken part in a TV series called *My GDR* and I've a new book for young people because we have found out that they don't know anything about the history of the GDR.
>
> In March 2007 I went public again. I took my notebook and gave a lecture to a class for advanced level students who were in Berlin for about a week studying. They also had a meeting with a vice chancellor. The students produced a report on the internet about their visit and their history class and at the end they say it was a very interesting trip but the most interesting was the lecture by Hagen Koch. In the Bundestag somebody said: 'how can it be that they found the ex-*Stasi* man more interesting than a vice chancellor?'
>
> ... [I held] a seminar in Berlin with young students from Israel, Jordan and Palestine. I told them about my past and The Wall's past. 'But what,' I asked, 'are the Israelis doing in Jerusalem? Our wall was 3m 60 and yours is 8m.' That put me in a position to say that building a wall separating people from each other is not the answer to the problem. I know from my own experience. I said, 'it doesn't matter how high the wall is, people will always want to overcome it. In your country, as it was here, there will be people thinking how to break through it. If not, they will fire rockets over it.'

The Israeli government protested about the talk, but how can I form the opinions of the young people?

Mrs Merkel went to China in September 2007. A weekly magazine there gave her visit two pages, two pages on the election campaign of Hilary Clinton and three pages about the work and lectures of Hagen Koch. They asked the question: you complain about human rights in China but what are you doing to Hagen Koch in Germany? So the Federal Press Office came here and they were upset because she had two pages and I had three …

Since Koch is guardian of The Wall, what does he think of the twin row of cobblestones?

Now they are incorporating little metal plates beside the cobblestones, BERLIN WALL 1961–1989, but they are positioned to be read from the West …

The cobblestones mark the outer Wall, but the real wall for the GDR was the inner Wall, because to the East *that* was The Wall: if you went to it you were arrested and if you got over it you would be shot. If The Wall had only been where the line of cobblestones is, Walter Ulbricht would have been finally right because he claimed he'd built a wall against evil capitalism – the anti-fascist protection wall – and it directly faced the West. I would have agreed with laying them where they are now if there had been signs saying: THIS WAS THE END OF THE FREE WORLD, but to say it was The Wall is simple, not accurate – it's a lie. So why put the cobblestones where the outer Wall was? Of course, whenever I suggest something is not really true people say: 'ah *Stasi!* You have to be against everything because you were the *Stasi.*'

As I keep saying, nowhere is more gripped by its geometry than Berlin, right down to a row of cobblestones, and it might be more accurate to talk about the Geometry in the Head. It leads, as such conversations so often do, to Checkpoint Charlie.

A tourist now simply cannot visualise what it was like.
'This is the intention.'
Should they have left it?
'In 1995 it was all torn down. We asked to rebuild it but this was refused – only art can be there. The Berlin Senate for Cultural Affairs decided. Like Bernauer Strasse, seen from behind. There, for artistic reasons, The Wall was made one-third smaller than it really was. They put up a six-metre metal wall beside it in order to make it seem even smaller. Why? If you look closely you

will see that everything is missing which was there. I protested because when children come they can touch the top of this inner Wall and they say "how come the Easterners didn't just jump over? Why didn't you flee if The Wall was so small?" I was told this is art. The artists who made this, a couple, come from Stuttgart. Their reason for making it smaller was that, when they came to West Berlin and looked at it from that side, they could see the inner Wall and it appeared very small to them.'

　　But that's not history, it's very misleading.

　　'It's art!'

Bernauer Strasse is not an ordinary, placid street and it does bear obvious resonance: the death strip. It's a kilometre long and has ten intersections with roads running across it. The Wall ran across *them*. If you are looking from the southern end, everything on the left was in the West, everything on the right in the East – a contradiction because while the Western side is fully built up there's not very much on the Eastern side except the overgrown death strip, a modern church within the death strip and by definition built after the fall, the section of The Wall Koch mentioned and in the distance some trendy apartments under construction. It gives the street an open, spacious feeling.

　　The third intersection is with Ackerstrasse. The Wall section is in fact 212 metres of the outer Wall, and it still faces the West from across the street. To the tourist its 12ft stance is a shockingly high, bare cliff-face, dehumanised and inhuman, and you really can't see over it if you are close. A square has been made: the outer Wall forming a front, the inner Wall a rear, with two metal walls forming sides like giant bookends. The metal walls are higher than The Wall and a tourist could be forgiven for thinking *they* were The Wall. Evidently some tourists do. The overall impression is distracting at best, hopelessly confusing at worst.

　　The Wall 1961–1989 came at you with a purity of purpose shorn of any architectural pretensions except the functional – one function, and only one, twenty-four hours a day for twenty-eight years. To confuse this is a very great feat of stupidity and a violation of genuine history, hence Koch's contempt for it, and my contempt for it, and Ms Kubisch's contempt for it.

　　Mr Mayor, tear down these metal walls. Mr Mayor, open up this precious, monstrous area again and let it speak for itself.

　　The inner Wall, which you can reach by sneaking past one of the metal walls, has been vandalised (sorry, rebuilt) in a subtly different way – the attempt at art which also earns Koch's contempt, and will earn that of Ms Kubisch and me in just a moment. It is lower than when it actually stood, the slabs have been positioned with enough space between them to be able to see through (which obviously the GDR would never have permitted) and, uncannily, a family are there inspecting it. A teenage girl reaches and is able to haul herself up easily. You can hear Koch saying *if you look closely you will see that everything is missing which was there. I protested because when children come they can touch the top of this inner wall and they say 'how come the Easterners didn't just jump over? Why didn't you flee if The Wall was so small?' I was told this is art ...*

Ms Kubisch and I explain this to the family but they seem dubious or, more likely, they are so confused they have no idea what to believe. This ought to be their history, their heritage and there for them to draw their own conclusions instead of new geometry being overlaid on old geometry until the meaning has been fatally diluted out of it all. They can't even get The Wall *into* their heads, never mind get it out.

This is made more poignant because Bernauer Strasse does resonate. In 1961 old, tall terraced houses lined the Eastern side and, as workers bricked up the windows to prevent flight, people jumped from upper floors with the West Berlin fire brigade trying to catch them before they hit the ground. The old black-and-white newsreel footage of these incidents is as standard as Ulbricht's words. The Church of Reconciliation stood not far from Ackerstrasse and, stretching the geometry as far as it would go, for some months after 13 August a door was left in The Wall so worshippers from the West could pass through it. Further up, Conrad Schumann the border guard, suddenly vaulted the wire and a photographer took one of the most famous photographs of all as he was in midair. Further up again, a famous tunnel was dug from the West, coming up in the basement of a house in the East. An American television company filmed people escaping through it and that joins the necessary footage of Berlin.

At least at Ackerstrasse now there is a long photo montage on hoardings which covers this territory and explains it, but because all the buildings in the East were levelled for the death strip so long ago, whatever Bernauer Strasse was before has gone and a strange, tangible feeling of emptiness lingers. The dark tarmac patrol strip which the border guards drove in their military jeeps still snakes its way up the death strip and, all unknowing, people stand on it to see part of the photo montage. There's a kiosk nearby where you can hire audio guides to The Wall. The two young men working in it had no idea the tarmac just *there* was the original patrol strip.

The photo montage contains details of a competition between artists because the idea is to extend the section of The Wall. Presumably each of these artists will strive to interpret *what it really meant* as it gets into their Heads. The competition represents an exercise which is as fascinating, maddening and complex as Berlin itself. You have to keep repeating: between 1961 and 1989 The Wall was exactly that, a wall, and the GDR was prepared to kill at it[11] to maintain its sanctity of separation. It came at you exactly like that at Ackerstrasse, through Checkpoint Charlie, along Leuschnerdamm and all the other places on its twenty-eight-mile journey.

The Berlin government was given 40 million Euros in 2006 to preserve it.

Mr Mayor, when you've torn down the metal walls and the bogus inner Wall at Ackerstrasse, re-build a complete section, complete with death strip and a watchtower, exactly as it was.

As Hagen Koch says, 'you have to tell history the way it was.'

You have to show it the way it was, too.[12]

Notes

1. At least three streets were renamed after officials killed by escapers: Streilitzer Strasse became Egon-Schultz-Strasse on 15 July 1966 (and reverted in 1991) after the border guard was shot by tunnelers; Behmstrasse became Helmut-Just-Strasse on 18 March 1960 (and reverted in 1993) after the police constable was shot in it by escapers; Schützenstrasse became Reinhold-Huhn-Strasse on 15 July 1966 (and reverted in 1991) after the border guard was shot by escapers.

Leaving the politics aside, this is how and why (courtesy of Ms Kubisch) Germans name streets as they do: If it is named after someone it is all one word, like Legiendamm and Leuschnerdamm. If it is a first and surname it carries hyphens, like Bruno-Leuschner-Damm or Karl-Marx-Allee. If it is named after a city or a place it is usually two words, the second word carrying a capital letter, like Dresdener Strasse, Oppelner Strasse, Lichtenberger Strasse, Strausberger Platz.

2. Strictly speaking, The Wall was opened on Thursday 9 November 1989, which is usually referred to as its fall. The dismantling took much longer and even weeks later Westerners had to go through Checkpoint Charlie, as they had always done. I tried to get through a new checkpoint at the Brandenburg Gate but when I brandished my British passport the customs man said 'no' and directed me away.

3. The number of districts is misleading in terms of who really got what, because some were large and others, particularly in the city centre, small. In reality, the Soviet Union was taking slightly less than half of the whole city. For the record, the districts were: Soviet – Pankow, Weissensee, Lichtenberg, Köpenick, Treptow, Prenzlauer Berg, Friedrichshain and Mitte; French – Reinickendorf, Wedding; British – Spandau, Wilmersdorf, Charlottenburg, Tiergarten; American – Zehlendorf, Steglitz, Tempelhof, Schöneberg, Neukölln, Kreuzberg.

4. The Wall's height meant that you couldn't really see over it except if you lived in high-rise apartments or, distantly, from certain places on the S-Bahn. This was all that most East Berliners had ever seen (apart from pictures on television). Whether these glimpses were tantalising or uninteresting, would

presumably depend on personal preference, although Westerners like me assumed Easterners would want to see the West. This impression was confirmed the night The Wall fell, the next day and then the weekend when a mighty torrent of Easterners crossed to see.

5. Any Westerner imagines that brands like Coca Cola are and always were ubiquitous. I went on a holiday to the Soviet Union in 1972 and, arriving in the hotel in Leningrad, asked for a bottle. They looked at me incredulously for even asking. Coca Cola represented the enemy.

6. *Goodbye Lenin* is a charming nostalgic study, a comedy which never descends to the comic although it is also (inevitably) charged with all manner of ironies. I have to report that Hagen Koch saw it and it didn't do much for him. I have also to report that Ms Kubisch did not regard it as nostalgic because, she says, that implies a desire for the past.

7. Rainer Hildebrandt (1915–2004) had been opposed to Hitler and served time in prison. He founded the museum which overlooked Checkpoint Charlie in 1963 and it grew into a vivid home for the artefacts of escapes (as which it remains). Hildebrandt became a propagandist for non-violent resistance all over the world and published extensively on that as well as The Wall. He loomed as a father figure, slightly eccentric, slightly innocent but right.

8. Interview in July 2008.

9. Lieutenant Oliver North, a U.S. marine, was involved in the Iran-Contra Affair when, during Ronald Reagan's presidency, he sold weapons clandestinely to Iran. He subsequently became a right-wing commentator, appeared on Fox TV and wrote best-selling books.

10. Ulbricht's words were used on tall posters on the Western side of The Wall pointing East so the population there could read them: NOBODY HAS ANY INTENTION OF BUILDING A WALL. Taken out of context, as this was, the words could scarcely be more ironic or damning.

11. Amazingly, a proper shoot-to-kill order was not discovered until August 2007 by a researcher working in *Stasi* archives in Magdeburg. It was dated 1 October 1973 and said: 'Do not hesitate to use your firearm, not even when the border is breached in the company of women and children, which is a tactic the traitors have often used.' Many GDR leaders had claimed such an order did not exist and its discovery seemed to open the way for the prosecutions. (The order was issued to a *Stasi* unit charged with preventing border guards from escaping, and at least thirty-seven are known to have been shot trying to do that.) Anyway, if such an order did not exist, why were the guards armed and why was there so much shooting? The *New York Times* claimed that 'according to historians, about 2,800 border guards crossed the border from 1961 to 1989', adding that between 270 and 780 people were killed by them trying to escape.

12. This is naturally a sensitive subject and in 2008 a short section of the original Wall was removed by contractors acting at night and in secret to make

space for a new environment ministry. Evidently, the section was put into storage, not destroyed. Some people regarded the act as sacrilegious and some as vandalism against a protected monument. As at February 2008, Berlin Wall Online was listing fourteen places where either some of The Wall or a watch-tower still stood. There seems to be more in the United States than Berlin, including a section in the men's bathroom in the Main Street Station Hotel and Casino, Las Vegas. For a full list see http://www.dailysoft.com/berlinwall/guide/berlinwall_us.htm.

2

GOD, A LITTLE DISTANCE AND THE FIRST ONION

If you stand by the lake at Leuschnerdamm you can see two churches built on the principal of ornate monumentalism, red brick upon red brick reaching towards heaven. One is straight ahead, the other at the end of a street called Bethaniendamm.

St Michael's, ahead, stands on an area of grass the size of a city block and is hemmed by tall trees from which it rises majestically. It is Catholic and looks, like all old churches, the sort of place city dwellers use to find a quiet corner for contemplation rather than go and sip the glass of chilled white wine on the jetty just over there. It has a tower above the arched entrance with, high up, three vertical windows and another taller tower at the back. A vast, green-shaded cupola sits on top of that.

Nobody worships there except in a small, restored chapel.

St Thomas's, some couple of hundred yards away, also stands in a grassy area, is hemmed by tall trees from which it rises majestically but has three towers, two at either side of the front and one circular at the rear. It is Lutheran and during the day the door in its arched entrance is open. City dwellers do find quiet corners.

The churches seem to represent timeless normality but for twenty-eight years they didn't. A bombing raid on 3 February 1945 tore the guts out of St Michael's and it remained a shell. Then The Wall came, isolating it in the East by cutting across just in front and dividing the congregation.

Bethaniendamm curves gracefully away from the lake towards the Spree and it has pleasant gardens along its length – they are slightly sunken. Until 1926 they were part of the waterway and frequented by the barges plying their trade from the Spree through the lake and on along Leuschnerdamm towards a big canal. A twin road, Engeldamm, runs along the other side of the gardens so you have access from both sides. There's a small children's play area, complete with climbing artefacts, and benches to rest weary legs. The area has the feel of an intimate park.

There are resonances everywhere despite the resolute normality. Both streets have their own geography and geometry although no photo montage is available to help decode either. All I'll say (to protect your sanity after the Leuschnerdamm maze) is that Bethaniendamm's pavement was in the West, the gardens were the death strip – of the same level, raked earth as the sunken gardens and lake – and Engeldamm was named, renamed and re-renamed. If you really do want to risk your sanity go to this footnote.[1]

A bombing raid on 22 November 1942 severely damaged St Thomas's and rebuilding only began in 1956. Then The Wall came, isolating it in the West by cutting along its side and dividing the congregation.

The Wall was firmly down here on earth but the religious communities – in Berlin, Lutheran and Catholic – ought to have been up there above it, and only answerable to the higher authority of their choosing. (The Holocaust had taken the extensive Jewish community, which declined for Nazi reasons during the 1930s to 75,000 before the war. Some 8,000 survived and the community is now estimated at 20,000. The Turkish community was exclusively in the West.)

Any wall bisecting a city will inevitably have a direct impact on everything, but it cut very deep into the religious communities: twenty-two congregations were divided.[2] The war left Germany a pulverised, traumatised country. A complete social rediscovery, personally and collectively, was necessary after the bestiality of the Reich. The Protestant and Catholic churches retained what has been described as an important degree of moral authority, and that enabled them to play a part in the rediscovery.

The Lutherans were most numerous among the Protestants, followed by the United Churches and the Reform Churches. Four months after the war ended they became a federation called the Evangelical Church in Germany, organised on a regional basis and without a hierarchy. Quite naturally it spanned East and West. The Catholic structure, which also spanned East and West, stayed centralised.

In the West the churches were independent of politics and considered so integral to the fabric of society that taxes were imposed on ordinary citizens to finance them. A vast majority paid. (The practice was to be banned in the GDR.) When the FRG was born, the Basic Law solidified the status quo, and in the coming decades the relationship between church and state would be unproblematic. When the GDR – atheist and seeking to impose atheism – was born, the Evangelical Church in Germany appointed an official representative to the government, although it did not intend to acknowledge the legitimacy of the government.[3]

The GDR's constitution, a deceptive document, proclaimed the rights which the churches would enjoy. This may have been because they were sure religion would die a natural death in a socialist-realist society and they didn't need to concern themselves with it, or it may have been that the constitution could be used against any external criticism. There was another factor at work, drawing on the Soviet Union's experience that if you overtly persecute religious communities it tends to strengthen rather than weaken them.

Of those who did go to church, Protestants outnumbered Catholics by about six to one. The GDR population of 17 million divided theoretically into 13 million Protestants and 2 million Catholics[4], and 2 million who, for whatever reason, were neither. Stefan Wolle[5] points out that the Association of Protestant Churches in the GDR had a membership of 5.1 million when The Wall fell, representing 30 per cent of the whole population. 'In its eight member churches there were 7,385 parishes with 4,704 rectorates of which 684 (14.5 per cent) were vacant. Each pastor was in charge of an average of 1,300 congregation members.' These statistics demonstrate the 'immense weight of Protestant churches' but they also demonstrate how far the GDR government's drive towards secularisation had succeeded: in 1950 some 80.4 per cent of the population were Protestant and that was cut to 'less than a third' in a single generation. Baptisms, marriages, confirmations and burials all fell consistently to 1989.

However, the GDR did not seize church property and, to the end in 1989, Protestants had their own news agency, five weekly newspapers (circulation 157,000) and printed 40,000 Bibles a year which they sold themselves. Wolle points out with exquisite irony that 'it is among the curiosities of the GDR, that ... the Holy Scripture may have been the only publication that was always available'.

I expect *Das Kapital* was, too.

The Catholic Church was restricted to cities and two regions in the countryside (Eichsfeld and Oberlausitz), giving it 6.1 per cent of the population. The end of the war brought an influx from the eastern territories, pushing the figure to 11 per cent before the long decrease. In 1988 the Church had 834 rectorates and pastoral care posts, and 1,068 priests, giving an average congregation of 1,030 to each.

I propose to give you the stories of four believers – three from the East and one from the West – in the hope that cumulatively they make a comprehensible mosaic of what happened and what is happening.

The first believer is from the East: Dr Johannes Althausen.

He lived in a spacious apartment in the Berlin suburb of Pankow before his death while this book was being written. He was a quiet, dignified old man and wore the cloak of the years lightly although he was almost blind. For what he had seen, and for what he was seeing, he no longer required eyesight. He spoke English studiously and softly, as if he was comfortable in it. He retained what he must surely have always had, presence.

He said:

I have nine grandchildren and two of them gave me a Christmas present.
They would accompany me on a journey to Paris, because of my sight. I
said, 'I travel wherever I want without accompaniment!' – but a friend was
living in Paris, I had never had a chance to visit him and I wanted to. It's a
big city and without eyes not so good. We decided to go. The granddaughter is 22 and studying in Kiel; the grandson is 20 and has just finished his
higher education here in Berlin. He says, 'I was born one year before the
Wende, I never had a chance to know the GDR.' He has a memory from his
mother about the GDR but he feels much more European. He'd never say
he concentrated on Germany.

   They got the tickets on the internet. It was their first time in Paris, too,
but it was no problem for them. It was very easy for these two young people
to understand French. They'd learned in school, of course, and they were
able to use it. It's good.[6]

Dr Althausen was a leading Lutheran in East Berlin who'd spent time in
prison, had a *Stasi* file and, because of an exquisite political joke (which leaden
GDR officialdom didn't get), had been able to travel abroad to religious gatherings. The idea, however, that his grandchildren bought him a trip to Paris
and accompanied him on it struck him as quite normal. The stretching of
their school French represented a deep satisfaction that they could do it. After
everything he'd lived through, he wasn't the kind to be openly emotional
about it but you could sense he delighted in their normality.

   Althausen traced the nuanced, uneasy history of church-state relations to a
series of external circumstances: post-Stalinism, shifting domestic priorities in
the GDR and a meeting in the 1950s between a political delegation and five
church leaders.

[It produced] a communiqué that demonstrated a measure of mutual
respect. We were quite attentive to it because, for the first time, it expressed
the church's readiness to respect the socialist path. Already there were stri-
dent critics among us who, like many today, characterised this step as an
impermissible concession and – or – as the first in a series of concessions.
One should guard against a one-sided interpretation, however. In the same
communiqué the state promises to respect Christians' observation of their
civic duties 'according to their faith, and within the parameters of the law'.
In this document, the state backed away from the Marxist denial of the continuing existence of Christians. The communiqué therefore demonstrated
mutuality. It became the foundation for many additional agreements over
the years and gave both sides experience of each other.[7]

In East Berlin there weren't many of those compromises, perhaps only this one.

The Catholic Church in the East was much weaker than in the rest of Germany because, as we have seen, the East was more Protestant than Catholic.

'This is very important to know,' Dr Althausen said. 'The West was industrial and Catholic; the East was agricultural and Protestant.'

He was

born in today's Poland, 40km beyond the Oder river. It was a little village. My childhood was very good. All the bombing and other aspects of the war went *above* us. We could see the planes but nothing happened in our village. I went to school at Frankfurt (Oder) although sometimes getting there wasn't easy. My father was the minister and he stayed until the end of the war. When we left in January 1945 – the Russian army was coming – he remained. He had a long, grey beard and could have said 'I am an old man' but since he was a very honest person he didn't. He said 'I am fifty' and at that age he could be taken to do work. He was imprisoned, transported to the Ukraine and he died there.

We had gone to a Berlin suburb. I was sixteen and I tried to attend school but it was a little bit difficult so I worked on a farm as long as possible – to the end of 1945 I was a farmer's boy. I was cautious because the Russians were always on the lookout for men who might have been soldiers in the German army. I got through that period and started my schooling again in January 1946. I finished in September and had the opportunity to start studying philosophy four weeks later.

Yes, I was always religious. It's an interesting question about how it all happened. I was a really pious boy. My decision to become a minister I took at the age of twelve, because of reading a calendar. Under each day there was an explanation of words from the Bible. I read it every night and I remember one night I found it so very interesting I thought I must study to understand the Bible better. It was my own interest. Was I influenced by my father? When you are twelve nobody knows how much comes from your father although he didn't say anything about me following him. When I see my grandson playing football he does it because his father is doing it, not because his father is saying 'play football'. This might also have been my position. It was quite clear that the family would go to the church service on Sunday morning, and so this was my *atmosphere*. Maybe it contributed.

His story is the sort which in any other country but the GDR would make it resonate as a freak, a former potential battleground, a site of genuine historical importance and, in the sane world, an impossibility. That it became ordinary and placid *is* Berlin.

My family had had something to do with the Jewish people. My father's grandfather in the middle of the nineteenth century became a Christian and he studied medicine in the Ukraine. My grandfather became a minister and his son – my father – again also. So the family had more Christians than Jews but, because of the Nazi laws, things changed and my parents had some difficulties, although nobody was killed, nobody put in a concentration camp. However, some of my father's brothers and sisters had to leave Germany because of the racial legislation. We children didn't know anything about the reasons – the only thing we couldn't do was take part in the Hitler Youth. We asked 'why?' We weren't really interested in taking part but we were interested in why we couldn't. My mother only told me the whole story in May 1945 when my father was already away and in the night you could hear the Russians moving around. The story changed my whole view.

Until that point, my understanding of my life was that I would stay on the path of normal Germans. At that point I found myself on the other side. At the same time the war was finished. I had a real difficulty understanding Jewish theology after the Holocaust. My personal solution then was to live a life of piety. My inner voice was saying I belong to Christ and Christ is among all of them, Jewish and Christian, Nazis and Marxists. This helped me later on.

After The Wall fell[8], Dr Althausen said:

When my political consciousness first awoke I was a student. My first critical struggle with the social and political conditions of the GDR took place as I assumed leadership in the student Christian fellowship movement. I was twenty-four years old. In early 1953, I was detained for five months in a *Stasi* prison. In 1952 – that is to say, three years after the founding of the GDR – Walter Ulbricht called for the construction of socialism in the GDR, so as to fight all ideological enemies more vigorously. There had been a general development towards a divided Europe, and the European Community was in the process of emerging, after Stalin's offer for German reunification in early 1952 was turned down.

There was no mistaking that Ulbricht's action would affect the church. Already in the fall of 1952 the first reprisals began. In early 1953 there was a wave of arrests, affecting about forty ministers.

I very clearly experienced my arrest as an injustice – as the kind of injustice Christians and church leaders experience often. At the same time, I was guided by Dietrich Bonhoeffer's thoughts.[9] His letters from prison had just appeared and would have been a little guidebook for many of us even without the reality of arrest. Soon it was clear what was going on. The *Stasi* intended, with the help of witnesses who turned state's evidence, to elicit statements that would justify restricting the church's possibilities. You could see through their method, and their arguments were threadbare. If you could keep your nerves, you could survive ... without damage and without accommodation. Historical circumstances began to change, too. The larger political realities necessitated a settlement between state and church. The reason for my arrest passed, and I and many others were set free.

In prison I had successfully resisted. At the same time I learned that for Christ's sake I could not despise others. The one who had suffered on the cross had prayed for his enemies. Above all, the experience had freed me from the pressure to resist, a pressure that I had found among Christians and among all of us in general – we had all been influenced by a Nazi upbringing. Now I was required to make my own judgements about how the church should live in this society. Why should I not also find opportunities for conversation with Marxists?

Reflecting in 2007, Dr Althausen added:

'The time in prison was a problem for me in terms of understanding the situation as a Christian in the GDR. I already understood that I was an outsider. However, I found myself in the same cell as other prisoners and I had long conversations with them each day and each night, and they were asking me – because of my life – even about my faith. These discussions brought us so deeply together that afterwards I felt much more obliged to those normal people than to the system. And I never saw them again.'

He was ordained in 1954 and 'I had a parish in Michendorf near Potsdam. I think there were 2,000 Christians but later on the number decreased very much.'
Was that because it got more and more difficult to be a Christian?
'That's a very interesting question. The situation of Christians and churches, even the church institutions, was changed once more. It had been of course at the end of the war but much more deeply at the end of the 1950s and the beginning of the 1960s because of the very quick secularisation. I started my Confirmation classes and the official legislation was saying anybody who does not go to the *Jugendweihe* cannot have higher education.'

The *Jugendweihe* was a secular ceremony replacing Confirmation for fourteen-year-olds, created in 1852. It was heavily adopted in the GDR in 1953 and has been described as youth consecration.

'I had the opportunity, I had the obligation, to talk to the young boys and girls: *be careful, your Christian faith is now at stake.* This was very hard work for me because most of them, almost everybody, went the other way. They thought of their future and a job and a career.'

The Wall gave the GDR government a free hand to rule absolutely, and without fear of the consequences. It could, and did, control every aspect of the society it was creating. Industry, education, art[10], medicine and sporting bodies[11] were all obliged to function as the state decreed.

The religious community in East Berlin was different from every other body in the GDR. It could not accept the state's demand for complete submission because it had already submitted to another higher authority. The religious community could not function, however, as if the state didn't exist. That led to a very Biblical situation: rendering unto Caesar that which was Caesar's, but knowing that Caesar wanted everything.

Dr Althausen felt 'the key words "accommodation" and "resistance" are more objective than the words "compromise" and "opposition"' for the situation 'because they more clearly express the dynamics between church and state.' The state and church *both* contained the faithful prepared to give their lives for their beliefs. Communist revolutions were always blood-soaked; communists had known exile and persecution, while the suffering of the Christian martyrs dated from Rome and the Colosseum. Both bodies insisted they had the truth and the way, making compromise elusive and a settlement ultimately impossible. The state had all the physical strength it needed, could intimidate and punish, but what use was that against the believers who came bearing no arms and wanted only to forgive those who trespassed against them, including the state?

Nor could any Christian – no matter how convinced of God's great purposes compared to man's ephemera, like a concrete wall – gaze from St Thomas's across the death strip to St Michael's, or vice versa, without reflecting that the division was having profound consequences. This was made more poignant because the Catholic and Protestant churches remained organisationally undivided from their Western arms and, on top of that, enjoyed connections with each other in the GDR.

In 1968 the GDR introduced a new constitution, again a deceptive document, changing little. It guaranteed all manner of freedoms but with caveats about how free people would be to exercise them. Subsequently, the eight regional Protestant churches in the GDR withdrew from the Evangelical Church in Germany and set up their own body with the idea of becoming the 'Church in Socialism'. It could only mean the churches were recognising 'the division of Germany and the reality of two German states'.[12]

The Catholics kept their own counsel although Dr Althausen was revealing about one aspect of that. 'As I became known as an ecumenist [promoting understanding among inter-denominations] I was invited by Catholic people, even by lay men, and I felt they were very good, deep connections. This took place in an institutional way; it was not just for the individual Christians.'

The new constitution

put the relationship of church and state on a new footing. [It] was a decisive point of departure legally. If the church had not been willing to respect this new situation it would have had to go into a kind of quasi-illegality. No one was interested in that path because it would have surely deprived the church of the possibility of interceding for the people. Instead, the church decided for the people.

Tensions reached a peak when the Evangelical Church in Germany concluded an agreement with the West German government to provide pastoral care in the West German military and to grant chaplains the status of civil servants. For the most part, members of the synods in the GDR withheld their approval. Nonetheless, the law was fully valid without their votes and prompted the government of the GDR to break off its relations with the Evangelical Church in Germany.

A state secretary for church questions, installed by the state, now took the place of the church's representative. The state's position was clear. The state secretary for church questions would act according to the needs of the state. The state would deal with the church as the state deemed appropriate.[13]

Both churches in the East experienced a steady erosion of their congregations although Dr Althausen never contemplated that they might wither completely 'because when you are living in a congregation and meeting people of the same faith all the time you couldn't think about that'.

But in the GDR it was very difficult to be a Christian and dangerous, perhaps. Did that make the people who were Christians more committed?
'In general, I'd say yes. I have to be very cautious in saying this because people could misinterpret it, but there were signs which showed it: for instance, a wonderful series of voluntary gifts for the church or a fantastic atmosphere in youth congregations. There were also many people in leading positions who were still Christians and did a lot of good work.'
Politicians?
'Not politicians.'
There must have been some.
'Maybe. I wasn't aware of them.'

From about the middle of the 1970s there was

increasing discomfort with the growing indoctrination of people in the GDR ... This indoctrination increasingly served to preserve the state's power and did not allow the underlying political problems to come to open debate. Everywhere in my world there were friends with whom we could discuss these developments – whether the *Stasi* were present or not was really secondary – but we did not find a way to demonstrate opposition publicly. Above all, what our experiences had taught brought us to the idea of wanting to make socialism better. In that respect, we were not the only ones. The leaders of the so-called opposition, even as late as September 1989, continued to speak in terms of improving the GDR, not eliminating it.[14]

Paradoxically, Dr Althausen

first applied to go to West Berlin at the end of the 1970s because I had been invited to make a speech and I got permission. I hadn't been there for fifteen years. I met friends who were still my friends. I got information about a lot of trouble in the 1960s and 1968 but I couldn't really understand it.[15] It was a quite different situation to ours so there was already, in spite of all the friendship, a little distance. Maybe that was because of my temperament, maybe because I could just go to the place where I had to make the speech then leave again.

I didn't really know about West Germany. I was there when I was studying from 1947 until 1950 and went back twenty-five years later. This was similar to the situation in West Berlin because I had friends from my study time. I had obligations in several parts of West Germany but this was for me a similar foreign country to Switzerland.

The whole question of freedom to travel, or more properly the absence of freedom to travel except to approved countries, became a running sore for GDR citizens and ultimately a cause of profound resentment.[16] Essentially their world was reduced to Poland, Czechoslovakia, Hungary, Romania, Bulgaria, the Soviet Union and Vietnam.

When you wanted to go to the West how technically did you go about that?
'There was a very clear way to apply for it, via the police station, and this application of course was sent to the *Stasi* as well. I needed some invitation from abroad. I started my work in the Berlin mission society in 1957 and in 1959 I became responsible for all the missionaries who were working in South Africa. The headquarters still remained in the GDR because, despite all the difficulties, it was easier to leave it there. Five times between 1959 and 1965 I asked for permission to travel to South Africa, which was politically an anti-communist country. I did not get it. I did receive an invitation to another part of Africa for a big ecumenical gathering – a gathering of all African Lutheran churches in Addis Ababa. I applied again and there was a church leader in East Berlin who had a way to the state people. He went to the *Stasi* and said "you should let him out." I was away for six weeks and went to Tanzania too.

'When I came back I got a visit from the *Stasi*. I had known that what I said in Africa was going to be reported to them. During discussions with the Christians at Addis Ababa I said "oh, you should have a socialist government in order to get your rights." I said it as a joke. I told this story to the GDR ambassador in Tanzania, and this was reported. It opened all the doors to me. From that point onwards I had no trouble in travelling! In fact, in the mid-1970s I had a chance to go to the United States and ordinarily that was almost impossible.

'What did I think of the United States? I was very impressed by the ignorance about Eastern Europe. What struck me was the Press who cut out certain parts of the world completely. There were almost no articles about South America and the word socialism seems to have been forbidden. This was very astonishing. I wasn't so astonished by the standard of living because I knew that already.

'A most important question, and one I was looking at, was race relations because I knew of Martin Luther King and the freedom marches. When I went to Chicago in the 1980s I had a chance to be involved in a discussion group including theologians from the GDR and West Germany. The group had a black president although most of the teachers and students were white. He wanted to show us black Chicago and so for one day we were put into a car and went to the southern part. This was quite an experience – [we were] the only white people there!'

The state was never far away.

'I remember in the 1980s I met someone from the Ministry for Education who wanted to negotiate about the theological training in the GDR. Later on I got information that everything I had said was put into a report and it went into my *Stasi* file. Later, when I read it, I found he hadn't understood anything I had said! In the government there was someone responsible – a lawyer – for churches and he had a little department with one or two secretaries. This person wanted to have regular talks with me because I was responsible for seventy-five young students who were going to become pastors. He was interested in holding ongoing discussions to find if anything was unlawful. These kinds of discussions were sometimes difficult because, again and again, he asked about costs and about people's feelings in the church. I thought it was not my responsibility to tell him everything, especially about specific persons, so I avoided any names in these talks.'

They must have realised they couldn't convert you.

'They made one more attempt, which was reported in detail. They came into my office just as our morning prayer was starting. It was eight o'clock. I had something to arrange with my secretary and I was in the secretariat. People from the *Stasi* came into the room and said "good morning". Then they were saying "your nephew is in the seminary" – which was right in the sense that he had been, but he'd gone. They wanted to know things about him and this was the point where I said, "oh, that's impossible." I stopped very suddenly and I said nothing else except "goodbye".'

Europe was about to say 'goodbye' to the *Stasi* and the GDR.

On the way to that, protest groups became more and more vocal, more and more public and ultimately more and more confident, but that brought 'one of the most dramatic situations that I can remember. The church had to save one of the so-called groups from the grip of the *Stasi*, even though in the church space that it was using it had smeared a wall with swastikas and other grotesque symbols. The church could with reason have abandoned the group to the state authorities but, for the sake of human worth, and for the sake of some of the concerns that the group represented, the church could not simply do so. The *degree* of accommodation and resistance became the question: how we help without betraying people.

'I do not know if an outsider can imagine such situations but they always occur to me when I attempt to put myself into the shoes of the church leaders who are accused of having gone too far in their contact with the *Stasi*. You have to examine each case very carefully and even then be cautious in your judgements. What in each case did an unofficial collaborator actually do? What constituted "regular" conversations with the *Stasi*? When someone says he hoped through such contacts to help others I am sympathetic, and I wish to believe him until there is proof of the opposite.'[17]

Nor should the role of the churches in providing 'free space' for the protesting groups be underestimated.

Where were you the night The Wall came down?

'I had a meeting 200km outside Berlin. I heard it on the radio. It was not so much freedom as the first night when I came out from prison: that was real freedom, more than I felt on 9 November 1989, but when I returned to Berlin and heard from my students what they did that night it was different. I was moved by descriptions of West Berlin but also moved that they were present for the morning service at eight o'clock the next morning. Everybody. No exceptions. I was very proud.'

Have you seen your Stasi file?

'Yes. Only one thing was not so good. In my work in theological education I had a lot of contacts with many *Stasi* people who wanted to get in touch with me. I had no reason to avoid or refuse them so we had some talks. I never thought about that after The Wall came down and had completely forgotten it until I read my file. I found the reports about these meetings. This was a really astonishing thing for me and I asked myself *are the reports accurate?* I had some difficulty remembering but in general I was glad because at the end of this report was written: *It might be good to remain in touch with him.* They didn't!'

Many people when they saw their file discovered that they had been betrayed by someone close.

'Not me. Nothing. Nor did I expect anything like that.'

Everybody talks about The Wall in the head. How long will it take for that to fall?

'For a certain generation it will never happen, but then I look at my grand-children and they have no wall any more. They are now in a position where they begin to take responsibilities. I think it will take ten years more because by then all these young people will have reached the middle of their lives and only known normality.

'What has changed? I know much more about the Western world. I got information about the time between when The Wall came between us — I simply lacked information before that. Secondly, we have a new type of soci-ety, a new type of life. Since 1989 very many things in Europe, and especially Germany, have changed. With regard to the church, anyone can go to any church they want anywhere. However, I never thought that everybody would be able to do everything they wanted. You couldn't in the GDR and you cannot today in this society. That is the background for my judgement. You have to be much more careful because you are free whereas in the GDR you were obliged to behave in a certain way. This freedom means it is much more necessary for everybody to be taught what their obligations in life are and what they are responsible for. What I learnt about democracy is that it is you who are responsible, not the state.'

The second believer is from the West: Pastor Christian Müller.

He came to St Thomas's in 1987, when he was forty-nine and found it

a very quiet area, actually. I was born in a village with a lot of pubs in north-ern Bavaria. We lived in the so-called *Zonengrenze*, the border area near Czechoslovakia and the GDR. I remember the uprising in Budapest as a seven-year-old.[18] The adults talked about it — we had no radio or television — and I was very afraid, so in a sense I had grown up with the cold war, the American soldiers with their chewing gum doing manoeuvres and so on. I never knew Berlin without a wall because it was already there in 1967 when I made my first visit. I found Berlin was an exciting city with the student movements going on which would produce the events of 1968.

When I moved to the city in 1970 we lived in the so-called better part of Kreuzberg, not immediately where The Wall was. For me it too was relatively normal, although I noticed that it was something different for my parents and my family. They wouldn't come to visit us for many years because they didn't want to travel through the Soviet Zone to get here. They were afraid.

I worked in different parishes and between 1979 and 1986 I was a priest for the homeless. Ever since I came to Kreuzberg I'd wanted to be at St Michael's and now I was. The congregation had obviously been separated for a long time, one-third in Mitte in the East, two-thirds in Kreuzberg. The ones in Mitte were re-congregated with a neighbouring church over there, St Petri Mitte, in 1965. When I came in 1987 we had meetings twice a year in East Berlin.

The story of these meetings reflected what The Wall brought.

The nature of Kreuzberg's population changed in the 1960s and 1970s. Many of the Lutheran population moved away, flats were cheap and Muslims – Turkish people – came as well as students and people who had a lot of big social problems. We had had a huge congregation but fewer and fewer people were coming to the church because of the shift in the population. Before my time the church decided to look outwards because of the social problems. We talked to the people. We had meetings with squatters and politicians. We strongly cooperated with the congregation of St Margaret's West, although it was Catholic, again because of the social problems. Actually we did more with them than with the other neighbouring Lutheran congregations.

St Michael's West and their divided congregation – St Michael's East – had a close relationship, they'd already met and St Michael's West initiated the whole thing. They invited us to the meetings which included St Petri Mitte.

What did we speak about? Every possible thing, although nobody thought The Wall would fall and nobody discussed what would happen if it did. It was very interesting to hear what problems they had and what their world was, and for them it was very interesting to hear what our world was. They were open-mouthed because we could discuss our problems so openly. In East Berlin the congregations were small and closed. They had pressure from the state and they cared a lot about maintaining their structure. The meetings weren't difficult and we also had individual contacts because we could go there.

In July 1989 there was a big GDR church meeting in East Berlin, a huge event. We went there with a delegation, a group of ten people from our congregation. You could sense something – movement. There were events for the young people and they discussed a lot, but these young people didn't think of The Wall coming down and we didn't either.

Within weeks GDR holidaymakers took refuge in the FRG embassies in Prague and Budapest, Hungary opened its borders and the refugees poured across into Austria, bound for the FRG's promised land. The GDR celebrated its fortieth birthday with, to external perception, great pomp and circumstance while the country was beginning to boil over.

You had the demonstrations on 7 October and we were thinking about the effects they would have on the GDR. For a long time we imagined they wouldn't have a big effect. I remember when Honecker was replaced by Krenz[19] I wrote in the parish magazine *Give Him A Chance*. I had a colleague who came from the GDR at the beginning of the 1980s and who looked after senior citizens. When the article appeared she said, 'they are all very irritated by it', so I went and the senior citizens questioned me. *How can you defend Krenz?*

Müller was trying to make the point that after the glacial, unyielding and aged Honecker, Krenz could bring change. It was an entirely reasonable point and can only really be appreciated by reflecting on how unyielding the whole Eastern bloc had been since 1945: seen from outside it rose like an iceberg.

St Michael's held monthly meetings and in November 1989 the meeting fell on Thursday the 9th.

It always started at seven o'clock in the evening and one of my colleagues, who lives nearby, was ten or fifteen minutes late although she was usually punctual. She said, 'I heard on the TV that something is happening in the GDR', although she didn't know quite what. We said, 'OK, OK, now what is the agenda for today?' The meeting lasted until eleven o'clock, I went home and went to bed but I woke in the night. I could hear a kind of humming. No lights, no rockets, just the humming. Only in the morning did I hear on the radio about the border being open.

I didn't know whether it would remain open but so many things were happening that we only thought from one day to the next. The underground was so crowded that I walked from home to the church. The first man I saw from the East was on the morning of the Friday at ten o'clock. He was sitting on the steps of the church crying. He said there were many people where he crossed and everybody was drinking Champagne. They'd given him some but that created a problem: he was a recovered alcoholic. He said, 'what am I going to do? What am I going to do?' We gave him coffee and something to eat and he went back. I hope whoever he is he's stayed dry.

Is it not strange that he came to a church?
'I think he had contacts with a church parish in East Berlin. Probably that's why he came here.'
Did you think that your congregation would be reunited?
'No – no real reunification. We are hoping it will happen in 2009. When The Wall fell some people came from the East to see where they had been baptised or married, but they were old people. One woman got married in

the church, had her children baptised and then The Wall came. She lived just over on the other side. She has resumed contact but she is not a member of our congregation. I think those who became members of St Petri would want to stay there because the pressure they had had over the years also held them together. Our intention until two years ago was to merge but nothing came of it. Maybe it's because of the reputation Kreuzberg has! Anyway, the national church is now reunited and actually only a few congregations were divided.'

What was it like for you, because The Wall was just outside for all those years and then it was gone?

'The Wall came down about a year later. Strange, it was. I remember it was some time in autumn and we had plum cake. The border guards were about to remove that part of The Wall with a big machine. We went outside and said, "we'd like to invite you for some coffee and plum cake", but of course they were border guards and there was a distance between them and us. They said they would have to ask their superiors. After a while seven or eight of them came and drank the coffee and ate the cake but the atmosphere wasn't very relaxed.'

Is the whole situation normal?

'It is getting more and more so. There are a number of people coming from Mitte or Friedrichshain who know the West but don't really know Kreuzberg. We had someone who was in a subsidised project by the labour office and lived 500 metres away in the East. She worked here and she was astonished at the number of Turks. She hadn't been to this part of Kreuzberg before.'

Do people from the other side come to the church on Sunday?

'Yes. The area over there has become one for people who are quite well off, especially from the West who have moved to Berlin. If they want contact with the church they come.'

Has the congregation got bigger since The Wall?

'In this part of Kreuzberg only 12 per cent of the population are Lutheran. You can say we have had a decrease but it has become slower. We don't ask everyone who comes: "are you a member of this congregation or that congregation?" When there are big festivals like Easter and Christmas you can see them coming across what was the death strip and the parents of a number of children in our kindergarten live in Mitte.'

There must be people living there from, say, Bonn who don't even realise there was a wall. It's just pleasant gardens.

'It's true they have other reasons to come. The flats are good and Oranienstrasse with its nightlife is not far away.'

In the church you have an exhibition of photographs of The Wall.

'It's rather a coincidence. The church was destroyed during the war and the rebuilding took until 1963. Because it would have the status of a protected building the work was done as close as possible to the original. They insulated the ceiling with asbestos but in 1985 we discovered it was coming down. We closed the church immediately and had discussions about whether we could really maintain it. Some people thought it would be a good mosque.

'We have a villa with a garden and a room for 120 people so the services could be there. The church reopened in 1998 and when it did we decided on a Wall archive. We had had a reunification present – a man from the East who was born and grew up in Alexanderplatz before the TV tower[20] was built. His family was large and living in one house. They wanted to knock it down to make room for the tower so the family were dispersed. He was trained as a miner but as a young man he had problems. By the time The Wall came down he was divorced and he went to Hamburg to start a new life. He failed completely because everything was much more difficult in the West than he thought it would be. He returned to Berlin because it's where he'd spent his childhood and he knew the place.

'He came here because we had a café for homeless people, where they could get breakfast. We got talking and I realised he was very motivated. He began to stay in a flat in the basement, he became a member of the congregation and he takes care of a lot of little jobs. He arrived around 1994 and when the church reopened in 1998 it became his centre of life. He's moved to Friedrichshain but he very often spends the night in the church. There is a bed in one of the towers. As a miner he was used to getting up at four o'clock in the morning and that's when he starts to do the cleaning. If the church is open later than seven in the evening, for a concert or something, he doesn't like that because he says it needs its quietness.'

He became a collector of Wall memorabilia, as well as the photographs, for those who come to St Thomas's to worship or out of curiosity and do not know what the gardens just there really were.

'The archive is important because many people come and see it, even tourist groups. Some walk and some cycle. They sit in the church and he talks about it all, showing them the photographs.'

The third believer is from the East: Pfarrer Gregor Hohberg of St Petri.

He estimates that there are about a hundred of the congregation left who couldn't continue at St Thomas's after 1961. The fact that they did not reunite is, he feels, more than 'to do with the East–West separation. The congregation at St Thomas's was orientated towards Kreuzberg and the congregation here towards Mitte.' In other words, the separation reflected the reality of the orientations which already existed.

Hohberg is an East Berliner and 'I have always been a Christian. Yes, it was difficult in the GDR but my family is a "minister" family – my father was a minister, my mother taught religion but only within the congregation, not in schools, of course.'

What do you think now, the twentieth anniversary approaching so quickly?

'My family and I think it was a huge slice of luck that there was the Wende. I was twenty-one when The Wall came down and I took part in the demonstrations at the Gethsemane Church [in Prenzlauer Berg].[21] It wasn't difficult for me to lead a normal life after, although I had never been to Western countries. I'd been to Hungary and so on. I was educated not by school but my family so I knew about places like Hamburg even though I'd never been. Through my parents I also knew the political systems both in the East and the West.

'I went to the West on 9 November. I was part of this opposition group and each day we were demonstrating. In the evening we'd watch television to see what was being reported about the demonstrations. I saw the Schabowski press conference. I took a bottle of champagne and went to the Brandenburg Gate but that was still closed. There were maybe fifty people. I went to Friedrichstrasse and there were about 200 people. We were told "no, not possible to cross, wait until tomorrow." We heard a rumour that Bornholmer Strasse was open so all the people went there. I went over the bridge[22] but I had a feeling that if I stayed I might not be able to go back and my family were still in the East, so I decided to return immediately. There were 20,000 people going one way over the bridge and one person – me – going the other!'

Hohberg did cross later that night and 'my first impression was of kind people and all the lights. The roads were small compared to the East. We bought a Coca Cola at the Ku-damm – very exotic. I remember seeing the morning newspapers saying THE WALL IS OPEN, which was unusual to me because here the newspapers were rather boring. I kept the newspaper. I still have it. I spent several days in the West because I had friends there. I went to the Gedächtniskirche [the Emperor William Memorial Church][23] next day alone and I prayed.'

Do you think The Wall opening was an act of God?

'God works through people.'

The fall caused the Eastern churches subtle as well as obvious problems. They needed, as someone has remarked[24], to 'redefine themselves' because they were 'confronted with the reality that the population was largely irreligious.' In short, they had to rejoin the mainstream, and this is what, according to a United Nations estimate, the mainstream looked like:

Total population	81,912,000
Protestants	28,197,000
Catholics	27,909,797

The reunification of the Protestant churches wasn't straightforward. In February 1990 those in the East were drawn between doing the deed as quickly as decently possible or maintaining some sort of separate identity. This led to a commission with representatives from both sides and six meetings. There were legal problems, financial problems, problems of whether Eastern diplomas and so on would have validity, and veiled words about political involvement. In November 1991 they decided on reunification and the church became one again.

By then, and amidst controversy, the Church Tax which had always existed in West Germany was applied to people in the East. Contributions had been voluntary before and it risked alienation in the East. The position of the Catholic Church in the East was quite different because all Catholic churches everywhere were organised in the same way with an unchanging hierarchy in Rome and a Bishop's conference for each country. It was only a question of merging the conferences East and West. This dispensed with the problems which the Protestants had faced and the reunification proceeded to a swift conclusion.

The fourth believer is from the East: Thomas Motter.

The fifty-seven-year-old stonemason was and is a leading figure in St Michael's. He lives in an apartment facing the gardens.

'When The Wall went up the congregation of about 1,000 was physically divided although about 85–90 per cent has always been in Kreuzberg. There was a transitional period during which some of those in the West maintained contacts with those on the other side and visited them – special events and the like. In the mid-1960s a new church was built in the West, about 400 metres from St Michael's in the East.'

Motter comes from a Catholic family with a strong faith which wasn't broken by The Wall. Before it was built he had attended a Catholic school in West Berlin, but at the end of the school holidays, on 1 September 1961, he had to go to one in the East instead, another casualty of The Wall. Other pupils there joined various East German youth organisations, but his life continued to centre on his church. His Christian faith had repercussions. He was banned from taking advanced exams.

What was the Wall's impact on you?

'Thank God you didn't think about it every day. If you had, you'd have gone mad. We would hear shots when people tried to escape' – between 1964 and 1989, he thinks ten made it.

When The Wall came down, did people from the West return to St Michael's?

'After twenty-eight years apart it wouldn't work. On both sides there was only a handful of people left who knew each other from before. On this side there were a lot of families with children but in Kreuzberg over there a lot of single people. Social structures were different. They had changed completely.'

There are no plans to rebuild St Michael's. Since 2001 Motter has been in an organisation involved in its restoration as a memorial. 'To revive it as a church would be too expensive, and the parish doesn't need one that big. Masses are held in a parish room in the former transept.'

As an active member of the church and a Christian youth movement the *Stasi* took a keen interest in him and his family. During the interview he produced his file, a ring binder containing photographs of his parents and 300 typed pages detailing meticulously his movements. There is even a map showing where he lived, the apartment marked by a triangle. Astonishingly the 300 pages represent only about half his complete file and he has applied for the rest. The 300 he has provide ultimately meaningless detail. For example, on page 136 you can read entries for 4 June 1975 timed at 09.37, 09.44, 16.12 and 18.05.

'What really surprised me was that the telephones were tapped and the conversations recorded.'

Many details, including names, have been blacked out under data protection in case they lead to incrimination, but Motter is sure he can work out who some of them were by the overall contexts.

In your heart can you forgive now?

'If I met somebody and I knew from the file that he had betrayed me I would have a short conversation with him. Maybe the forgiving would come later.'

Curiously, in the aftermath, church membership in the East fell despite its role in unification as refuges from the raging storm and subsequently as mediators between state and people. One estimate suggests the Protestants lost 5 per cent of their membership and the Catholics 4 per cent, although as time passed the rate of decline slowed.

The East remained, however, largely a Godless place.

The magazine *Der Spiegel* (No. 52, 1996) pointed out that when former GDR citizens were asked if they believed in God only 20 per cent said yes compared to 51 per cent in the West, although the percentages had long been falling in both places.

The *Jugendweihe* survived because it had enduring popularity, although it became controversial when politicians played a part in it, which church officials claimed violated state neutrality in all matters religious because the *Jugendweihe* was atheistic – a demonstration in effect against religion.

Lurking behind it all was the sensitive and complicated matter of how much the churches had compromised with the *Stasi*.

The reunification had an unforeseen effect: the place of religion nationally became a subject for debate, something which had not happened before.

Pieces from an old wall ...

The situation was the GDR saying 'we will kill religion. If you want it you can't have anything else in terms of higher education, job, and the rest.'

'It was a difficult situation for the churches in the GDR,' Dr Althausen said. 'Many people today say that in the Eastern part of Germany there are very few Christians. The GDR was the starting point of this and it is more than fifty years now, so this is the third generation who have known it' – or rather not known it.

Birgit Kubisch grew up without basic Christianity or stories in the Bible playing any real role in her life. She was aware of the Bible and had friends who went to church but religion remained remote from her, as it did for most GDR citizens.

'I knew what Christmas was and I knew that it had to do with the Bible,' she says. 'I knew that the Bible existed. I had seen a copy, yes, yes, yes, but I had not read it. I knew that many things in everyday life had to do with the Bible but I couldn't say what. I couldn't have told you about the importance of the church in the GDR or how many people went. Although I knew people who went, it was something marginal in my life.'

Stefan Wolle[25] has expressed this eloquently: 'The position of churches in the GDR was characterised by an elementary discrepancy. While as institutions they had largely been pushed towards the margins of a secularised society, their building stood centrally in all towns and villages. At least on Sundays their doors stood open, and who passed through entered a strange world. While outside traffic blustered in the heat it was cool and still inside. In contrast to the ubiquitous symbols of the GDR, there were other signs and pictures inside, the meaning of which was not taught anymore in school, and that aroused curiosity. On the book tables in the lobby lay documents that were not available in the bookshops, in the showcases events of the parish were indicated that sounded strange and mysterious.'

Andreas Glaeser points out that 'the GDR maintained such major holidays as Christmas and Easter, wisely attempting to secularise them [following a trend that was visible even in the Weimar republic] rather than abolish them. Still, Socialist countries tried to produce their own rhythm by introducing new holidays.'[26]

Ms Kubisch, reflecting, says: 'I am trying to catch up, because I like to go to churches and see them. They tell you a story but there are so many gaps in my knowledge that I don't get all the stories.'

It also has a timelessness, and you can be very quiet in a church – be absolutely yourself, whatever you feel about it. In our lives it has always been there. Every village in England has a church. Whether you want to go to it is your choice.

'We didn't have that and, even if you don't have a relationship with it, when you go – for me at least – you can feel a beauty. Whenever I go to a church, maybe I don't understand but, well, when I was in Paris I went to St Denis. It was a Sunday morning, ten o'clock, Mass. It was very moving to witness it.

'I knew there was a Mass at ten o'clock on a Sunday but it didn't come naturally to my mind. When I heard the singing I said to myself *oh yes, of course, Mass*, but I wouldn't have thought about it at eight o'clock in the morning.'

Perhaps the situation in the GDR army, the NVA, reflects the official view which could be enforced. 'Of all the communist militaries, the NVA had been one of the most strictly anti-religious. The environment was dramatically opposed to that of, for example, the Polish army, where hostility toward religion was tempered by the presence of chaplains. When it came to individuals with strong religious convictions, believers often found themselves serving in *Baueinheiten* or construction battalions – a very unattractive place for a young man to do his military service.'[27]

The boundary of the Mitte district formed a dog-leg traffic island as it reached towards St Thomas's, and it was easier to build The Wall ignoring this. It left the island physically marooned on the Western side but legally still belonging to the East.[28] Westerners used it as a dumping ground for rubbish and only delicate East–West negotiations allowed this rubbish to be removed twice a year.

In the 1980s a Turkish Berliner, Osman Kalin, was gazing from the window of his apartment overlooking the island and thought *that's interesting*. He shifted the rubbish, made an allotment a few metres wide and began to grow vegetables in what someone has gloriously described as guerrilla gardening. Others murmured about a Garden of Eden.

Osman put a fence round it, built a garden house and the West Berlin authorities couldn't touch him because if they went in amongst his onions, kale, sunflowers, pumpkins and cabbage they had invaded the East.

One report suggests that the GDR welcomed Osman as a 'victim of capitalist circumstances' although, of course, he was exploiting socialist circumstances.

One day two armed border guards appeared.

'Who do you think this land belongs to?' they demanded to know.

'It's mine,' Osman said.

'No, it is the GDR's.'

'But I've been here a long time.'

They retired East for consultations, returned two weeks later and said 'you can stay'.

He gave it a number, Bethaniendamm 0, and his sunflowers grew as well as they had ever done back home in Anatolia. They were evidently higher than The Wall and needed 'beheading' because they were blocking the view, although whose view is not at all clear. He planted an apricot tree and ventured into zucchini.

He had ambitions and started to construct a two-storey 'house' beside the allotment using recycled material. It was constantly enlarged and occasionally burnt down. He'd got two concrete armchairs flanking a concrete table outside and if he was in the mood he'd sit there watching the world go by.

Another Turk, Mustafa Akyol, asked if he could have some of the island to make into his own allotment. Osman agreed and Mustafa started growing, but his onions spread into Osman's side and Osman's onions spread into his side. They fell out and needed to build a mini-wall – a wire fence – to separate the territories.

Irony doesn't get near it.

The land remained in Mitte until 2004 when Kreuzberg absorbed it and the mayor attended, extending an official welcome to Osman, now an eighty-two-year-old semi-recluse with a long beard and a heart complaint.

The Wall, its watchtowers and shoot-to-kill, held Mitte from Kreuzberg for twenty-eight years, just as it held the congregations of both St Thomas's and St Michael's apart, but without it Osman Kalin couldn't even have planted the first onion.

Yes, irony doesn't get near it.

Notes

1. Bethaniendamm was originally Bethanienufer and its twin Engelufer because they flanked a canal, built in 1852 – hence *ufer* for shore. It was filled in 1926 and made into a park – hence the transition to *damm* for the two roads. In 1951 the GDR could not resist the urge to rename the latter Fritz-Heckert-Strasse after a politician of the 1920s. The gardens were levelled to make the death strip. The Wall ran along Bethaniendamm but not the pavement, which Westerners could use to wander down to Leuschnerdamm, on to the bridge and Kreuzberg. The Wall also ran along Fritz-Heckert-Strasse but not on the pavement, allowing residents there access through their front doors. In 1991 Heckert became a non-person and Engelufer became Engeldamm.

2. These twenty-two were divided to different extents, as the table shows. P = Protestant, C = Catholic, F = French Reformed, R = Reformed Bohemian.

Church / Congregation	Place	District
Heiligensee congregation (P)	Heiligensee	
Martin-Luther congregation (P)		Pankow / Wedding
St Augustinus (C)	Dänenstrasse	Prenzlauer Berg / Wedding
St Sebastian (C)	Gartenplatz	Wedding

Versöhnungskirche (P)	Bernauer Strasse	Mitte / Wedding
Golgotha congregation	Gartenstrasse	
Gnaden congregation (P)	Invalidenpark	
Dankeskirche congregation (P)	West	
Dreifaltigkeit (P)	Mauerstrasse	
Liusenstadtkirche (F)	Kommandantenstr.	Mitte / Kreuzberg
Bethlehemkirche (R)	Mauerstrasse	Mitte / Kreuzberg
St Michael's (C)		Mitte/Kreuzberg
St Hedwig (C)		Mitte/Kreuzberg
St Jacobi (P)		
St Thomas (P)		
Luisenstadt congregation (P)	Sebastianstr.	
Jerusalemkirche congregation (P)		
Georgenkirche (P)	Alexanderplatz	Mitte
Osdorf (P)		Near Teltow
Stahnsdorf cemetery (P)		Near Teltow
Güterfelde cemetery (P)		Near Teltow
Klein Glienicke chapel (P)		Potsdam / Berlin
Heilands Church (P)		Potsdam / Berlin

The Versöhnungsgemeinde had 492 (7 per cent) of its congregation living in the East, 6,500 (93 per cent) in Wedding, in the West. Osdorf was a village which almost completely disappeared. The Stahnsdorf and Güterfelde cemeteries had been used by East and West. The Klein Glienicke chapel was near the border between Potsdam and Berlin. The Heilands Church was a church in no-man's-land.

Source: Dr Christian Halbrock, *Zwischen Himmel und Mauer, Geteilte Berliner und Brandenburger Kirchgemeinden nach dem Mauerbau vom 13 August* 1961 (Between Sky and Wall, Divided Church Berlin and Branden burg Church Congregations after the Building of the Wall of 13 August 1961).

3. Dr Johannes Althausen was the Director of the Paulinum School for Pastors in Berlin, known for his theological leadership.

4. *The GDR*, Childs.

5. Stefan Wolle in *Die heile Welt der Diktatur – Alltag und Herrschaft in der DDR* 1971–1989.

6. Interview with Dr Althausen in July 2008. Other parts of the chapter incorporate a speech he made and where, with his kind permission, I have quoted extracts they are indicated in footnotes.

7. Dr Althausen's speech, in Cincinnati in 1992, was entitled 'GDR churches between accommodation and resistance' and given to the Christians Associated with Relations in Eastern Europe.

It was established in the 1970s as a counterpart for an Eastern European group which was called Christian Peace Conference – more or less an idea from the socialist point of view. When this European group was established in the 1950s some of the West European people were very much involved in it. [The *Stasi* got to work undermining it.] In 1974 the Americans invited people from four countries to visit the United States, Washington to San Francisco, to describe Christian life in socialist countries. I was one. It was quite an experience.

His 1992 speech was 'translated from German by John P. Burgess, a friend who studied in the GDR during the 1980s. He was present and asked if I could give it to him then he did the translation. And that's how it was published in the United States, appearing in their Newsletter of December 1993.'

8. Althausen speech.

9. Dietrich Bonhoeffer, a passionate anti-Nazi and pacifist, was hanged by the Nazis just before the end of the war. He has become an international symbol of resistance and a guardian of Germany's conscience.

10. By definition the GDR government had a much harder time controlling dissidents but could make life very uncomfortable for them – writers refused publication, for example. The more serious of them were either expelled to the West or *sold* to the West. A definitive study of the whole subject would require another book.

11. Paradoxically, Germany fielded a unified team at the Olympic Games from 1956 to 1964, then competed separately as the GDR and FRG.

12. *The GDR*, Childs.

13. Althausen speech.

14. Ibid.

15. This is a most revealing statement because in the GDR and the rest of the Eastern bloc the 1960s, and particularly 1968 – young people asserting themselves, flower power, mini skirts, student unrest physically challenging the existing order, anti-Vietnam war protests – happened in a much more muted way. In August 1968 the Warsaw Pact invaded Czechoslovakia, which was liberalising under Alexander Dubček, repeating what it had done in Hungary twelve years before (see footnote 18 below). Ulbricht had been calling for this for several months and GDR forces took part in a supporting role. It was given no publicity: the notion that German soldiers should be marching into Czechoslovakia, as they had done in 1938, would have been appalling imagery and as it was provoked revulsion within the GDR although, of course, that was given no publicity either. For more on this, see Chapter Eight.

16. The GDR was utterly cynical about its pensioners, allowing them to emigrate to the West because they were unproductive – and the West would be paying their pensions. Other GDR citizens who did manage to get permission

to travel to the West could find themselves in an awkward position when they returned. If they waxed lyrical about what they'd seen and tasted they risked resentment.

17. Althausen speech.

18. The Hungarian uprising of 1956 was a pivotal moment in post-war European politics. The Hungarians demanded neutrality and attacked the secret police. The Soviet Union invaded to crush the uprising.

19. Egon Krenz succeeded Honecker, who resigned on 18 October 1989. The following month Krenz ordered the opening of The Wall, dooming the GDR.

20. Alexanderplatz, an old marketplace – originally a cattle market – which was rebuilt and reshaped after the war. The TV tower was constructed on it between 1965 and 1969. At 368.3 metres high (1,208ft) it could be seen from all over Berlin, East and West.

21. The Gethsemane Church deep in East Berlin became one of the focal points of protest up to the fall of The Wall. Members of New Forum and Democratic Awakening met there daily. Vigils were held, candles burnt outside.

22. Bornholmer Strasse, in the district of Prenzlauer Berg, was one of seven checkpoints between East and West Berlin and, because it was in a built-up area with a lot of apartments, attracted a huge crowd demanding to cross on 9 November 1989. The bridge itself (over railway lines as well as The Wall) was humped in shape, adding to the mystery for those who had never been to the West before: they couldn't see what was on the other side.

23. The *Kaiser-Wilhelm-Gedächtniskirche* (Kaiser Wilhelm Memorial Church) was built between 1891 and 1895 at the end of the Ku'damm. An Allied bombing raid in November 1943 destroyed it except for the west tower, which survived as a gigantic stump. It was left like that after the war as an eternal reminder and became one of the enduring symbols of West Berlin.

24. *Contemporary Review* 12/1/2000, Dr Solange Wydmusch.

25. *Die heile Welt der Diktatur – Alltag und Herrschaft in der DDR* 1971–1989, Wolle.

26. *Divided In Unity*, Glaeser.

27. *Requiem For An Army*, Herspring.

28. The 'island' was by no means unique. The Lenné triangle protruded into West Berlin not far from the Brandenburg Gate but, for the same pragmatic reasons, the GDR preferred a straight Wall and left the triangle physically in the West. There was always the danger of unexploded bombs from the war because the West couldn't go onto it to check. The triangle became overgrown and abandoned, then was absorbed by the West after a territory agreement.

3

WINDOWS ON THE WORLD

Leuschnerdamm and Bethaniendamm have been returned to anonymity. In everyday life they are just ordinary streets. Checkpoint Charlie can never be anonymous because the name remains so potent it keeps the tourists coming. When they reach the old intersection they find themselves in a place which is anything but ordinary.

The well-travelled among them may have gazed at the Statue of Liberty, the statue of Jesus overlooking Rio de Janeiro, the Tower of London, the Arc de Triomphe, Rome's Vatican and Colosseum, the Taj Mahal, Sydney's opera house or any of the other global attractions. When they reach Berlin they may gaze at the Reichstag, the Brandenburg Gate, the television tower looking over the East, the bomb-broken spires of Kaiser Wilhelm's church (*Kaiser-Wilhelm-Gedächtniskirche*), the Olympic Stadium and any of the other attractions.

Checkpoint Charlie is different. The tourists are looking at an attraction which no longer exists. I can think of only one other example anywhere, and to reach that you walk a few easy minutes from Checkpoint Charlie towards the Brandenburg Gate. There, in another anonymous side street, you'll find a small segment of grass marking the location of Hitler's bunker. It no longer exists either, in any real sense.[1]

In Berlin, history is all too often what you cannot see.

The tourists who mill and wander at Checkpoint Charlie do at least have some clues: on the Western side there's an Allied hut as there used to be, there's the museum beside the hut showing the escapes, as it used to do, there's the sign saying YOU ARE LEAVING THE AMERICAN SECTOR. There's also a huge hoarding of two soldiers in front of the hut which wasn't there and looks particularly irrelevant.

Everything on the Eastern side – The Wall, the watchtowers, the enormous customs and passport facilities – has gone as if it had never been. Instead

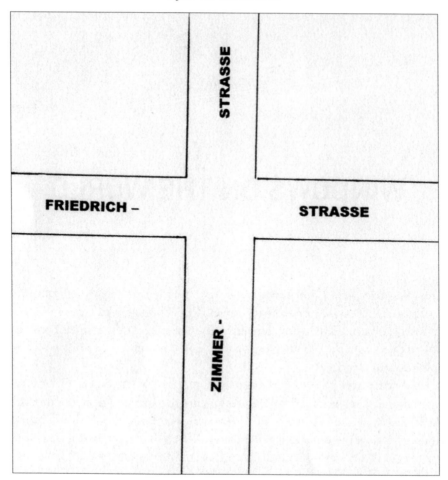

Map 5. This was an ordinary Berlin street junction like a hundred others.

there's a series of hoardings depicting what the checkpoint looked like in its various phases, evolving from a crude roadblock in 1961 to the sophisticated construction of 1989. The mood of the checkpoint has gone too, never to be recaptured: if you were coming towards it from the West you rounded a corner into a street full of shops and a café at an intersection. Beyond it, suddenly, you saw The Wall and the watchtowers with their guards wearing dark glasses. The contrast of shopping street to armed watchtower in such a short distance was genuinely shocking and decades later people can vividly recall the first time they experienced it.

The London *Sunday Telegraph* was reporting in August 2007 that the whole checkpoint area had degenerated into 'a seedy tourist trap which uses actors posing as border guards in a failed attempt to recreate its legendary past'. The article quoted a former US Army colonel called Vernon Pike, a check-point commander, as writing to the Berlin city government saying: 'the use of

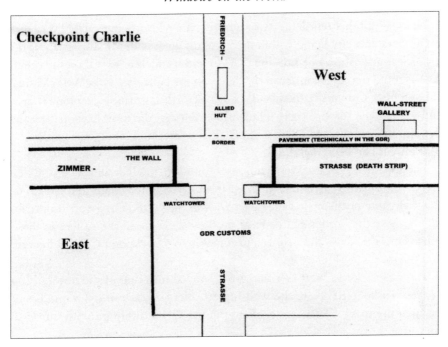

Map 6. It became convoluted and unique: Friedrichstrasse bisected, Zimmerstrasse the death strip. Note that the GDR boundary was the northern side of Zimmerstrasse but The Wall was constructed just back from that.

fake soldiers is an unacceptable spectacle which is inappropriate for the location and its historical importance.' A British tourist was quoted as saying he'd anticipated it would resemble something out of 'a cold war spy novel, but it is more like grotty Disneyland'.

There were moves by leading European politicians, including Mikhail Gorbachev, to establish a cold war museum on the site because a generation had arisen who'd been born after the fall and couldn't relate to The Wall or find very much of it to try and relate to.

The intersection is on Friedrichstrasse, a broad north–south avenue, and Zimmerstrasse, a side road. The Wall bisected Friedrichstrasse – putting the northern part in the East, the southern part in the West – and ran along Zimmerstrasse. Here the geometry and geography were even more precise than Leuschnerdamm. It was more dramatic too because in Zimmerstrasse some houses had survived the war and now found themselves in the West, but with the pavement outside their front doors in the East.

If only it had been that simple.

Because The Wall would require maintenance from time to time, the GDR carefully constructed it back inside their own territory, leaving a narrow strip outside The Wall which was still their territory. The workmen and border guards could go there without actually leaving the GDR.

This was not theoretical nicety or bureaucratic pedantry but carried very real importance in a city living within demarcation lines, with the Warsaw Pact and its nuclear arsenal on one side and NATO and its nuclear arsenal on the other. The slightest transgression across the lines – in the same way as the West clearing rubbish from Osman's traffic island – might start the escalation everyone feared, and wise judges surveying the whole planet felt that the most likely trigger for the Third World War would be an incident at or around Checkpoint Charlie.

If only it had been *that* simple.

The inhabitants of the Western houses found themselves with The Wall's 12 feet and the narrow strip outside their front doors. They could step out on to the strip quite normally but they were now in the GDR. They were ordinarily safe because the border guards were on the other side of the 12 feet so these inhabitants could use the strip as a passageway to Checkpoint Charlie, the café and the shops.

Peter Unsicker, a West German artist, moved into one of the houses on 9 November 1986 to create the Wall-StreetGallery, a place of open minds and challenging images – images challenging the GDR although with universal meaning.

'Of course I was attracted here because The Wall was outside, or rather I was attracted by the street because it is much more difficult to visualise The Wall in your head than just the concrete in front of your face. Gorbachev was talking about perestroika and glasnost and I thought *okay, let's do it.*'

What Unsicker wanted to do was use a mask to make a face and fix it to his side of The Wall.

'I went to Checkpoint Charlie and crossed to speak with these people. I wasn't making a secret out of it. I wanted to have the thirty-six square metres in front of my house. They couldn't believe it. They took my passport. It was a bit naïve in some ways but I thought it was the way to manage it.'

You must imagine the border guards' reaction when a soft-spoken, delicate-looking artist arrived quite normally wanting their Wall for his canvas and quite possibly preparing to use it as propaganda against them.

He went home, put the face up and that caught their attention.

How did they know?

'I guess The Wall was always watched from the West side by, I don't know, secret service personnel or whatever. A lot of people photographed it and nobody knew where the photographs went but later a friend looked in the *Stasi* archives and there was a photograph from the Wall-StreetGallery taken from a roof. Seven soldiers came to take the face away. They didn't knock on the door.'

The act of knocking would have meant leaning out of the GDR (and the Warsaw Pact) and having physical contact with the West (and NATO).

'They just took the face away. I stood in the door taking photographs and they were shooting videos. The Wall was mad but all this was even madder. If you imagine it: one guy with a hammer would be enough to break the face but they couldn't be sure that he was going to be coming back so they send a second man to watch him, but both were workers and they needed a higher military presence, and someone to watch the higher presence – an officer who just stood beside them. There was the soldier with the video camera and another with a Kalashnikov. I don't know how the command structure worked. I only know what I saw: seven of them. We had a man called Mick, a Briton, living here. They didn't know he was British! He told them where to go and there was a fight. Mick had to go to hospital later. If they'd taken him back to the East it would only have been trouble for them.'

Other artists, some of dubious provenance, painted on this outer wall and it became a vast jungle of graffiti. 'There were a lot of stupid provocations,' Unsicker says, 'but they'd say "don't mention my name". The rest of the artists, they did it at night-time, sneaking around, because of course they were afraid of getting caught.'

Were you not afraid?

'If you really take seriously what you do, anything which gets in your way would be a scandal – a scandal for me. I think I was the only one who said to the border guards "Okay, you can have my name and I live just there."'

How many artists have seen their own work physically destroyed as your face was?

'A lot. Too many. If you look at 1933, how many of the big writers saw their books thrown on the bonfire?[2] How many sculptors who did Lenin and Stalin statues saw them come down?'

Unsicker remembers another incident – still putting faces up – where the border guards stood directly outside and he stood directly inside. 'They said, "if you don't return The Wall to its normal condition we will close your windows." I said, "come on in, let's have tea together", but they said, "you stay on your territory, we stay on ours." If any of them had stepped inside my door, the one behind would have shot him, of course' – for the crime of fleeing the GDR.

The phrase 'close your windows' is exquisitely Berlin because, as Unsicker insists, 'some people said "this is the border line" and some said "no, this is it", but nobody knew exactly.' If Unsicker opened his windows outwards they may well have gone into the GDR, allowing the border guards to close them because they were removing them from GDR territory rather than trespassing into the West.

These days Zimmerstrasse has only the twin row of cobblestones marking where The Wall went. Like Leuschnerdamm and Bethaniendamm it has been returned to anonymity and even the proximity of Checkpoint Charlie doesn't alter that. The tourists wander down it without, surely, any idea of what they are walking on and everyday traffic passes up and down what was the death strip.

It's incredible to think just beyond your doorstep was a foreign country that suppos-edly hated us. What has taken its place?

'A united Berlin, which I appreciate very much. It's fantastic to go over to Friedrichstrasse [in the East] to meet my friends who I had before but were divided by The Wall. I would like that to open up into a European idea, making the reunification just a start, although I don't know. Of course it's great that all these bureaucrats who hung on the division are gone – there was a lot of bureaucracy – and this is really something.'

What do you think now? You have an open mind, you have an open door.

'It's no big change in one sense because I always had an open door. Everybody could come in and after 9 November 1989 it was overcrowded, a big party. Now it's very interesting because there are a lot of Chinese people coming along. To *work on what has been spoiled* is an old Chinese idea from *I Ching*[3] and we tell them about this. I show them the Chinese symbol – "oh, yes", they say. They understand what it is. Just a few days ago a young Chinese student was here and I said "*I Ching.*" He had never heard of it! At the same moment on the radio there was a Hungarian dance by Brahms and he said "ah, Hungarian dance", so the Chinese knew Brahms but not his own culture, which was chopped away during the Cultural Revolution. My idea is to bring back the *I Ching* to China and the idea of the Chinese wall to Berlin – the Great Wall was never built to keep the Chinese in [but invaders out], like any town in old Germany. There are a lot of walls *inside* people, too. Please let us live in peace.'

The gallery is a place of suspended, controlled chaos, bohemian as you would wish bohemian to be, eccentric and by the nature of its artefacts open to whatever ideas anybody prepares to bring along. The artefacts mingle with Unsicker's creations: there are interlocking moulds of faces made out of Trabant parts, tea cups with a wall down the middle of each, a tower of tiny metal figurines. 'There are 365 which means one for every day of the year, and if you look closely they don't push down, they help each other up.' The twelve Apostles have been made out of telephone cables *and* six of them are women.

'When I first came here I thought of *I Ching* – *work on what has been spoiled* – and said to myself, "it fits here." I was surprised by how well it fitted. Now I know this much better: it is incredible how it fitted *and* fits.'

The fall brought a specific problem to Unsicker, the army of 'wall peckers' who arrived with hammers and chisels to chip off chunks as their souvenirs. The hardened concrete did not submit easily and the noise of them nearly drove him out of his mind. 'I thought I can't stand it any longer.' He chal-lenged one of the peckers, a female teacher, and she said, 'but it's so satisfying.'

There was at least one amusing moment, too.

'One day a black American, a huge man, came along and started pecking. I opened the door and said "please could you do it a bit further away." He said, "you're only saying that because I'm black. If I was white you wouldn't try and chase me away." So I closed the door and after a while I opened it again. I said, "let's put it this way: because you are black you are allowed to do it here." He said "hmmm" and disappeared.'

I think true reconciliation will come when Germans learn to face the past, not keep taking it away. Lenin has been taken from Leninplatz and it's called something else, Checkpoint Charlie has been taken away …

'This is the point. In the intervening years since the fall I thought shall I leave? It's not easy here but, because everything has gone away, the Wall-StreetGallery stays. That's not just because of The Wall. We are right in the centre of German history in the twentieth century – the Gestapo headquarters down there, Göring's Air Ministry across there, Hitler's bunker over there. We are exactly on a line, for example, with the Holocaust Memorial and the Jewish Museum and when I found that out I said to myself *okay, that means something.* I will go on.'

Claudia Croon, from Cologne, is Unsicker's partner. She's 58 and says 'I came to Berlin in 1977 after my philosophy exam to experiment with new ways of living. I grew up in a very bourgeois family and I knew there were levels of accepting things. Rich families have many aggressive aspects and my generation – the generation of 1968 – tried to develop a different kind of being. Berlin was the only city in Germany which was not comfortable. All the rest had the same structures [prosperous, organised, safe]. In Berlin, when you walked through the streets, you had to develop your own being, learn to investigate yourself.'

Did you go to the East?

'The things which are very strange also have a certain attraction. For me, the people in the East were always less egocentric. I went to Leipzig as well as East Berlin; fascinating for me because the people had a kind of spiritual simplicity which wasn't superficial. They had a different way of being together, of understanding each other, of helping each other and listening to each other. I love music and that must have much to do with the fact of listening. When you talk of politicians – everywhere – they very rarely have the capacity to listen.'

Especially, she might have added (but didn't), in the GDR.

She talks of *Wahrnehmung* which translates as *I see and I take note.* 'Here at the Gallery we are on an international stage, so to say, with very many people passing by who are interested in history – the ones who are not only fascinated by Berlin but have eyes to see and ears to hear. They come in, we have dialogue and we hear the opinions of people from many places. The gallery is a place of artistic dialogue. Strange people come sometimes and they have strange ideas. We are what I call the coloured corridor.

'I love humorous things and there are very many very comic situations: those who do not know that The Wall was literally at the front door, and people who have a bad conscience that The Wall existed. It's really crazy. If you are discussing history I prefer the Indians and Australians because, for me, they are the most open-minded on this planet. To discuss German history with Germans is always complicated because it is so complex and you have the bad consciences: families weren't open, weren't prepared or not able to exchange views.'

Is that changing?

'We are coming to very superficial kinds of exchanges. I give piano lessons and one of my pupils is a "brain trainer" for industry – he helps them develop the right way of thinking. We have many logistical systems in our brains covering how we integrate. It would be very fine if our politicians and industrial leaders discovered their artistic side because they could accept more and love more. The artistic part enriches every human life. I know every politician would say "yes" but never do it ...'

How many people come in from the East?

'It's difficult to say in quantity. There are groups from the East passing by and we have contact with friends in the East, very open and engaged people in GDR times and today. When you want to change something, to transform it, you have to begin by being able to listen and revisit ancient knowledge. We have wonderful friends coming from the East.'

But what about ordinary people from the East?

'More and more I get complications with the word ordinary.'

Nobody's ordinary but I mean somebody who lived in an Eastern suburb, worked in a factory, wife, two children, had an apartment, saved up and bought a Trabant. He didn't know or care much about art, he didn't know much about West Berlin. Does he come in now?

'There are very many people in the East who are very depressed and I understand it more and more because their belief systems have been destroyed. Not everybody wants or is able to find the spiritual, especially after living in an atheistic country like East Germany. That's why there are people coming who had normal jobs during The Wall time and who had their own ways. People who want to meditate in a very special, open way. We are not ideological, we have no political position. People who long for this are happy about it. They can say anything they want.

'I know scepticism is very profound, even in myself, because I have very many experiences but I think we are together on this planet to learn. What is love? It has nothing to do with *Befriedigung* – satisfaction. As the Bible says, love other people as you love yourself – but love is giving and love is extending and love is growing.'

The tourists do wander quite normally along Zimmerstrasse. Some gaze through the picture window into the gallery and the artefacts of peace arranged there. Do they know what to make of it? Do they realise what it is intended to convey? Do they understand where they are standing?

John le Carré, in his seminal novel *The Spy Who Came in From the Cold* – it surely begins at Checkpoint Charlie, incidentally – wrote of an activist's meeting in the GDR where only seven people came and 'they were evidence of the inertia of the uncapturable mass' who stayed away.

Are the tourists the *uncapturable mass,* and all Unsicker's talk of *I Ching* and Croon's talk of love merely verbal gesturing? I don't think you can measure it like that. The Wall-StreetGallery and its like are important because the moral landscape would be much bleaker without them, whatever impact they may or may not have.

It's a close parallel to those who find quiet, personal places in St Thomas's at lunchtime.

It's ever closer in that both had The Wall thrust at them, both lived in the most abnormal circumstances and both today look like it never happened.

That Claudia Croon can speak of love quite naturally – without irony, without symbolic load – seven paces from where the shoot-to-kill was in force day and night distils just how far Berlin has come in two decades.

The beauty, or tragedy, is that you'd never notice.

At Checkpoint Charlie a small procession of Trabants put-put-putters by – evidently they're for hire, or you can take chauffeured trips in them – and the cheap, sour exhaust their two-stroke engines pump out is the purest nostalgia.

Roman Polanski,[4] the Polish-born film director who came West, caught this sentiment perfectly when he was going back, through Prague, for the first time in fifteen years in 1976. In Prague he saw 'streets filled with shabbily dressed people, the characteristic stench of low-grade gasoline and cheap tobacco. [It] all came back with a rush.'

Polanski was recapturing the characteristics of the whole Eastern bloc and he might just as easily have been describing Warsaw, Budapest, Bucharest, Sofia, Moscow or East Berlin.[5] The perils and limitations of centralised planning were evident in each and they produced a resignation among the population. You couldn't change anything and you couldn't leave so you lived with it. Of all the bloc economies the GDR's was the most successful so that those who did manage to get permission to visit the West would be doubly shocked.

First, they experienced the reverse of Polanski in Prague because the rush was well-dressed people, modern cars with petrol which didn't smell, full shops and restaurants. This moment was so profound that Markus Wolf, a *Stasi* specialist in penetrating the West, trained agents not to head for the shops and ogle when they were sent over for the first time, thereby giving themselves away.

Second, when they got home they experienced a sensation of how grey everything was. It had always been like that, but while they lived with it they simply hadn't noticed. Now they had that lethal perspective: comparison.

Anytime between 1945 and 1990 you only had to glance at East Berlin to read a chapter from Hitler's war. Despite the most extensive rebuilding programme, large tracts were left to make do and mend. These long, cobbled avenues lined by four- and five-storey buildings looked as if the war finished a moment ago. Balconies rusted, the stonework (often bearing the chip-marks of bullets of 1945 from the street-to-street fighting) needed cleaning and restoring, the angled pelmets over the windows had sometimes fallen, and crumbling cement exposed the old bricks behind.

It may have been because the Trabants and Wartburgs were so small, it may have been that the avenues seemed deserted, the occasional person walking head down[6], or it may have been the absence of advertisements and neon and shopping arcades, but it felt empty. East Berlin proceeded at its own pace.

That has changed completely. It still looks Eastern – the avenues, the high-rise workers' apartments (some bearing the original tiles, like kitsch), the architecture which constantly dwarfs human beings – and will continue to look like that for generations. Within that inevitable constriction you can barely recognise the place. The battered buildings have been restored, painted and are highly desirable residences. The Wartburgs and Trabants have disappeared – hence the procession of Trabies at Checkpoint Charlie as something of an event – but there are so many new cars you can't find a parking space any more. The full range of international cuisine is here, discount shops hustling for trade and mini-markets with their endless special offers.

East Berlin looks like the East and feels like the West. Bersarinplatz, named for Nikolai Bersarin who was a Soviet commander and played a leading role in returning Berlin to everyday life in 1945, used to be Baltenplatz but hasn't been returned to that. Workers' apartments hem a roundabout.

Heike Herrmann lives in one and it reflects typical Berlin East or West: to reach it you go into a courtyard surrounded by tall buildings, search out her name on the panel of residents by the door and press her button. There's a distinctive buzz as she answers the button and the door clicks open.

You go up a stone staircase to the studio on the first floor, spacious and uncannily like the Wall-StreetGallery. It, too, is a place of suspended, controlled chaos, bohemian as you would wish bohemian to be, eccentric and by the nature of its artefacts and paintings and drawings, open to anything except politics. That's not sinister. Herrmann just isn't interested. She terms the studio a workshop.

She was born in the GDR town of Halle in the south and moved to Rügen, the island in the Baltic. 'Maybe it's the same as in England. When you live on an island you are automatically isolated in a way and, when it becomes too small for you, you want to leave.' She moved on through a couple of towns 'always to study or to learn something new. I came to Berlin one year before The Wall fell. I came to be a rebel' – a joke, evidently, because she adds: 'Not against the system but because I was occupied with myself and finding out who I was. I worked as a designer in the fashion institute in East Berlin.'

Was it difficult to come to Berlin?

'It was, because I had been the director of a big ceramic factory company in Rügen. I was unemployed when I left, which was unusual in the GDR. Did I want to go to the West? I was very much occupied with art and ideas, and anyway The Wall was fixed. It was there and you knew you couldn't go so it was something you didn't think about. There may have been interesting new designs in the West but you didn't really think about that either. I read a lot.'

To explain the world in which she grew up, here is an extract from a speech by Hartmut König, Secretary of the Free German Youth Central Council – the FDJ, the official GDR youth movement – in 1982.

The crucial development in our literature and art, and with our greater ability to understand society today, is the exploitation and true-to-life portrayal of the dialectic of our socialist evolution. And not for its own sake, either, but with the clear aim of advancing social consciousness and the thoughts, feelings and actions of people for socialism.

Not much room for movement then in the artistic community, until The Wall came down.

'The first time I went to the West was immediately, the morning after The Wall opened. We'd put all our luggage in the Wartburg because we were planning to visit my parents in Rügen. We had breakfast about six o'clock and it was then that we learnt what had happened the night before. We drove to the Bornholmer Strasse checkpoint because we were curious. I was pregnant. We approached the checkpoint and it was completely empty of cars and ordinary people. We showed our identity cards and asked if we could go in the car. The officials had a look in the boot and saw all the luggage there. They said, "ah, more of those people who just want to leave" but we said "no, we are coming back and we are going to Rügen!" When we got to Rügen people came and rang the bell and asked what it had been like.'

Well, what had it been like?

'Strange.'

That's a very graphic way of covering the distance, and difference, between East and West as it presented itself on Friday 10 November 1989. It would have been just as true of any West Berliner going the other way for the first time.

She met someone working on a Cologne newspaper who invited her and her husband to visit, so they did, although they took fuel in cans because you couldn't buy that kind in the West. 'Cologne was beautiful.'

Not everything was beautiful though. 'The opening of the border destroyed my marriage because my husband changed. Sex shop, sex shop! And work, work, work! He's got his own company now and makes a lot of money but I don't care.' She moved about 'but I kept my flat in the East so I could come back. I have always been independent and I never wanted to be dependent on a man.'

She met her partner Fulvio at an exhibition at the East Side Gallery, that
lingering remnant of The Wall. 'At the time he was painting and he wanted to
help me as an artist. I have three children: Carlo, 21, Florian, 18, and Elisa who
is 12. Carlo's father died in an accident, Florian's father went when The Wall
came down and Fulvio is Elisa's father. Three children, three different fathers
… much trouble in the family and many problems with social security. 'Why
do you have three children and three fathers?'

'So I met Fulvio and went to Italy and I am used to living there for two
or three months at a time. It was only when I got there that I thought about
it all and tried to cope with it. I still don't understand why anybody should
be kept in a limited area [like the Eastern bloc] but of course what you don't
know you don't miss. There was the border, you knew it and even mentally
you didn't climb over it.

'I had a dream when I was a student. I always wanted to study in Italy but
you couldn't do it. Three years ago I went, funded by the European Union,
although it was extremely difficult to get the money. I attended a three-month
course in restoration techniques and that fulfilled the dream.'

What do you think twenty years later?

'I still cannot understand the political reasons for holding people
prisoner.'

You can now paint and draw anything you want. You couldn't do that before.

'Not true. I always painted what I wanted. I am an 'easy' artist – I paint
easy topics. Why not political? I had so many other things to think about like
my family. Until some years ago money didn't matter to me. I didn't have to
earn much, I could live on a little, but now we have a house in Rome, one
in Sardinia and the workshop here. It all costs. You have to work to finance
your basic needs and you don't have the time to get engaged in bigger things.
I don't like it that way. I want to sell one of the houses so as not to have too
many things to take care of. I don't like being solely occupied with how you
earn a living and have food on the table. In the GDR you didn't pay much
rent, 200 marks each month, maybe 150.'

And now?

'One of the big sorrows: 1,300 Euros. I don't know how much that would
be in East Marks. Maybe a million! Maybe 10,000 – you cannot really compare. This was a designated artists' area and the others pay 1,300, but since I
am registered with the labour office I get part of the money from them. I also
have had some trouble with the bakery downstairs and I get a rate reduction
for that. When the baker moved in and rebuilt the place he had to install
insulation but he didn't. He starts work at four o'clock in the morning and we
can't sleep because it's right underneath.'

In conversation you can barely imagine that Herrmann spent half her adult
life being, as she has put it, held prisoner.

'When I was sixteen I had big problems with my mother. My mother is different; she doesn't accept all the changes. She teaches geography and languages, English and Russian. She found it much more difficult to live after The Wall.'

Carlo says he does not regard himself as East or West, he has no prejudice. Is that the future?

'Yes. European. I believe his is the generation which will just grow up thinking of themselves as Germans or Europeans. Even among the three children there is a difference. For instance, the little one – Elisa – goes to a school where the children learn Spanish and part of the lessons are in Spanish. [Birgit Kubisch, interposing: 'My friend Marina's husband is Spanish so they are entitled to send their son to a Spanish school.'] For Elisa, Honecker and the GDR and The Wall have no meaning but Hitler somehow does. He is always there. He is in the newspapers every day.

'As a family we travel a lot and the children have friends everywhere. For several months during the year we keep on travelling from one place to the other and when I say "tomorrow we go to Rome" they aren't even excited. It's like a bus ride.

'Carlo speaks fantastic Italian and did his university entrance exam in Spanish. Elisa even says "I can go to Rome on my own". They speak four languages without problems and they can switch from one to another. I don't find it easy to switch but this generation does.'

Bienvenido. Bienvenu. Benvenuto. Willkommen. Welcome, boys and girls, to the future – your future.

Pieces from an old wall …

Heike and Fulvio had a dinner party in their studio apartment on a Saturday evening in winter 2008. Those invited: Ms Kubisch (a native East Berliner, Mitte actually); her fiancé Axel (from Osnabrück, a model West German community and British military base); Richard Piesk the Engineer (East, see Chapter Nine); Ms Kubisch's friend Marina (another Eastener, and the one she's just mentioned in the Spanish context) and her Spanish husband; the author and a fellow journalist, John Woodcock, along for the trip. In mid-meal a man from the apartment upstairs (East) arrives with his son, who in a moment will play the piano in the corner of the room charmingly: a kid with talent and a future. Heike (East, of course) takes her place at one end of the long dining table and Fulvio brings all the gestures and sounds of Italy to the other end.

The conversation was a truly wondrous thing, moving in and out of different languages up and down the table as various limited vocabularies were stretched and stretched. Think the United Nations with not enough interpreters and you'll get it. Such a gathering would have been physically impossible in this apartment before 9 November 1989, and dangerous even if it had been possible. The *Stasi* noticed.

Now it's just another dinner party in a capital city, much feasting on that
international dish, pasta, and much quaffing of that international beverage, white
wine. Much laughter too, sometimes gales of it sweeping up and down the table
as the white wines stretched the vocabularies much further than they could go.

Afterwards, Richard and Axel settle down in the kitchenette to watch football on television, Germany playing Russia. That's one *Wessi* and one *Ossi* on
the same sofa enjoying *their* team against the country which from 1945 to
1994 occupied Richard's GDR and threatened Axel's FRG.

It turned out to be just another football match, actually.

Any chapter called 'Windows on the World' ought to include what happened to the GDR press, radio and television – which cumulatively must
have a much greater impact (forgive me) than artists, whatever their talent
and insights, if only in terms of frequency and numbers. *Junge Welt*, reflecting the Free German Youth organisation, sold 1.4 million copies a day. *Neues
Deutschland*, reflecting the government, sold a million. Both were rigidly controlled or more properly strangled. 'News' was frequently decided days before
and presented from on high. Neither newspaper in its traditional form had
the remotest chance once the captive audience had gone. *Junge Welt's* circulation fell to 50,000 and some speak of 20,000; Neues Deutschland was into
the 2000s selling less than 50,000. One GDR newspaper, *Berliner Zeitung*, did
survive and prospered despite passing through several hands.

The GDR broadcasting authority (*Rundfunk der DDR*) tried a variety
of tactics to stop GDR citizens watching Western television – including
jamming and turning aerials to face east. They even produced a children's
programme mimicking the one in the West but with a subtly different ending
so that, at school, young children could be asked about the particular ending
they had seen – revealing whether they'd been watching Western TV.

Eventually an accommodation was reached. GDR citizens could watch
Western TV (although it didn't reach Dresden, known as the 'valley of the
clueless') as a way of trying to satisfy, however obliquely, ordinary people's
desire to travel.

After unification it all merged with the West.

In January 2009 a British company was producing facsimile editions of
Hitler-era newspapers so that the present generation of Germans could see
what their parents and grandparents were reading. They included Nazi daily
Der Angriff (The Attack) and *Der Kämpfer* (The Fighter), ironically the newspaper of the SED.

As Heike the artist says, for her daughter Elisa 'Honecker and the GDR and
The Wall have no meaning but Hitler somehow does. He is always there. He is
in the newspapers every day.'

Yes, and here he is again.

Notes

1. Hitler's bunker, under his Chancellery, comprised thirty rooms on two levels protected by four metres of concrete. After the war the Soviet authorities made a determined attempt to blow it up and largely failed. In 1959 the GDR made their attempt and what remained was a grassy knoll in the death strip. This was levelled during construction work for modern apartments and, in the way of it, a few sections saw the light of day for the first time since the war. They were destroyed or resealed. There's nothing there now except an information board with a map on it..

2. On 10 May 1933, in front of the Humboldt University in what would become East Berlin, Nazis and students burnt books considered 'un-German' by authors including Freud, Einstein, Thomas Mann, Jack London and H.G. Wells.

3. *I Ching* (Book of Changes) is a classic Chinese text which seeks to find order from events which happen by chance.

4. *Roman* by Polanski.

5. I have not included the Albanian capital Tirana because it was remote, isolated, largely unknown and living in a different time dimension, even compared to the rest of the Eastern bloc. Private cars, for example, were all but unknown, as well as virtually everything else which makes life tolerable.

6. Ms Kubisch objected to this. 'I don't remember people walking with their heads down.' That may be because she hadn't seen the West, thronging with citizens in their fashions and their super-confident *look-at-me* body language. It may equally be that to a Westerner (like the author) the Eastern pedestrians appeared frumpy and dumpy in their stout clothes, and seemed to be averting their gazes rather than draw attention to themselves. I suspect we are both wrong: some did and some didn't; East – and West.

4

RECLAIMING 1933, AND 1945, AND 1989

The property ladder in Berlin doesn't go upwards; it goes backwards until it reaches 1933 when it stops. There is a good reason for this: the dead hand of Hitler lies upon it, and although this was followed by the dead hand of Soviet occupation and the dead hand of the GDR, you have to have a cut-off point if you are going to undertake something of unimaginable complexity: restoring property to its original owners after up to eight decades. The cut-off was 1933, when the Nazi anti-Semitic legislation became law and Jewish property was liable to confiscation.

The dead hand of Soviet occupation was more profound in its impact than anything in the Hitler era. An author, A. James McAdams, summed this up by writing:

> Under the pretext of engaging in 'land reform' in their occupation zone, Soviet authorities undertook the sweeping and, in many cases, brutal confiscation of nearly one-third of the landed property of the area that would eventually become the GDR. Some of the occupation regime's measures were directed against identifiable war criminals and former Nazi leaders and their sympathisers. Others were directed against the Prussian nobility, or Junkers, even though most representatives of this class had been killed during the war or in its immediate aftermath. But in numerous other cases, ordinary citizens became the targets of expropriation merely because their land-holdings were deemed extensive enough, in Marxist terms, to have contributed to the system of monopoly capitalism and reactionary politics that gave rise to fascism.

In practice, anyone who owned more than 100 hectares (approximately 247 acres) was vulnerable.

Often with little more than an hour to pack their belongings and with little hope of ever being compensated for their losses, thousands of landowners were deprived of farms and estates that had been passed down through families for generations. Many were then forcibly resettled to other parts of the Soviet occupation zone – ostensibly so they would not get in the way of Moscow's land measures.[1]

Beside Bersarinplatz, where Heike Herrmann lives, workers' apartment blocks do hem a roundabout. The GDR government built them and they might well stand on land owned by a Jew who fled for his life in 1933 and whose descendants now live in New York City. The descendants have been careful to keep the deeds, of course. Equally, the apartments might well stand on land owned by people who fled Communism before 1961 – when The Wall staunched the flow – and who have been careful to keep the deeds too, of course. *Grandfather's shop was just there. Our back garden was just here.*

Perhaps this applies only to part of the land which an apartment block stands on, perhaps several parts, perhaps none.

Now imagine a private house owned by a Jew who fled, enabling a German to buy it from the Nazi government. The Soviet authorities requisitioned it after 1945 but vacated it in 1949, when the original German (or his relatives) reclaimed it. The German lived there until mid-1961 when he fled West (perhaps fearing persecution, perhaps sensing The Wall which was coming). The GDR allocated the house to one of its citizens, who moved in, began paying rent and looked after the property until 1989.

Who owns it?

An article in the German Law Journal of 2004[2] approaches this with almost breathtaking understatement.

> After a restitution claim had been lodged, the relevant property office had to analyse the substance and feasibility of the claim. In some areas, like the suburbs of Berlin and central areas of cities, multiple claims seeking recovery of the same pieces of land to different 'prior' owners were sometimes encountered.

Now imagine 2.3 *million* claims, of varying degrees of provenance, from Germany and all over the world trying to reclaim all manner of property all over the territory of the GDR from 1933 onwards. Now imagine the combinations. Now imagine the ambiguities, the assortments of documents, the missing papers. Now imagine those who didn't have an authentic claim but did see the main chance. It could have become a forgers' festival, the ultimate forgers' festival.

Leuschnerdamm is complicated because of the geography and geometry, just as the Wall-StreetGallery and the apartment blocks Heike Herrmann can see are. In 1990 the unified German government found itself in a unique position: it could finally end all this *and* at the same time give restitution to those who had felt the live hand of Hitler. It was – forgive me – a monumental undertaking, but if they could do it they would take the maddening complications out of Berlin, making living in it and finding your way round it a more normal experience than it had been since the war. In short, they could cleanse the sins of history and do something of practical value for the future at the same time.

They applied very German methodology to the problem and they were going to need all the methodology they could get. As early as 1990 the West German Central Association of House, Apartment and Property Owners was predicting that at least half a million of the 3 million who had fled the GDR since 1949 would be coming back, and they'd have been careful to keep the deeds.[3]

Dr Ellen Händler is the Press Officer for the BADV (Federal Office for Central Services and Unresolved Property) and explains that it had two branches, each of around 800 people, and looking after more than property. She's a jolly person, something she surely needs to be. Everyone else in the Federal Office needs to be too.

Nobody ever thought that this would happen.

'Yes, and that applied to either side, the East and the West. There were no concepts and it had never been tried before,' she says cheerfully.

We are sitting in a conference room opposite the Alexanderplatz, a wide square and once a symbol of East Berlin modernity with its giant TV tower (topped by a revolving restaurant), world clocks, railway station, bookshops, restaurants and deluxe hotel. One of the bookshops is in a modern-looking bloc and I ask, as a sort of probe, whose land that had been built on.

'Actually,' she said, 'it's original.' The bombing and then the street fighting of spring 1945 somehow spared it so the problems of claim and counter-claim haven't arisen.

The TV tower (*Fernsehturm*) was different. It went up between 1965 and 1969 and at 365 metres (1,198ft) could be widely seen across Berlin, including the West. No doubt Walter Ulbricht[4] who ordered it to be built intended that, as well as proving East Berlin was a real capital – it's the sort of thing real capitals have – on solid foundations. There was a problem, however: when the sun shone on the stainless steel dome it created the shape of a cross. Ulbricht, promoting a quasi-aggressive form of national atheism throughout the GDR, certainly didn't intend that and Berlin wits named the tower 'Saint Walter' or 'The Pope's Revenge' (*Rache des Papstes*). The *New York Times* reported in May 1990 that a Swiss citizen, once of Berlin, did own the land (I seem to remember he had been a jeweller, or his family had had a jewellery shop) and told an interviewer 'I don't want a television tower', which was ominously ambiguous because it could mean *I don't want the tower, you can keep it* or *I don't want this tower on my land, take it down*.

The TV tower was a simple example of potentially horrific complexity. There were other early reports that Easterners now lived in dread of the Mercedes, BMW or Audi with FRG plates arriving, circling slowly, stopping outside the house they had been living in since the mid-1950s, getting out and coming up the path bearing documents which look suspiciously like deeds.

All this began, Dr Händler explains, 'in 1985 with Gorbachev and Perestroika, and that brought an opening within the GDR. People said "we want a different kind of socialism". So first of all it was a change within the GDR, and only in 1989 when The Wall came down were people talking of a reunified Germany.'

Again there were no concepts for such a thing, although Western politicians had long mouthed platitudes about it (because they were sure it wouldn't happen and they wouldn't have to face the consequences, but it was a good, perhaps necessary, thing to mouth), surveys seemed to show that West German youth thought the GDR was a foreign country (in the unlikely event they thought about it at all) and the notion of reunification had been written out of the GDR's own constitution in 1974.

In terms of practical politics, then, reunification did not exist and with each passing year it seemed to have become more and more of a chimera as the two Germanys appeared quite content not to be reunited. In retrospect, which is when everything becomes clear, this view carried two fatal flaws: nobody ever asked the GDR citizenry what they wanted, and hardly anybody sensed a catalyst was coming. The GDR economy, the one factor likely to maintain its existence apart from the Red Army, was beginning to break down.

Because there were no concepts, Dr Händler says, 'is one of the reasons why it was so peaceful. Nobody was prepared. That was a fantastic solution: the borders were open, people could go and come back, and no shots were fired. Only later did you see concepts developing about how the unification could be.'

The moment you say 'we have to have a united Germany' you also have to say 'we will tackle the property problem'.

'The problem was that there was the treaty of 1972 which clarified the relationship between the two Germanys. This treaty did not cover property.'

This was the Basic Treaty (*Vertrag über die Grundlagen der Beziehungen zwischen der Bundesrepublik Deutschland und der Deutschen Demokratischen Republik*), signed in December 1972, which meant in effect that the FRG recognised the GDR. It was a direct result of Willy Brandt's⁵ *Ostpolitik*, a way of working with the realities of Eastern Europe. The Basic Treaty gave the GDR the legitimacy it craved, and within two years Australia, Great Britain, France, Holland and the USA recognised it too. The way had been opened for both German states to join the United Nations, which happened in September 1973.

Clearly, however, property was too contentious to be covered and if you think in terms of the subsequent 2.3 million claims you can see why. The very nature and structure of the GDR, with its appetite for the state owning property, precluded it. The GDR had expropriated a lot of land and collectivised farming for, as far as the government was concerned, eternity just as they intended to govern for eternity. The notion of returning land was as dead as reunification.

The fall of The Wall suddenly exhumed both.

'Only through the collapse of the GDR was it possible to do this,' says Dr Händler.

As the two Germanys moved back towards each other from late 1989 into the early 1990s they needed a Unification Treaty and, says Dr Händler, 'immediately the question arose about property, meaning who to give property back to and who to compensate.'

Dorothea Wiktorin of the Department of Geography at Cologne University has described it.

Three months before German reunification in October 1990, the basis for a social market economy was laid. The Economic, Monetary and Social Union on 1 July 1990 set the course for privatisation of state property and the introduction of prices determined by actual supply and demand. Since the first negotiations concerning a possible reunification of both German states took place ... a central question [was] how to deal with the national property in the GDR that covered almost 40 per cent of the national territory (BMBau 1994, p. 33).[6]

Right from the beginning it was beyond question that the increase of private property and the introduction of a real estate market were central to a policy which aimed to create a unified legal and ideological system of property relations. To promote private ownership and further encourage private sector investment, state property was to be sold to the private sector.[7]

The Property Law was decided in September 1990 and, at the same time, it became a GDR law because the GDR still existed. After 3 October 1990 it was made law in the whole of Germany, the only law that applied in both German states. It dealt with three stages: from 1933 to 1945, from 1945 to 1949 and the GDR stage from 1949 to 1989.

You can see the logic behind the Property Law. Every other aspect of reunification could be settled between the FRG and the GDR quickly and amicably, provided the Allies agreed – and there was every indication they would – but property couldn't *because it didn't belong to any of them*. The property was, this time round, not for politicians to dispense but for the people who owned, or had owned it to reclaim.

The two Germanys and the four Allies met in the so-called 2 + 4 talks (spawning a cryptic barb: *what do you get when you add 4 and 2? Answer 5* – the GDR might as well not be there because nobody's paying any attention to it).

'During these talks,' Dr Händler says, 'the principles were laid out. Originally we were only dealing with the property problems in the GDR from 1949 to 1989. The first problem we encountered was the expropriation by the Soviets between 1945 and 1949.'

This, at least, had a straightforward solution. Because the Soviet Union was legally in control of its Zone and Sector, whatever property it had seized was deemed to have been within a legal framework, rendering it immune from claims. Reportedly, this was a stipulation by the Soviet government before they would agree to the Unification Treaty and you can see the logic behind that. If they didn't, they'd leave themselves open to who-knew-what, involving who-knew-what restitution.

'A decision was reached that there would be no restitution for these expropriations,' Dr Händler says.

A further and more momentous decision was reached that restitution must 'cover the period 1933 to 1945 because in the GDR there had been no basis for restitution of Jewish property seized then. The philosophy behind it was that the GDR said "we are not the legal successors of the German Reich so we are not responsible, we are only responsible for the people who live in the GDR".'

This had been a neat way for the GDR to render itself immune from the who-knew-what restitution by saying *it was nothing to do with us*. It not only saved the GDR a lot of trouble but a lot of money too.

'One factor which had to be considered was that the constitution of the GDR said all the property of the state would never become private again. That led to cases like one I know,' Dr Händler says. 'A man had his house seized by the Nazis. In the GDR he lived in the house again but it was considered property of the state – the constitution forbidding it to become private. He had to pay rent. As a result, he received a compensation pension and he still gets it today, so by living in the GDR he actually got more: there was no compensation for those who'd had similar experiences but were not living in the GDR. This had to be tackled.'

Nor, of course, was it so simple. Dorothea Wiktorin has written that beside people dispossessed without compensation were 'those owners – mostly inhabitants of the GDR – [who] had a legitimate claim to their previous property' but had been forced to give it away because of debt.

It was later transferred into national property. These cases were especially frequent in the late 1970s and early 1980s.

In view of the disproportion between income and expenditure in the housing sector, ownership was often seen as a burden requiring investment, without an adequate financial return. ... in the GDR, rents in all sectors were maintained at a very low level and were highly subsidized by the state. The rents varied from 0.80 up to 1.25 East-marks per square meter, which was approximately 4% of the average income in the GDR. On the other hand, average costs for maintaining the property came up to 7 East-marks per square meter (Schönig 1994, p. 80). As a result, private property, especially apartment houses, became dilapidated more and more and the owners gave it away to the state – often as a last resort.[8]

There's a curious and unexpected byway here. Up to 1952 a huge number of people moved out of the GDR, but if they left everything behind they were not automatically dispossessed. Their property was put under state administration but it remained theirs until the end of the GDR. 'The funny thing was,' Dr Händler says, 'that if somebody else moved in to the property, the rent was paid into a state administered account, and when the original owner came to the GDR – perhaps to visit relatives – he could withdraw the money and buy things. It meant that for forty years nothing had been done to maintain the property because there was no money.'

The dilapidation, particularly in the old quarters of Berlin and Leipzig, struck any visitor immediately and forcefully, and here is one of the explanations.

Claims for restitution (*Rückübertragungsansprüche*) had to be lodged before 31 December 1992 with an Open Property Office – there were 221 of them. The claims had essentially to be that a house or land had been seized and no compensation paid. If compensation had been paid, however low and regardless of when, the claim failed.[9]

Let's use the Alexanderplatz as a working example: to one side it is empty but people had to have owned houses, apartments and shops there up to 1949.

'There were Jewish houses – bombed – and nothing was built there during the GDR,' Dr Händler says. 'It used to be a huge parking place. No money! They would have been expropriated in the GDR but the owners would have received compensation, so if the GDR decided to build a shopping mall on it the compensation had already been paid. It's the same everywhere in the world. If a government wants to build a road or houses or a shopping mall or whatever, it can expropriate the land in the public interest [in Britain, compulsory purchase].'

This explains how the other part of the Alexanderplatz was built on.

If a house or land had been sold under the laws of the time, it remained a legal sale and the claim for that failed.

These two factors offered simplification before the real action began.

The Property Law functioned on 'three basic principles,' Dr Händler says. 'The first was restitution before compensation. The second was investment before restitution, which meant that somebody who would invest in a property would have priority over someone who only wanted compensation. The third was that we needed an agreement between those who now lived on the property and those who wanted it back.

'The consequences of these principles were 2.3 million applications for restitution from all over the world. About 98 per cent are now settled but the remaining 2 per cent are really difficult. The hardest period is between 1933 and 1945 because there are only a few survivors who can talk about the families. For all the Jewish property for which there were no applications there is an organisation, the Jewish Claims Conference, which gets all the compensation.'

There must have been a lot of people who tried to make false claims. They thought 'I can make money, I can apply, I can say we owned this'.

'We are very thorough and we only offer restitution if somebody can really prove they are entitled to it. First of all, we see if the person applying really has been affected by, literally, what you can call a damaging measure against them. That means not all property in the GDR will carry restitution or compensation, only those which are linked to the division of Germany. The most important document is an official one where it is laid down that you are the owner of the land [the deeds].'

What happens if I left the GDR in 1960 because I didn't like Socialism?

'If you sold your house to somebody else – a private person – and took the money to the FRG you wouldn't have a claim. You could only claim if you were forced the leave the house.'

How does anyone prove that?

'It has to be dealt with from case to case but you do have to prove you were forced to go.'

Before The Wall went up, the leaving was often a matter of choice?

'We really research it. If you sold the house in 1956 and only left in 1960 then probably you weren't forced, but if we see there is a time connection between selling and leaving – a short time – that might change things.'

What if I say 'I was threatened'?

'You have to prove it; you have to have eye witnesses, for instance.'

Did you go to the Stasi files?

'Of course. We went everywhere. There were Jewish address lists and Jewish expropriation lists from the finance authorities of the Nazis. Yes, we have Nazi archives. We have everything listed.'

Jewish claimants, or their descendants, didn't have to prove this forcing. The historical evidence, which assumed a legal form with the anti-Semitic laws of 1933 and which assumed a form the world can never forget after that, would make any proving an obscenity. They have to prove the property was theirs, that's all.

From 1933 to 1939 every level of government passed a whole armoury of legislation and regulation tightening, then removing, all civil and human rights for Jews. In 1933, for example, when the 523,000 Jews represented less than 1 per cent of Germany's population (160,000 were in Berlin), Jewish doctors were forbidden from working in Berlin charities. Jews were forbidden from working for the government, being admitted to the bar or holding editorial positions in the media. Naturalised Jews lost their citizenship.

From 1933, 37–38,000 Jews read the wind and got out, some tragically to other European countries which the Nazis would conquer. By the end of 1939 some 202,000 were still in Germany and 57,000 in Austria, then part of the Reich. In 1941 Jewish emigration was declared illegal, trapping the then remaining 163,000. And the Holocaust was at hand. By war's end, some 8,000 Jews contrived to survive in Berlin but the traditions and culture of centuries had been murdered in cold blood.

No wonder survivors or their relatives wanted back what was theirs.

'Can I give you a case history? I can give you hundreds! In the 1920s the S-Bahn railway system was built in and around Berlin, making the outskirts accessible. There were huge fields. Rich Jewish people bought them up and divided them into plots. They sold them to ordinary Berlin families who, with credit, could build houses. Now from 1933 on the Jews were persecuted. The ordinary working family kept on paying without knowing that the money didn't reach the Jews' accounts – the Nazis had confiscated Jewish property and got all the money. In 1945 they had it taken from them by the Soviets. Some of the land was available because the owners had moved away, and the Germans from the East, what is now Poland or Silesia, were given a piece of land. Then the GDR comes, some of these working families went to the West and somebody else had the house in, say, 1952.

'Here restitution at one level is not possible because buying it in 1952 was legal. At another level, under law there can be no rightful purchase before 1945 – meaning everything bought before 1945 was illegal, so this goes back to the Jew. One piece of land, three different cases: the original Jew, the man whose payments went to the Nazis, the man who went West in 1952.'

Someone once said that the GDR's policy of taking property under state control was the equivalent of making an omelette. Nobody in future would be able to unscramble it. This might have applied particularly to the collectivisation of farms. If the GDR towns struck the visitor as dilapidated, the countryside conveyed openness: the fields were enormous and seemed to stretch to the horizon. This was the collective in operation.

'The farming is a very exciting topic because it was a very interesting development,' Dr Händler says. 'First of all we had the land reform from 1945 onwards and every farmer would get a piece of land as his working property.

He was not allowed to sell it but he could use it free of charge, no rent. From the beginning of the 1950s there were machine and tractor stations. It meant the farmers could rent big machines and all could share them. That was the first stage towards collective farming.

'There were three stages of collective farming. The first was using the machines together. The machines were too big to be used on the small fields so they put the fields together, not always voluntarily. The second stage was to put the animals into joint farm buildings. The third stage was that the collective would own the animals and the machines.

'That was called the Collective Property. The farmers were the owners because they put their property into the cooperative, but after the fall of The Wall many of these cooperatives were destroyed. Some of the farmers wanted their piece of land back and now they could get it. This is how the Collectives broke down although there were clever people who said "we were much more profitable when we stayed together". The problem was that the West German Farming Association really saw a competitor in these cooperatives because they were much more productive. They tried to destroy the cooperatives. A big number still exist but others were sold by the farmers.'

And that's how parts of the omelette were unscrambled and parts remain scrambled.

Of the 2.3 million how many succeeded?
'A total of 25 per cent got restitution, 25 per cent compensation and 50 per cent were refused because they hadn't suffered injury or couldn't prove they had been the owners. The first claims were for 1933 and most from 1933 to 1945.'
Will you go on forever or is there a moment when you say enough?
'We hope to have finished the 75,000 outstanding cases by 2020.'
And The Wall?
'Here you have Berlin, here is The Wall and it goes through Berlin, and this is The Wall land. These pieces of land were expropriated according to GDR defence law, and with that law there was compensation. All those who had their property expropriated received compensation. If they couldn't find the owner because he had already left for the West, there was still compensation, but it was put under the administration of the state. Sometimes the cases were not dealt with properly at the time and that is why there are single places where people have lodged a claim.

'Now there is the next stage: the Wall law which says that all those who were covered by this have special dispensation to buy the land back – for instance in Bernauer Strasse. They can buy it back at 25 per cent of today's market value.'
How would they know exactly which bit was theirs?

'They had to prove it, because in the deeds there would be a record saying it had been expropriated according to the defence law. So on the one hand they can buy it back for the 25 per cent, but if there is a public interest' – it's needed for a road, an apartment block, a factory or whatever – 'they can sell it for 75 per cent of the market value. Never before have you had a law like this!'

In practical application to Dresden, Dorothea Wiktorin writes: 'Often the sizes of the empty areas were so enormous that actually only professional development corporations instead of numerous private landowners were able to create and finance a sustainable urban concept.'

Some Westerners got their property back but hadn't lived in Dresden for decades and had no intention of leaving their homes to go back there. Others, former GDR citizens, simply lacked the resources to take on the necessary restoration. 'In Dresden, like in other cities of East Germany, approximately 90 per cent of the old owners sold their former property to the highest bidder. The purchasers were mostly professional real estate agents from West Germany.'[10]

(Dresden is a complexity within the overall GDR complexity for several reasons, some unique. See Chapter Ten: The Word in Stone).

There are a couple of postscripts, both from Dr Händler, and both, as you might imagine, surprising.

'We also administer paying the compensation funds. Up to now [winter 2008] we have paid 6 billion Euros. Of course the question is: where does the money come from? The first source was the *Treuhand*, the organisation which sold the state property of the GDR. All the money went into the compensation fund. The second source was that if someone had gone to the West he was compensated by the West Germans for the property he'd left behind. If he reclaimed the property he had to pay back the original compensation. We have not spent people's taxes because of the two sources. Now it will start, however, because there is not enough money left.'

The second: 'One thing has to be said, and it is that the GDR, especially during the last years, had relationships with Jewish organisations in the USA trying to solve the property problems. There was an agreement between the GDR and the USA to try and solve the problems. Also Sweden, Denmark, Austria, Finland in the 1970s – but not with Israel for political reasons.'

The GDR never had diplomatic relations with Israel, which on the surface was both inexplicable and, in the context of German history, a scandal and a disgrace. The GDR government, however, made a distinction between Jews and Israelis.

'This approach, stemming originally from the theories of Marx and Lenin on nationalism, class struggle, and the "irreconcilable struggle between socialism and imperialism" also served to counter accusations of anti-Semitism. In this context, a specific relationship, or responsibility of the German people to the Jewish state, was denied.'[11]

Israel, backed by the Americans, was portrayed as an expansion oppressor in the Middle East (and therefore imperialist), which gave the Societ bloc ample excuse to align itself with its Arab neighbours. Individual Jews in the GDR were regarded as citizens like everybody else.

The FRG would pay enormous reparations to Israel for what the Nazis did. The GDR said, as they said about the property, *nothing to do with us.*

Stalin had been suspicious of Jews (as well as everybody else) and was preparing to kill Jewish doctors over an alleged plot when he died in 1953. That echoed into the GDR where, according to the Central Council of Jews in Germany:

> [the] police raids and persecution were halted, Community members detained in prison were set free and most of the Jews who had been expelled from the ruling party were rehabilitated. The communities, now smaller in number, were given grants to renew their synagogues, run a home for the elderly, set up a kosher butcher and maintain the Jewish Cemetery in Berlin's Weissensee.
>
> In the 1980s the GDR leadership opened up further, although it did not cease its anti-Israeli propaganda with its underlying anti-Semitic prejudice. It was only after the political revolution of 1989/90 that the new de Maizière government acknowledged 'co-responsibility for the humiliation, deportation and murder of Jewish men, women and children' and 'this burden of German history'.[12]

It was time, high time, to right these wrongs, just as it was high time to return property to the people who owned it.

Pieces from an old wall …

'East Berlin contained hundreds of memorial plaques put up by the GDR, as well as dozens of stone and bronze monuments. Everyone in East Berlin encountered some of these either in daily life or in official ceremonies. The GDR worked hard to make its memorials a part of its people's consciousness and identity.'[13]

These were inevitably anti-Fascist, lauding workers' movements and worker heroes or celebrating the GDR. What to do with them?

'It was above all Western conservative politicians who wanted to ratify their triumph by sweeping away the Communist past.'[14]

There were undercurrents. If the Western conservatives had their way they risked rising resentment in the East, where people might or might not care for the monuments but would not care for *Wessis* bossing them about yet again, but hadn't exactly this been done in 1945 when every vestige of the Nazi era was removed?

It dissolved into a mess: anything to do with border guards went, and so, amidst much acrimony, did the huge statue of Lenin in Leninplatz just off Karl-Marx-Allee. The statue, as the *Berliner Zeitung* said, 'has become the symbol of GDR history'. It was eventually dismantled and the area renamed United Nations Square. It feels very empty these days.

At the end of Unter den Linden, the Palace of the Republic had been built on the site of the old Berlin castle – whose remnants were blown up by Ulbricht in 1950. The palace was intended to be the GDR's nerve centre. Some said its modern glass façade was completely out of keeping with the sombre stone buildings around it. Some said it had too much asbestos in it and was a danger to public health. The palace went, torn down in 2008.

The bronze statues of Marx and Engels, placed in the park beside the palace, remained, although, as Berlin wits pointed out, they were facing away from it. *Nothing to do with us.*

Two Soviet war memorials – one in the West and within site of the Brandenburg Gate, the other a giant soldier holding a sword, cradling a child and trampling on a Swastika in parkland in the Treptow district – remained because the treaty which the Soviet Union accepted for German unification stipulated that they should. To reach the soldier, you walk past blocks of granite, set at regular intervals, with quotations from Stalin carved into them.

You won't find anything Hitler said carved into granite, or anything else, anywhere.

Stalin won.

The fate of the monuments can't ever alter that.

Notes

1. *Judging The Past In Unified Germany*, A. James McAdams, Cambridge University Press, 2001.
2. *German Law Journal*, Vol. 5, No. 1, 1 January 2004, 'Lost Information and Competing Interests in Restoring Germany's Dispossessed Property – The Recent Decision of the German Federal Administrative Court' by Hanri Mostert.
3. *New York Times*, 1 May 1990.
4. Walter Ulbricht (1893–1973), son of a Leipzig master tailor, fled the Nazis and spent the war in Moscow. He and a small group flew back to Berlin just before the end of the war to take control. He was First Secretary of the ruling SED until Honecker deposed him in 1971. He retained a strong Saxon accent,

an absence of humour and a propensity to make monumental speeches but, unlike the Soviets, he did not kill his opponents.

5. Willy Brandt (1913–92) was born to an unwed mother in Lübeck. A socialist, he spent the war in Norway fighting the Nazis, was mayor of West Berlin when The Wall went up and became FRG Chancellor in 1969. He had to resign when an aide was found to be working for the *Stasi*. His *Ostpolitik* proved controversial at home but won him the Nobel Peace Prize.

6. Some estimates suggest a third of the GDR land area was under government (or if you prefer communal) ownership.

7. The role of landownership in the transformation process in East German cities. Illustrated by the case study of the inner city of Dresden by Dorothea Wiktorin in www.wlu.ca/viessmann/html_pages/series_online.htm.

8. Ibid.

9. '*Volkseigentum* [people's property] refers to property, mostly of an industrial or agricultural nature and including land, buildings, installations, machinery, raw materials, industrial products, copyright and patents, which was expropriated for public purposes after the establishment of the German Democratic Republic in 1949 and during its forty-year existence. In most cases extremely low compensation, if any, was awarded.' *German Law Journal*, Mostert.

10. Wiktorin, op. cit.

11. Angelika Timm, 'The Burdened Relationship between the GDR and the State of Israel', Israel Studies, Vol. 2, No. 1, Spring 1997, pp. 22–49, Indiana University Press.

12. Central Council of Jews in Germany at www.zentralratdjuden.de/en/topic/134.html.

13. *Ghosts of Berlin*, Ladd.

14. Ibid.

5

TAKING YOUR MEDICINE

At some point a housing estate matures into a residential area. It must be something to do with the trees and bushes which grow, the gardens which are so individual and need so much creating, the personalised houses which require time to evolve and settle. Dr Wolfgang Bringmann, once a leading figure in GDR sports medicine, sits in one such, decorated inside and out by his artefacts – in fact he sits on delightful period chairs which might be a hundred years old and will certainly last another hundred.

It was said my fellow workers would not trust me any more so I replied 'Okay, if it's like this let's have a public meeting and ask them' – but of course there was no meeting. It was when this began that I really realised how much I was observed. For instance, we lived as we live now. Somebody in the Party said that as a chief executive I must not have this old furniture – the old garbage – but instead have socialist monuments, like model tanks and pictures of political leaders. You have to remember that when you were a member of the Party such things were discussed within the Party. Misbehaviour was dealt with by the Party, not within the institution where you worked. Anyway, the people I worked with said they wanted to keep me and that enabled me to stay.

Dr Bringmann is like so many other former GDR citizens: affable, approachable and blessed with a merry sense of humour. In manner and appearance he's not somebody you'd pick out in a bus queue and this makes his life story seem even more amazing – just like so many other former GDR citizens ...

His terraced house is in the borough of Treptow-Köpenick, specifically in the district of Adlershof, which places it firmly in the old East. The streets are narrow, some cobbled, giving the area a cosy, middle-class feeling. It's all neat and quiet and respectable.

Dr Bringmann's house, incidentally, has had a tortuous history which would be extremely familiar to Ellen Händler and I don't propose to go into that again here. Suffice to say Dr Bringmann owns it but not the land it stands on, although if nobody claims it within a couple of years he will own that too.

Dr Bringmann was born south of Dresden in 1934 in what is called Saxon Switzerland, but moved to a place in Brandenburg called Doberlug, with a population of 10,000, when the war came.[1]

The bombers which flew to Berlin all came over the town, British, American. The town didn't have too many air defences so that's the way they came. I could see the planes, one formation after another. It was always the same time, twelve o'clock at night. One day there were clouds and the bombers unloaded their bombs to be lighter: 240 fell on Doberlug. The Russians came in 1945. I was joining a queue at the baker's to buy bread and I saw their tanks coming down the street. The Russian soldiers didn't behave very well. They robbed flats, they drank, they molested women and raped them.

I went to school there and did my *Abitur*. I had two wishes, to be a doctor or a conductor. My father didn't want me to be a musician so it was medicine. In the GDR, if you had studied something like that, 80 per cent were students from workers' families and 20 per cent from white collar families – a deliberate policy.

When I had done my *Abitur* I had to go into the army for two years. For me it was not like punishment, I thought it was a normal development. That was 1955 so already the GDR was six years old. I took up my studies in 1957 and studied until 1963 – six years. One year before I finished studying I had already finished my doctoral thesis. In 1963 I started as a surgeon.

Bodo Radtke, the East German journalist who you treated, never forgave the West for luring doctors by offering more pay just when East Germany was weak.

'Many doctors went, all the highly qualified people. Me? I had a family, I didn't have relatives in the West and it didn't occur to me. I never had the idea because I didn't feel bad in the GDR. I was promoted, I had a very good professional life – and if you feel you have to help people it doesn't matter whether it's in the East or the West, the north or the south. Later in the GDR of course there were problems with politics and I saw it as an imperative to help those people who were weaker. [We'll be coming to this]. Of course we realised there were a lot of problems.

'I started as a surgeon but after three years I had to give up because I got eczema and I could not wash my hands with disinfectant before surgery. I became a general practitioner and then did my doctoral thesis in sports medicine. It was really a profession in the GDR and you had to learn it for four years. I was in Neubrandenburg[2] and then I was promoted to be the sports medicine chief in Berlin. A total of 220 people worked in the Sports Medicine Institute, 70 of them doctors. I also gave lectures at the Charité Hospital [the main hospital in East Berlin] and edited a journal called *Science and Sport*.

'I worked in the field of sports therapy, dealing with it from a scientific point of view, which means the application of sport in curing illness. There were twenty-three institutions in Berlin and sports medicine was divided into several branches: one took care of sport in schools, another sport for everybody – the general public – and another general competition sport. Sports clubs – for instance water sports, ice skating, swimming, soccer clubs – were all taken care of. I led the research into rowing. There was a big department analysing sports performances. It was all a huge field of work. I was not only interested in high performance sports but also in the general sports everybody could do.'

So far, it was an entirely orthodox and commendable career but, as with so much in the GDR, shadows spread in the background.

'I have never been an enemy of the GDR but I have always been critical of certain things. That's why I didn't become a professor – because the Party in Berlin would say no and they had to agree. Yes, it was necessary to be a member of the Party. You weren't asked. There was no other way and it was a normal thing to be. That's how we felt. Of course we didn't agree with everything – the fact that you were a member didn't mean that you agreed with everything.'[3]

'I had an important position but it did not entitle me to travel. There is a specific reason for it: I was registered as somebody who was a little bit critical, and so the *Stasi* categorised me as not being too reliable.'

If you applied to go, the Ministry sent the request to the Stasi *and the* Stasi *said 'he doesn't go'.*

'Everything was fed through the *Stasi*. In the beginning I was allowed to travel, which meant I went to the Summer Olympic Games in Munich in 1972, the World [Soccer] Cup in West Germany in 1974 and the Winter Olympics in Innsbruck in 1976.'

And of course 1974 was the one …

'It was the first time I had been to West Germany.'

Did you feel you were in a foreign country?

'Not really. Of course when you are in a country for a short time you don't really get to know the places, the people or the special things about it.'

But if you are in Milan for even one hour you know you are in a foreign country.

'Yes. I didn't feel that West Germany was a foreign country, because from inside myself I felt very sad that Germany had been torn apart. I was the doctor for the tourist delegation but they were not tourists, of course. There were 800 of them. We were called waving elements – we were given little flags and we all had to wave together.'

The FRG was drawn in Group A with Chile, Australia and the GDR. On 22 June the two Germanys met in front of 60,000 people in Hamburg. Both had already qualified for the next stage, which cleared that away. The match was always going to be more, anyway, and that's one of the great understatements.

How did you feel about Germany playing Germany?

'Again, I was a little sad. When Jürgen Sparwasser scored the GDR goal we were ordered not to wave so the other spectators wouldn't notice us and there wouldn't be any fighting. No riot! Then at the end of the World Cup there was the final in Munich where the FRG beat Holland 2-1 and I was very happy. I jumped up and shouted "goal, goal!" for Germany – and all the other 800 tourists sat in silence.'

The Stasi *thought you were unreliable. Was that just your general attitude or was there something specific?*

'There was no specific occasion; it was just my critical attitude. In my own institute at least thirty people worked for the *Stasi*. As the chief executive, of course, I was observed all the time. Everything critical I said was written down by somebody and, from 1980, there was no travelling any more.

'Normally about thirty people from the institute were allowed to travel. Every January for years and years I had to write a judgement on each of these thirty people. For instance, I had to say whether they were politically reliable or not, and that there was no danger they wouldn't come back. I had to write this down. I gave my judgements to the Sports Executive and they would immediately be given to the *Stasi*. From 1980 I knew it was pointless to ask so I didn't, and that's when I knew they did not trust me any more.'

The concept that Dr Bringmann could judge how reliable the thirty were but that he himself, doing the judging, was unreliable is very GDR.

'Another example of the *Stasi* – the doping. In my institute there was doping in the high performance sports, of course. We weren't the ones who said "let's do this", it was a central provision and it came from above. There was no private doping, it was centrally regulated and controlled. Nor was there specific Berlin doping, say – it was a government decision. The term doping was used but not with the sports people, who would be told they were getting vitamins. It meant publicly – for the public – there was no doping.

'I don't want to talk myself out of it, but I was against it. This was also known to the *Stasi* – that I opposed it. The drugs were obtained from above and everyone involved was categorised as holding a secret. Those doing the doping in my institute had secret books which were locked away. Since I wasn't considered reliable I was not a holder of the secret so I, as the boss, didn't know who was doping. I was very satisfied with that!

'When all the sports medicine executives met there would be a point on the agenda that was called doping. I had to leave the room and go for a walk; I wasn't allowed to stay for that item. Suppose we were meeting in Leipzig.

One of the people under me – who did hold the secret – had to travel down for the item, which might last half an hour, then he went back to Berlin and I went back into the meeting.'

Can you give an example of why they thought you were unreliable?

'Yes. In the 1980s there was a South Korean passenger aircraft which flew the wrong route and went over Russia and it was shot down. There was a meeting at the institute and during it I said "this is an irresponsible, inhuman act".'[4]

At this point Dr Bringmann's wife Inge, who had passed around cakes and coffee before the talking began and then sat silently right through (except for laughing gently a time or two), suddenly exclaimed 'thank God we have over-come all this.' She paused, her thinking moving on to post-1989. 'We didn't go and have a look at the *Stasi* file; we don't want to know anything about it. We suspect certain people, we know certain friends who might have been but we don't want to know exactly. We don't want to discover more. Yes, we are still friends because we cut all that off and made a new beginning.'

What Inge said is only this paragraph of simple words you've just read but they cover a lot of terrain, past, present and future – and when a gentle, patient woman like her raises her voice, listen.

Dr Bringmann insists: 'I was always *expected* to react differently so I always reacted in a way they didn't expect from someone in my position. For instance, if sports officials had run into trouble I'd try and protect them.

'I want to add something about the *Stasi* having observed me for long years: I know somebody who started working in the institute as a personnel chief and he came from outside. I didn't employ him. I know he came from the Party and I know he came with only one task, to write everything down that I said. They really did write down everything I said.

'In 1985 there was an intrigue against me and overnight I lost my position. It started with the Party in Berlin. I had friends who confirmed that there was an official resolution saying "he must be liquidated" – since I was well known and diligent they tried to force me to move away from Berlin. My friends prevented that. One of them came and said "continue working and don't leave the Party, don't apply to leave the country. If you do this it will definitely be the end for you. Do not do it." So they gave me a job in the central sports medicine leadership, and all the other positions I held which didn't have to do with Berlin I could keep them all. Many people would ask "why are you not the chief executive of sports medicine in Berlin?" and the only response I could make was "it had to be".

'From the day I was pushed out of the institution I stopped going to any meetings, I stopped going to the socialist demonstrations and I stopped wear-ing the Party badge. Some of the officials said "you are not dressed correctly" because I didn't have the Party badge. Shortly before The Wall came down I found the courage to leave the Party.'

The night The Wall came down, what do you think the man who said you should have socialist monuments was thinking? 'This is not good news'?

'Yes! When it all came to an end there were a lot of discussions. I thought of something which, unfortunately, did not come true. I said "it's wonderful luck that it is in my lifetime I can take part in forming a united Germany" – but we were not in a position to do that. It was taken away and done by the political parties, done from the West, not by the people.

'Anyway, now The Wall comes down. It was a very specific development afterwards that the executive layers in all the Eastern institutions were dismantled. Since the Party had no influence any more, they were all changed. The trade unions voted off the person who got the position after me. He was replaced. In November 1989 I was re-elected with 99 per cent of the vote, but sports medicine in the GDR was being ended. I got a new working contract from the West Berlin Senate – to dismantle the institute.

'Until 3 October 1991 I did that and took everything to the garbage dump. That was everything, even completely new electro-cardiac machines which had not been unwrapped, medical equipment, office equipment, laboratory equipment. I spent 44,000 D-marks in transport costs! I had three people to help me with the whole thing, a secretary, a driver and an economist.

'I'd say it was political. It was the spleen [anger] of the West Germans, who didn't want anything from the GDR.

'I was very sad. When I came to Berlin originally we were 36 people in sports medicine and in the end 220, so you can say it was my life's work. We were a highly specialised institute. Physically I built it all up and physically I took it to the dump. It had to be stripped bare, in the same way as when you sell an apartment. Even the dust must be gone! The German word is *besenrein*, completely empty and clean.

'What I did do, in a little bit of opposition again, was to keep a bit of the equipment so that some of my former workers could continue their careers. It saved fourteen or fifteen surgeries. The scientific journal was closed.'

Dr Bringmann faced a further problem. 'I had written those reports [on people's reliability if they travelled] and given them to my superiors and they had given them to the *Stasi*. So when I had to make up my mind what to do after the *Wende* it was clear to me that I could not apply for a job with a state organisation. I could not keep my mouth shut in the GDR and not here, either, and as soon as I got into trouble they'd find out there are these documents. Then they'd accuse me of being *Stasi*. That's why I opened a general practice in Mitte. It is what we call a domestic practitioner.'

You were not just a doctor, you were a counsellor.

'Yes, naturally. People had special problems, like they were unemployed and had never imagined they could be unemployed – many, many, many of them. In the East it was a relationship of trust between doctor and patient.

I tried to talk to them, support them. Sometimes I'd transfer them to a psychologist and sometimes I tried to help them personally. I have contacts so maybe I'd know somebody who could help them, but I have to say there have been enormous cutbacks compared to the GDR. In the GDR we had a completely free health system and now we have typically two-class medicine. Actually there are three: the person with normal insurance, and it is getting worse and worse and worse for them. Then there is the privately insured person who is a little better off and then there are those who have a lot of money and who can buy everything.'

Dr Bringmann points out that 'we rented this house in the GDR for 64 East Marks a month and the state would subsidise it.'

But subsidise it with what?

'Remember I had 225 workers at the institute and I earned 2,000 East Marks. Today it would be the equivalent of 15,000 Euros for the same kind of work and responsibilities. When I give a lecture today I get maybe 300, maybe 400 Euros and in GDR times I got 25 East Marks. The money they saved like this they put into subsidies.'

But it's not enough money to buy the modern drugs that get better all the time but cost more all the time.

'We had the modern equipment.'

That equipment will be out of date in two years or whatever and you have to have more money to buy the newest equipment.

'It was much slower in the GDR. The drugs were very cheap and we had about one-tenth of the drugs that we have today – today we have too many. There are about twenty companies producing the same kind of drugs.'

It's almost twenty years now. What do you think?

'I can say that I have been successful again after the *Wende* because it was not a big change for me in terms of my own commitment, my own energy, my own initiative. I have always been like this. I found a lot of new fields I could work in – specialising in laser therapy – and I am as active as I have been before. I'm a part-time doctor now and lecture twice a week at a school for physiotherapy. On Wednesday from 7.30 a.m. until 6 p.m. I work in a practice. On the weekends I often go to seminars – and to Austria, Switzerland, within Germany. I have been to Costa Rica this year. To travel, all I need to take is my passport! As a whole we are satisfied.'

Is that true of the people who live around here?

'If I had to do a résumé I would say the Federal Republic of Germany is different but not better. There were good aspects in the GDR, like the social services, the security people had, the safety nets. This is not good here, but the quality of life – like travelling – is far better. In the GDR the people were much more trusting towards each other, they supported each other and today I don't know the neighbours. There is no togetherness in society.'

Was the ordinary person who just wanted to go rowing or play football better off in the GDR than they are now?

'Yes, yes, because the places where you would go to row or swim were subsidised by the state and open to everybody, and if they found someone who was very talented they could progress.'

Does that not happen now?

'The ordinary person who wants to play sport doesn't have much money. You didn't have to make contributions for children. Everything was free of charge.'

This demands examination, especially in the medical field, because nothing is cost-free. In Dr Bringmann's example he was underpaid for lectures and that money went into subsidies. The underpayment was his cost. It's a question of political philosophy how you evaluate this method – personal loss, communal gain – and the story of the Western democracies since the war has been how, and where, you hold the balance. The GDR didn't really do balances at one level – you build The Wall or you don't, you shoot people trying to cross it or you don't, you take all industry under state control or you don't – but ultimately it did have to try it and balance the funds available and what they were spent on.

Eric M. Katz wrote in 1994[5]:

> The GDR, as a centrally planned economy, operated a single, State-managed social insurance mechanism that provided comprehensive health care benefits to virtually the entire population. Workers paid a flat 10 percent of gross wages, up to a total of 60 GDR Marks monthly, for an insurance scheme that included comprehensive health care benefits as well as pension, disability, and other protections. The State-controlled workplace contributed an equal amount and the State itself guaranteed the fiscal health of the plan and all benefits. High-wage workers (more than 600 GDR Marks per month) were permitted to secure an expanded benefits package for an additional 10 percent deduction. Dependents were automatically covered, as well as those in retirement or on disability, resulting in nearly universal coverage.

Katz added that the GDR 'pharmacy distribution system was well-developed' with over 1,600 retail pharmacies and 400 dispensaries. It had a pharmacist for every 4,100 people, about the same as the FRG, but the 'number of available products was lower, however, with only about 2,000 formulations on the market, including about 200 homeopathic drugs and 450 non-prescription preparations'.

In the 1980s the cost of drugs rose inexorably, an outpatient costing 232 East Marks in 1985 and 295 when The Wall fell.

Overall, the two Germanys spent about the same pro rata on health care.

Life expectancy in the GDR was 69.9 for men and 76.0 for women, 72.2 and 78.9 in the FRG.

GDR infant mortality was 0.92 per 100 in 1986, FRG 0.85 (although it had been 7.2 in the GDR in 1950, and its fall to 0.92 was proportionally greater than the FRG's).

The GDR had 2.3 physicians per 1,000 people, the FRG 2.6.

The GDR had 10.6 hospital beds per 1,000 people, the FRG 11.8.

It led to a conclusion.

> If the GDR enjoyed a similar volume of health services to the FRG but had much lower health expenditures per capita, then the prices of health services must have been much lower in the GDR. ... it is not clear ... that the health care system of the former GDR did not work. Improvements to health status in eastern Germany seem to have kept up, more or less, with those in western Germany, despite the fact that the standard of living grew much more slowly in the East.[6]

Reunification involved creating 199 new statutory funds like the 1,138 in the FRG instead of the GDR's blanket cover. The funds reflected, in premiums and benefits, the FRG's.

Dr Ulrich Bartel, with spontaneous contributions from his wife Anne, explores aspects of all this because he was a leading GDR gynaecologist at the Charité Hospital in East Berlin.

He lives in Eberswalde-Finow, a town near the autobahn which snakes up through the countryside to Stettin and the Polish border. Finow would, in GDR times, have been one of those sleeping, silent communities gathered round a badly maintained country road with, likely, mud from tractor tyres on it. Eberswalde is no longer like that, and you can tell before you reach it because there's a supermarket on open land, shimmering with promise, and the obligatory vastness of a car park in front of it.

The Bartels met at a university carnival in 1968 and married in 1974. They have a very pleasant, spacious detached house with a long garden, a therapeutic swimming pool for a daughter badly hurt in a traffic accident, an abundance of fruit trees. Other spacious detached houses surround it. Eberswalde could be anywhere in the West.

Dr Bartel was 'born in 1947 in the south part of Brandenburg, the Soviet Zone. That was two years before the GDR was founded so I grew up in the GDR. I never went to the West. Why a gynaecologist? I always wanted to study medicine and I knew I wanted to operate on people. I started studying in Dresden then Berlin. I qualified in 1972 and had the choice to do my national service, which was obligatory, as a soldier or work as a military doctor. I was lucky to be able to do that.

'I was twenty-seven when I started work at the Charité, which was next to The Wall. In the beginning there was only one building where you could see across it. The big Charité building was finished in 1981 and could see The West but it was far away. Somehow you lived with The Wall and didn't really think about it.'

Anne: 'I had never been there and I didn't want to go there. I wanted to see other countries but West Germany, no. It was only in my thoughts sometimes – I could go to Bulgaria, Russia and Poland and I went. This was enough for me.'

You thought West Berlin was a foreign country, which you could see but not go to and suddenly it came to you, bringing big, big change.

Anne: 'The change was bad, the change was difficult although one thing you didn't have was a language barrier. Actually, we found out it was the same language but it wasn't the same language.'

Ulrich: 'The difference between the Charité and the West wasn't so big. When The Wall came down I went to work in a clinic in the West for five years and the difference wasn't that striking.'

But in the West people doing research could contact each other all the time, exchange ideas, go to conferences, send each other letters. You couldn't.

'We had access to Western literature but, except for a few people here, no human contacts were allowed. I was not one of them. I only went to the West once, four weeks before The Wall came down – Amsterdam – but people came to conferences and meetings here. I applied twice as a private person to see some relatives on my father's side and twice I was refused.

'I was invited to Amsterdam. It was the only way to go – you needed an invitation. I got a little money from the Dutch. I went by train and I liked it a lot. The prostitutes [in the shop windows]? That was a new experience, that was something you wouldn't find in the East! You knew that there were prostitutes in the East but not in public. When I saw them in the windows I felt a bit strange. Unpleasant. When I went to Hamburg later I had the same feeling. I didn't like it at all. It was part of the contrast with East Berlin but it happened very quickly in the East when The Wall came down, in Oranienburger Strasse.

'When I went to Amsterdam I had no idea The Wall was going to open, but looking back I remember something strange. In 1988 I went to Hungary for a gynaecologist's congress and there I met someone who had visited us professionally in the Charité. He said "have you heard that Hungary is going to open the border with Austria next year?" – so in Hungary there was already a rumour that it would happen. When I got home I told Anne and she said "then we will not be allowed to go to Hungary anymore".

'We knew the problems would grow and it was going to be more difficult if they closed off Hungary to get to the other countries down there like

Bulgaria. It was clear to me that if they really opened the border to Austria that would be the beginning of the end. The night The Wall fell I was working on a dissertation, sitting at the desk. I understood the GDR was finished, nothing to be saved. No rescue.'

Anne: 'I was resting in bed. Our little daughter came to me and said "mummy, they've said during the football match on television that the people are on the streets singing." None of the usual people were at my local garage. I asked someone where they'd gone and I was told "to the West!" Then my big daughter said "I'm going to the West, I'm going to the West!" I said "no, no, it is very dangerous – maybe it is a trick. The *Stasi* guys, they want to know who is going", so we went together through the Invalidenstrasse checkpoint.[7] I can't say what I thought. There were so many people, and some of them congratulated us. There was champagne and flowers. One man gave my daughter 20 D-marks as a gift. I can remember standing in the flower shop – this was November – and they had roses and everything, whereas in the winter we would only have certain kinds of flowers. And of course there was fruit: oranges and peaches, and we didn't really know that. Somebody offered to take us in their car to a bank to get the 100 D-marks welcome money. We bought a Barbie doll for the younger daughter and a jacket for her too. Then we went home.'

Ulrich reflects that 'somehow you had grown to be immune to the West being over there. You knew a different country was there but somehow you had grown to accept it, and accept it was just not possible to go there, so it was very strange for me when I did go there, and hard for me to describe.'

What was the first change for you professionally?

'Getting the possibility to work in West Berlin. I hadn't applied for a job and it was rather a coincidence that one came up. People were leaving the Charité and I knew there were going to be a lot of problems. By this time I had become a senior physician. I went to Charlottenburg to work in a clinic. The operations were the same, the techniques were the same, the equipment was better and was different but your own hands don't change – and they are the most important thing.

'There was a transition time before hospitals in the East were run like in the West. All the administrative things were difficult, financial issues.'

What about an ordinary doctor in, say, Magdeburg?

'You wouldn't have had such a big choice but the essential drugs would be there in the GDR.'

After 9 November you did have the choice.

'It was difficult to sort out the overwhelming choice of drugs and medicine, difficult just to find your way through this jungle. Only later did you notice that some of the drugs were very expensive – but not in the beginning when it was more or less a question of finding your way through.'

You were a specialist and you could read Western literature. You knew about the research and developments but the doctor in Magdeburg, he didn't know.

'The pharmaceutical representatives, they came very quickly to sell you things. Very quickly they came, in cars.'

Medicine ought to be above politics but is it?

'Unfortunately not. It should be. There is the problem of finance. In the GDR there was finance for research areas and other things. We also got foreign currency for research. The money to finance the research was certainly very difficult but a patient would get all the treatment he needed. I think there is an underlying disappointment that today maybe you don't get the treatment because it is too expensive.

'After The Wall came down there was a political cleansing, everything was *tumbling*. It was a very distressing time. There was the ethical commission and professors and others – senior physicians, bosses – were cleared out for political reasons, although most of them found something new.'

One source put it like this:

[the] institutional challenge is extending the old *Länder* health care system based on statutory health insurance to the new *Länder*. Achieving this goal has meant a complete overhaul of the GDR's state-run and highly centralised system; the introduction of insurance funds, private insurance, and voluntary organizations; and the training of physicians to become fee-for-service entrepreneurs, rather than salaried state employees as they were under the old system.[8]

What do you think now?

'I find it good that the division has been overcome but, looking back, I would have wished that both systems had more time to grow together. Speaking as a physician, if you leave out all the ideological things – the political questions – there were many things in the GDR that were good. It's not really an issue of comparing the GDR with the West but rather the whole development.'

Anne: 'I was always very well treated in the East, above all from a human point of view. I never had the feeling that a physician would be in a position not to give me the best treatment. Now I don't have private insurance and only recently I found myself in a position where my doctor told me he cannot give me the drugs I need because I haven't private insurance. This is a question of human dignity. You wouldn't have this in the GDR. You would not think of money in terms of your medication. I am speaking in terms of equal treatment. If the GDR couldn't afford a drug, nobody would get it. It was difficult in the GDR, of course, and there were privileged people [like the *Stasi*] but you would not have the experience of going to your doctor and have him say "I cannot give you the drugs because you don't have the right insurance". It couldn't happen.'

Ulrich: 'What the politicians seem to neglect is that we have a two-tier medical system, and the cost of the drugs and the insurance means the gap widens all the time.'

What about adjusting to the West in general – say, the shopping?

Anne: 'I adapted but you don't really have the experience of success![9] There is everything! You can buy whatever you want. However, in this region we have an unemployment rate of 20 per cent, more than 20 per cent and only the big supermarkets survive. All the little shops are gone. You see people going round saying "what is the cheapest that I can afford?" – not for the luxuries but the basic things. We had to learn about advertising – new things which might not be good but people trying to sell them to us. Certainly after The Wall came down you'd step into a lot of traps.'

Do you feel just German now?

Ulrich: 'Yes, I would say so.'

Anne: 'I feel a human being – a German, but with different roots.'

If we had a magic wand and waving it would take you back to 8 November 1989, do you want to go?

Anne: 'OK, 9 November follows 8 November! But I miss a lot of things that were good in the GDR in my childhood and youth. You felt protected, no [street] drugs and everyone had a job. Nobody was left alone if they had a problem. There were measures taken by the state if somebody was an alcoholic and mechanisms to integrate people back into everyday life who had just come out of prison. I miss the warmth of the people and the feeling of responsibility towards each other. Take my granddaughter. Maybe her parents will have to tell her she can't go to that school because they can't afford it; she'll have to go to another one. In the GDR everyone had the same chance. You couldn't buy the education of your children.'

In everything there is a plus and a minus.

Anne: 'There is a bit of nostalgia, of course, but now there are also things I like. I can travel although I know that many people can't travel because they don't have the money. Meanwhile, in the West things have changed as well: many factories have closed down and there is unemployment.'

That was the plus and minus, that was taking the medicine.

Notes

1. Initially there were two neighbouring towns, Doberlug and Kirchhain. They merged in 1950.

2. Neubrandenburg is an ancient city west of Berlin on the shore of Lake Tollense.

3. People who have not lived under a totalitarian regime do not confront, and therefore fully comprehend, the compromises which must be made to sustain a career. In the 1930s, thousands joined the Nazi Party because it was the only way to advance. It did not make them Nazis in the true sense, although it did make them guilty by association. In the 1950s, and especially the 1960s (after The Wall), thousands joined the Communist Party in the GDR because, again, it was the only way to advance. It did not make them communists in the true sense, although it did make them guilty by association – if you believe the Party was something bad. Separating the believers from the fellow-travellers was never going to be easy, in 1945 or 1989. In 1945, and subsequently, the GDR was extremely thorough in prosecuting (and banishing) members of the Nazi Party. The West was more lenient (and arguably pragmatic) – and echoes of that were heard in Iraq when Saddam Hussein was deposed and the Iraqi army disbanded, leaving – literally – a terrible vacuum.

4. A Korean Air Lines Jumbo jet was shot down by a MiG fighter in September 1983 after it strayed into Soviet airspace over Sakhalin Island. All 269 passengers and crew died and the incident produced a worldwide storm of protest. The Soviet government claimed the plane had been deliberately flown into Soviet airspace at the behest of the Americans to test Soviet response capabilities.

5. *Health Care Financing Review*, Spring 1994, by Eric M. Katz.

6. *Health Care Financing Review*, Spring 1991, by Jeremy W. Hurst.

7. This was more than strength in numbers. Nobody knew if the opening of The Wall would be permanent, last just this one night or be rescinded immediately, marooning any GDR citizen who happened to be in the West. They might be refused readmission or be readmitted into the embrace of the *Stasi*. At least if a family went they'd be marooned together, not separated.

8. *Germany Current Health Care Issues and Outlook for the Future*, http://www. photius.com/countries/germany/society/germanysocietycurrent health_ care_~1375.html.

9. Success in terms of beating the shortages, the queues and the lack of goods by finding something desirable – and getting it.

6

THE OTHER HISTORY LESSONS

That November in 1990, the autobahn from Frankfurt (Oder) uncoiled, just as it had done from the 1930s, across the Brandenburg Plain towards Berlin some 100km away. It followed the gentle contours of the land rather than being rammed through, wide and level, in the modern way.

The sky-blue Trabant which put-put-puttered along it, past typically slumbering GDR villages – Biegen and Briesen, Langewahl and Rauen – had teachers in it and they were travelling towards their future and a great mystery. They were very active teachers who had organised activities for the children at their own school and they were going to West Berlin to learn.

'It was a time without rules and the school authorities had to form themselves,' Kerstin Paust-Loch, one of the teachers in the Trabant, says. 'The staff of teachers sat down and started to think about the future. There were no instructions coming from [East] Berlin – well, maybe there were orders but if there were we didn't know about them, so we discussed what kind of school we would become. We didn't have a clue what the West German school system was like. It was completely different and all I knew about it was what my cousin told me.'

They had already telephoned schools in West Berlin to ask if they could come to have a look, and the schools were delighted to help.

'We visited different kinds of schools. The people were all very friendly, they welcomed us and showed us around. They explained what a Gymnasium was.'

They learnt it was a state-maintained secondary school which prepared students for higher academic education. It might be one of three kinds, classical, modern or science and maths.

'They explained that trade unions did some further education courses in West Berlin and West Germany so you could go on them. When we got back we really had information about different kinds of schools and we told our colleagues about everything we had seen. Then when we had talked about it we decided our school would be a *Gesamtschule* [equivalent to a British comprehensive].'

At this point you were able to choose?

'We believed we could and we were lucky. The politics were orientated towards the *Gesamtschule* because the Social Democrats were the ruling party in Brandenburg and they decided the region would be mainly *Gesamtschule*. My colleagues said "you have found all this out and we want you to take over the school as deputy director".'

In fact it became Friedrichsgymnasium. Of that, more in a moment.

Paust-Loch is a lively lady who laughs a great deal and you can tell in a moment she loves teaching for itself. More than that, she is one of those people – the kind from the GDR you hear so little about – who saw opportunity in chaos and did something about it, specifically in the sky-blue Trabi down the autobahn.

As in so many other fields, optimism was about to be tested, perhaps to destruction, because the two Germanys had naturally and inevitably evolved their own educational systems. Each reflected the demands and mentality of its parent state. That meant, in practice, their approaches were polar opposites and – again as in so many other fields – nobody had even contemplated putting them together never mind planned for it. And now you know why Paust-Loch speaks of a time without rules. For a GDR teacher to find herself in this situation was intoxicating but frightening after the centralised system she had known, which had lots and lots of rules.

The FRG educational system was organised to give the *Länder* sovereignty. Children started at six and from grades one through four attended elementary school (*Grundschule*) with a common curriculum. They separated by ability, or what their families wanted, into three streams, *Hauptschule, Realschule* or *Gymnasium.*

The *Hauptschule*, usually grades five to nine, taught the same subjects as the other two but more slowly. The *Realschule*, usually grades five to ten, was the path towards schools which teach job skills. The *Gymnasium*, usually grades five to thirteen, was the path towards a degree, the *Abitur* and university.[1]

The GDR educational system was highly centralised, rigidly controlled and designed to serve the needs of the state. In 1959 the 'ten-grade general education polytechnic high school (*Polytechnische Oberschule*) became the standard or compulsory state school. Since 1966, after successful completion of the polytechnic high school, pupils who fulfilled certain selection criteria could transfer to the expanded high school (*Erweiterte Oberschule*) which led to the *Hochschulreife* (higher education entrance qualification) after grade 12.'[2]

Ursula, a teacher trainer, explains that 'the GDR teacher was responsible for her children, for the achievements, for the success of her children. She had to take the rap if children failed to reach the class objectives. It was not the children but the teacher who had to demonstrate how she had looked after these children, how she had helped them and so on.'[3]

The GDR inherited seven universities[4] and many colleges, including technical, art and music. Rather than found new universities it concentrated on what have been called specialised higher education institutes. These were markedly smaller than in the FRG (in 1990, 2,500 students against 6,400) and reached by fewer students than in the FRG (13 per cent against 25 per cent).

Education did reflect the demands and mentality of the state, which directed students into courses answering the needs of the economy rather than the humanities. The higher institutions had a favourable ratio of teachers-students (1:6) measured against the FRG (1:15).

'The general conditions were, in some respects, more favourable for students in the GDR. Nearly all students received a scholarship and had the option to live in student accommodation. Students were expected to complete their course of study in the time allocated without changing their subject. Because of these conditions, the number of graduates was relatively high, and in this context "higher education in the GDR seems much more efficient than in Western Germany where 30–40 per cent of the students do not graduate".' (Bieber, 1994, p. 63).[5]

The educational system was, then, the polar opposite to the FRG.

'The task of the whole of education consisted in forming young people to become *convinced socialist citizens* according to the programme of the former socialist party (SED). This meant that the teachers … should see their job as a political task for the working class.'[6]

Another source uses almost the same initial phrase. 'The task of the higher education institutions in the GDR was – as the Decree on Higher Education of 1970 states – to educate and train "highly qualified specialists with a profound socialist class consciousness". Students were in general trained for specific professions and in this respect higher education institutions can be seen as training institutions.'[7]

This was reflected in teacher training which, since 1982, had been five-year courses at university for secondary teachers and training colleges for elementary school teachers. This, too, was centralised and the courses contained Marxism-Leninism, teaching itself, physical education, sport and Russian (with English as a second choice). It promoted close relationships between schools and universities while connecting theory with practicality.

The advantages of this are obvious but it was all to be swept away and the FRG system swiftly imposed.

Ursula gives this a human dimension, explaining that the teachers 'quickly realised' that their responsibility to and for the pupil was no longer required. They had become 'conveyors of knowledge and the educational virtues' but 'the efforts on behalf of each individual child … [have] largely been lost and the result is that the school and the job of the teacher have lost out.' Ursula gives the motive: political.[8]

It is a sentiment echoed by Dr Marlis Dürkop-Leptihn, retired president of the Humboldt University in Berlin. 'Inspired by the opportunities for reform presented by German reunification, some of us actually thought for a time that the restructuring of East German universities would represent a chance to renew the West German university system as well. In retrospect, this proved to be a romantic view of the situation that greatly overestimated the scope of action available to reformers from the East and West.

'Every day, highly motivated reformers from the East had to struggle with the insults and humiliations which resulted from the economic collapse of the GDR. The East German universities themselves served as poor examples for future reform: they had strictly limited access to higher education, were restricted by a dual-structure of scholars and political party, and had severed the international ties of their students and professors. On top of this came the terrible state of university buildings and equipment.'[9]

Kerstin Paust-Loch was born in 1954 in 'Karl-Marx-Stadt, now Chemnitz' – saying this makes her giggle. 'It was Karl-Marx-Stadt when I was born so that's where I was born.'

Are you a political person?

'Oh! Actually yes, because you cannot be apolitical in my profession. I am always dealing with young people, and young people ask questions.'

We are sitting in the apartment she and husband Rudolf share in a residential area of Frankfurt (Oder). The suburb looks prosperous these days, the buildings well-maintained, the gardens neat. There's a sunken lake opposite where people have little summer houses. Down the street there's a chic coffee house.

'I began as a teacher in 1977 in Berlin – Prenzlauerberg. I taught German and a little history to pupils who were between twelve and nineteen. I was happy. We came to Frankfurt (Oder) in 1979. That year our second daughter was born and in 1980 I started working in a school here. It's the school I still work at. I had pupils between twelve and sixteen, mostly teaching German.'

Did you think The Wall was going to come down?

'I could not imagine it. I had never been to the West – not allowed. My husband, yes, he had been.'

Rudolf managed it because he was researching a biography of Karl Georg Büchner (1813–37), dramatist and writer of prose from Darmstadt. 'I went to an archive in Darmstadt one year before The Wall came down. I was allowed to buy a ticket. There was an exhibition and I had written an article about it which appeared in Darmstadt. I was paid 500 D-marks.

'That was the first time I had been to the West and I was then forty-eight. Well, it wasn't exactly the first time because I'd been there in 1960. I'd started as a student and I was studying German theatre. I went on a very cheap night flight from Tempelhof to Hannover to visit a friend and I stayed there about four weeks. I hitchhiked through western Germany. In 1961 I went to Hannover again and then Rome. A few days after I came back The Wall went up.

'I got to Darmstadt at night and the exhibition had already closed. I had a rucksack and I stayed about 10km away. I had a "secret" address[10] of a person from long before and I walked through the countryside to get there. Because I knew their name I had someone to ask for. I got lodgings.

'In Darmstadt I thought how beautifully they had refurbished the old castle because there had been a huge amount of bombing. I was very sad to find that Büchner's birthplace had been destroyed during it and they hadn't retained anything. Terrible to see this. The aristocratic castle had been put back in order but Büchner – all gone. Darmstadt had a lot of culture.'

Kerstin wanted to accompany him, of course, but 'I couldn't go, no. It wasn't difficult when he came back because he was very good at describing the things he'd seen. I thought I'd get to the West, yes, but as an old age pensioner. You did have the possibility of going if you had family there, and I had an aunt and a cousin in Düsseldorf. There was a very intensive contact between us but I had accepted the way it was: they would come here if we wanted to see each other. They came. I didn't ask for permission to go because there wasn't really an occasion, a big anniversary or anything like that.'[11]

When you were teaching history you were teaching a very specific version of history.

'Yes, in a certain way. It was about all the workers' movements and all the revolutions that led to the workers' movements – the French Revolution in 1789, for example. No English Revolution!'

At school, did you get asked questions that you couldn't answer?

'Yes, of course there were, but I always tried to find answers.'

I'm not thinking just about political questions but, say, sex.

'Naturally.'

And drugs – 'what are they?'

'Yes. Questions about everything.'

What about the West, because there was no escape from the fact that West Germany had really been a big success.

'We were in a bilateral world and that was a part of the lessons, but they were also about telling the pupils about the advantages of the GDR, like the social justice system. These were the lessons where there were a lot of questions.'

How could you answer them?

'You develop a strategy [much laughter]. If you had a good relationship with your pupils you could be very open. Well, relatively open. For my part

I had a gentleman's agreement with the pupils so if there wasn't somebody [like an inspector] at the back of the class we would be open, if there was we wouldn't.'

What if somebody asked about The Wall?

'We had a lesson on The Wall. It was in the curriculum and we called it the Anti-fascist Wall' (*Antifaschistischer schutzwall*).

What about specific questions like 'if it's to keep people out, how come we can't cross it? They can come here on holiday but we can't go there ...'

'One of the questions asked very often was "if there is so much unemployment in the West why don't they come and work here?"'

And your answer was?

'I'd say something like "I don't really know!"'

You must have realised you were not telling the truth about The Wall.

'I didn't really have the feeling that I wasn't telling the truth.'

But it wasn't an anti-fascist wall.

'Maybe, but it is also a fact that there were a number of Fascists left in 1960–61 when it was built. Of course it was difficult and The Wall wasn't really a solution. You can't keep people apart. Well, it did do but not forever.

'I was ironing when The Wall came down. My feelings are difficult to describe. We had been worrying during the weeks before because on television we had seen how GDR people threw their children over the embassy gates [in Prague] and all the young people were leaving the country. It was very shocking to see this. History became a mechanism: something happened, you couldn't really control it and it all happened very fast. I heard Schabowski's famous sentence and I said to my husband "you will see, we will be one Germany again" and he said "no, that won't happen, that's not going to happen".'

Rudolf confirms that 'I didn't believe it was the end, because the living conditions of the people were not bad enough to terminate the whole thing. That's why I didn't believe it would happen. Of course we had shortages – fruit, for example – but I didn't really think this was a reason. We'd be doing the dishes, we'd be talking and we'd say "if the stagnation goes on something will happen" but I thought if there is still a chicken in the farmer's pot there won't be a revolution.'

'He's the clever one, I'm more emotional,' Kerstin says, 'but I got it right [laughter]. In the 1980s there'd been a lot of hope and I was certainly optimistic because I thought there would be changes. We had had stagnation before. Maybe it was because I was not so materialistically orientated – I was a school teacher.

'I didn't really think that the West would come and take over. I am a bit starry-eyed and Rudolf is more critical. I thought it would be a victory of reason and that aspects of the East – like kindergartens – would be incorporated.'

('There were a lot of aspects to think about: crèches, for example, and the position of women in society as a whole,' Rudolf says.)

'We'd been preparing for the fortieth anniversary of the GDR and everything was quite normal. I had the fifth grade at the time and you wouldn't talk so openly because they were so small – you had a very child-adapted version of explaining things. I remember one pupil, a girl, who came back from West Berlin and she brought a kiwi fruit. None of us had seen a kiwi fruit before. I said we must divide it so everybody gets some because the girl wanted to show off. The pieces were very small.

'I noticed the pupils started to change, big changes after The Wall. They wouldn't come to school on Saturdays and I think the parents were behind it. Although we were just teachers, maybe the parents thought we were officials. It didn't affect me personally but it was something I could sense in my team. They suddenly said they were being treated differently by the pupils.

'In a certain way it was more difficult because the pupils came with questions I hadn't thought of before like *what will happen? What will become of us?* There was a lot of anxiety.'

At this point the sky-blue Trabant set off towards Berlin to search out some answers.

'It was all a big adventure. In the GDR we had one publishing house for school books and now suddenly you had a hundred. They all came to the school bringing copies of their books. We took them, said "thank you" and those were the first books we worked with. They were not too different. I am speaking about German lessons. In the GDR we had quite a good school programme.'

A lot of the words must have been Western words.

'Not really.'

In purely academic terms, what were the changes?

'Geography: the map was bigger! Languages: more English. I learnt at a Russian school and never taught English. You could choose Russian and most of them didn't choose it anymore so the first foreign language at my school was English. We had a problem because we didn't have too many English teachers.'

Were you retrained at any point?

'Not really, not in the sense of a complete change. I started in the 1980s and there were a lot of things we had done before The Wall came down – project work, for example – so we didn't have to change the whole system. We carried on with many things. I was always dealing with human beings. That was the constant.'

But suddenly you weren't teaching about the Russian Revolution.

'Of course it was still a topic.'

And what about Hitler?

'Still a big subject. There were left-wingers and right-wingers who adopted strong positions, especially in the 1990s, and we had big problems with that. For me it was the right wing which was the problem. It was only latterly that

I dealt with Hitler. It was always a topic in the GDR because we had a lot of anti-fascist literature and we didn't have to bend in any way.'

Did you feel when the people from the West came they were listening to you or they were just going to do what they wanted?

'From time to time I had the feeling West Germans wanted to explain our own history – the GDR history – to us. I felt they were talking about a different country to the one we lived in. It was hard for all of us and the worst for me was that the educational practices of the school were questioned. One thing is that you just make the children learn – the new system – and another is that you educate them. Some teachers left for this reason, retired, got jobs in the economy. They couldn't cope.'

What do you think now when you look back?

'Germany had a unique chance to become a country where you could live very well, live peacefully and have social justice. Germany has had problems in history with becoming a normal country. It has always been difficult for Germany to decide what kind of a country it wants to be, especially in terms of the social problems that will come. I know this from my talks with the teachers, the parents and the pupils. Especially here in this region you have a lot of social problems – a huge gap between the very rich people and the very poor people. That was not there before. There is a problem of aggression. We have no drug problem but a little alcohol problem.

'Only recently we went to the cinema with the pupils to see a film about an American teacher applying fascist methods in school. The pupils think this is good and normal, a kind of experiment that works. Could this happen again, like the Third Reich? Twenty years ago I'd have said "no" but now I think it is possible, and not only in Germany.'

Rudolf, pursuing this theme, adds: 'A trend towards autocratic dictatorship is still there internationally. I come from Silesia. My father died in the war. I was only five when my mother, brother and myself came to Chemnitz. It was a struggle for our mother to bring us through the hard times. I was able to study and I know it would not have been possible in another era. It was one of the main merits of the GDR to break the educational privileges of the bourgeoisie. Of course, there were also children of doctors and so on but the majority of my fellow students were from the working class. Up to now [since unification] there has been a kind of equality of chances for people to go to a *Gymnasium*. I have a feeling that this is changing at a very rapid pace and more come from a well-off background.'

If you could have it back, would you?

Kerstin: 'No, although it is a testing question.'

Rudolf: 'You cannot go back. What you have to do is draw the essence from history. It's only after twenty years that you are able to draw this essence and decide what was good and what was bad.'

Kerstin: 'Nobody wants it back in the absolute sense.'

Marion Drögsler, now chairman of the *Arbeitslosenverband Deutschland e.V*, an umbrella organisation for unemployed people, was a history teacher in the GDR. 'Of course we had the school books and there were many things written about historical events, especially from more recent history. We were told how to evaluate events but I didn't always stick to the teaching programme. I was teaching sixteen-, seventeen- and eighteen-year-olds. They asked many questions and we discussed a lot. I was also a citizenship teacher and we discussed East and West a lot. The discussions were open. Officially it wasn't wanted but I did it with the pupils because they wanted it – and I wanted to talk with them, to discuss with them. We had whole lessons about political matters and their opinion of them. I can say the director of the school may not have wanted this. I was a pupil in the 1970s, but only in the 1980s when I started to teach were we allowed ourselves to ask these questions. Several efforts were made to dissolve my seminar group because we asked too many questions but we kept on. That was also the way I taught. I think it is true that the 1980s were different from the 1970s, more open, and not only towards capitalism but how we could improve here.'

Dr Rüdiger Wenzke was a GDR military historian. 'It wasn't that we couldn't write about things. We could write about everything but it was demanded that we write them in the way that they were seen politically. You couldn't be critical. It had to fit in the official picture. If there were difficult topics to cover, your superior would talk to you about them and if it should be written this way or that way. If you'd just done it yourself it would certainly have been thrown out.'

Were there things that you couldn't write about at all? Stalin and the Gulag?

'You couldn't write about that at all.'

What about the Nazi-Soviet pact [of which more in a moment]?

'These things were taboo. Only in the second half of the 1980s would some historians approach such topics, but very carefully. They did begin to discuss it. This was in the time of Gorbachev, *perestroika* and *glasnost*. Of course we would deal with the Hitler-Stalin Pact and we knew all about it. We had Western literature and television but from the point of view of publishing things, that wasn't possible.'

When The Wall came down, within a short time you could write anything you wanted. Was that sudden freedom difficult?

'No, that was beautiful!'

A former GDR officer put the restrictions like this: 'from the totality of the inheritance of German military history, events, personalities, behaviour, and achievements, only those which had a lasting impact and which speeded up social progress during that period were selected.'[12]

To the outsider, German history appears to be a sequence of events which the Germans wished had not happened or, refining that, wished had happened in another way – unification, for example. To apply a single, rigid interpretation to the sequence involves emasculating the sequence itself because the events don't allow it, and you end up changing the events or ignoring them.[13]

The SED leadership demanded that historians conform in their writing to vindicating the Party's actions past and present. This entailed constant rewriting to accommodate the political changes of direction.[14] It meant the version of history taught in the GDR was truly a polar opposite to the FRG.

Dr Falk Pingel of the Georg Eckert Institute for International Textbook Research in Braunschweig is an expert on the subject. 'History as presented in textbooks is always selective because you can't give, so to speak, the whole picture. That is impossible. So every history textbook reflects mostly a national perspective, say a Western European perspective or a liberal or whatever perspective.'

If I was reading a West German school history book would Hitler not be treated from several different aspects?

'Hitler is not a good example! It's very clear what he did – a brutal dictator who committed mass crimes – and there is hardly ever any other perspective. There might, however, be different perspectives explaining how he came to power and how he could exert such an amount of power and why so many people were willing to follow him. There isn't just one explanation for that.'

But in the East they minimised Hitler. They basically said 'Hitler was nothing to do with us'.

'Yes.'

They certainly didn't accept that ordinary people in Leipzig and Dresden and East Berlin wanted him as much as people in Dortmund and Duisburg.

'They were of the opinion that they had installed a system which would never again run the risk of turning into a dictatorship. That was just the case for the West, where it might.'

There's also the pact between Stalin and Hitler.[15]

'That was a most difficult thing. It wasn't just that it wasn't explained, it wasn't mentioned at all, and it triggered the Second World War, it enabled the Soviet Union to occupy parts of Poland. This pact is not mentioned because they didn't acknowledge that it really had been signed.'

The Nazis and their National Socialism were 'depicted as a perversion of the capitalist system. It was obviously not compared to Stalinism and very little was said about the concentration camps and their victims. Dissident movements weren't mentioned either. Of course the fact that Poland was now where part of Germany had been was mentioned because it changed the geographical map [and so could not be ignored]. They explained it as being due to German imperialism expanding to the east. The same conception was in the Polish books at that time: that the Germans expanded to the east – which is partly true because it started, at least, with the partition of Poland at the end of the eighteenth century – and then expanded even more. According to the Polish view, all this was originally Polish territory so they were just getting it back.'

In the West we like a lot of ideas, we like people who ask 'why are you saying this?' but in the GDR there was no possibility of that.

'There was no open discussion. They were not offered different opinions in the textbooks, there was just the Marxist interpretation. It couldn't be questioned, at least in the books. The teaching in the GDR depended to a certain extent on the teacher. The teachers had a certain amount of room for manoeuvre to discuss things. Students sometimes questioned the official interpretation and it was up to the teacher how to cope with this.'

A whole generation passed through their educational system knowing nothing else.

'I wouldn't say that. They had access, certainly in the last ten or twenty years of the GDR, to West German TV – no doubt of that – and people know what's going on. They knew that they were deprived of much of the news in the world and they sought to get their own knowledge about it, not just to trust what was offered to them in the official newspapers. Part of my family lived in Dresden and through family visits they had contact. Elderly people [the pensioners] could travel from East to West and vice versa. In Berlin, as a Westerner, you could move to the East easily: the time it took depended on how long the queue was to get on the train! So information went around.

'In the 1980s we had a big research project on the history and civic text-books in the GDR. We were constantly in contact with the historians in the GDR and we had conferences where we invited academics from the GDR to come over. For many of them that was the problem, because only those were allowed to travel who did not openly resist the regime. In a sense, however, we had a dialogue and a sense of understanding what was happening there.'

That must have been very important because after the Wende *suddenly you have a whole school system which was completely different to your own.*

'That was a very, very big problem. We did a lot of teacher training imme-diately after the opening up of the borders. Braunschweig is very close to the border.'

In the GDR all education was designed to reinforce the state, and in the FRG to teach knowledge, to think about what you want to think about.

'That's right and that takes a long time to change. Many GDR students and teachers were fed up with having to march and demonstrate their loyalty to the regime, fed up with the official ceremonies and celebrations. They had to go to them but as soon as they had the freedom to act in another way they accepted it and they were happy about it.'

There was an immediate problem after the Wende *in that the GDR school history books were all useless.*

'That's right. We even had problems finding some for our library because they just put them in the garbage or burnt them or whatever. They were no longer interested in these books. They were provided with West German textbooks and in the beginning they were more or less enthusiastic about them. The books were graphically more enjoyable, they had coloured pictures and illustrations and the texts were more readable. They enjoyed that. Then they discovered the Western-orientated view on the GDR. Most of them didn't admit to themselves that they had lived in a dictatorship and, of course, in West German textbooks you found passages about the terror of the *Stasi*. That was something that many of them didn't really accept. They had the impression that the West German presentation of the GDR did not reflect their everyday lives so then they became sceptical about using these kinds of books in the classroom.

'The publishers quickly brought out new books but they were just new editions of the ones written in the West in the 1980s, with an added chapter on reunification. It wasn't at all representative of the idea East Germans had of their own history. The repressive nature of the communist regime was emphasised, along with East Germany's membership of the Soviet bloc. Reunification was presented as a positive thing, without mentioning the dashed hopes of those from the East.'

Walther Funken of Volk and Wissen, the GDR educational publishers since taken over by Cornelsen of the West, has said:

In the mid-1990s, the education ministers of the Eastern *Länder* ... began to push for change. Many teachers in the East requested that we come up with a less biased textbook and we did in 1995. It wasn't a matter of writing a textbook for people who were nostalgic for life in the old East Germany but of presenting in a more subtle way all the aspects of East German society through individual portraits. For example, one chapter compares the different roles of women in East and West German societies, noting the large number of them in the East's workforce and the political and historical reasons why women in the West tend to stay home.

As Dr Pingel points out, once Cornelsen had taken over Volk and Wissen the East 'hadn't any further chance of producing their own books. They just had to accept Western books and these were imported, so to speak. We researched that. It took until the second half of the 1990s to find joint teams, meaning teams of Eastern and Western German authors writing in the same history textbooks.

'Every pupil got the same books, meaning somebody in Dortmund and somebody in Dresden would be getting them, although like in Great Britain

1. Hagen Koch, The Wall Man, uncensored. Here he holds his controversial book and DVD. (*All photographs taken by Birgit Kubisch unless otherwise stated*)

2. Leuschnerdamm: the black tarmac fillings in the cobblestones were supports for an early version of The Wall. To the left was the death strip and the East, to the right – including the pavement – was the West.

3. The view towards the lake today, St Michael's Church in the background and Leuschnerdamm on the right.

4. The lake, flanked by the curve of Leuschnerdamm. This was the death strip – and not very long ago.

5. St Thomas's Church.

6. St Michael's Church, which looks so imposing from the front reveals, side on, the bombing devastation of 1945.

7. Pastor Christian Mueller with St Thomas's Church in the background.

8. The Guerrilla Garden, opposite where Pastor Mueller is standing. The house was in the East although The Wall ran behind it.

9. The late Dr Johannes Althausen.

10. Claudia Croon in her natural habitat, the Wall Street Gallery.

11. The geometry of the Wall-Street Gallery. Everything from its windows was legally in the East although The Wall, marked by the twin row of cobbles in the road, was the physical demarcation.

12. Checkpoint Charlie straight ahead, the Wall-Street Gallery building on the far side of The Wall. (*Courtesy of Hagen Koch*)

13. Heike Herrmann in her natural habitat.

14. Reasons to be cheerful in the East: Dr Ulrich and Anna Bartels, accommodating the Western health system and staying true to themselves.

15. Reasons to be cheerful in the East: Kerstin Paust-Loch the teacher and Rudolf her author husband still smiling despite their reservations.

16. Erich Honecker's house in the Wandlitz compound, pleasant and secluded but scarcely a mansion.

17 & 18. Bernauer Strasse: the most bitter division. People stand on the former death strip reading about it (the West is to the left).

19. The bogus and misleading inner Wall – the vertical slabs straight ahead.

20. The prize-winning 'wall' which is meant to represent The Wall.

21. The real thing, just round the corner in Bernauer Strasse itself.

22, 23, 24 & 25. The extraordinary legacy of The Wall almost two decades later. This is no-man's-land in the city centre being reclaimed by nature – before the bulldozers and planners get at it.

26 & 27. The Holocaust Memorial, redefining simplicity. The Brandenburg Gate is a short walk one way, the site of Hitler's bunker a short walk the other way.

28 & 29. At the bunker site tourists gather in front of an information board but no sense of what it was remains, just a very ordinary emptiness.

30. Richard Piesk, the Easterner who went looking for the new normality – and found it.

31. Dresden, the Eastern city which went looking for normality in its own past – and found it.

32. The Zwinger Palace, now one of the glories of Europe.

we have a wide variety of books on the market. Teachers have a choice. It may happen, however, that in Dresden and Dortmund they use the same book.'

Brandenburg, for example, has revisited its curriculum (last done in 1991) and offers a portrait of everyday life in the GDR as well as an examination of the Nazi era, the Holocaust, a comparison between Nazism and Stalinism and the peoples' revolutions of 1989.

Pingel says that a majority of German historians now agree on a common version of GDR history but, because the generation now at school has not, by definition, lived through the history they are learning, 'the textbooks discuss the rise of the 1989 citizens' movements and use a range of sources and accounts to show how young East Germans experienced reunification. This open way of teaching doesn't present a single truth, but various points of view. It seeks to encourage debate in the classroom.'

Did the GDR schoolchildren have more difficulty adapting than you had anticipated?

'That's difficult to say. In the beginning a lot of teachers – in particular for history and civics – were replaced by West German colleagues or by teachers who had formerly taught mathematics, or those more or less objective disciplines, because all those who could have been in cooperation with the *Stasi* were no longer allowed to teach. It took about two to three years and then almost all of them came back to school, so mostly the teacher body remained the same. The methodology of teaching didn't change much or only step by step. After the first phase of opening up and a certain enthusiasm about the Western view, many of them didn't go totally back to their old views but something like a mixture.'

I'm wondering particularly about the GDR history teachers and if they didn't find it more difficult to adjust than the pupils.

'Yes, in principle the older people have more problems than the younger ones in adjusting. Most of the younger teachers – and students – were ready and learnt very fast how to adapt, how to behave, how to advance. If you want to advance in society you have to adapt and you have to understand.'

Let's just say a forty-five-year-old in Leipzig who had been teaching history for twenty years and then suddenly he or she had to stand up and say 'actually, what I've been teaching you is mostly wrong'.

'Some had severe problems admitting that. There was a big debate between leading historians and what was called the GDR methodology of history – that means how to teach it – and there were some joint conferences at the beginning of the 1990s where people spoke out and complained about the impact of their Western colleagues on the way they now had to teach history. Some accepted it, others did not.'

(Discussing how GDR teachers had to move from their version of history to the other one in only a year, one Eastern history teacher, Andrea Schwärmer, has said: 'many of them didn't know how to explain to their pupils why yesterday's truths no longer held today. Those teachers lost all credibility and had to resign themselves to leaving the profession.'[16])

Where are we now?

'All the opinion polls show that there is still differences in the concept of history and the evaluation of the present state of affairs between the East and West parts of Germany.'

Has a generation come along which doesn't remember?

'It's still true that the youth of the GDR have a more positive view of the GDR than the West Germans.'

The very young generation don't know and don't care.

'Now it's about twenty years ago so those who are twelve or fourteen were born after unification and it's not any longer their personal history, although it is still connected to their parents and grandparents and so on. There is still, I would say, at least a family impact. This plays an important role, in particular when parts of the family still suffer from unification: they don't have a job, or they don't have a well paid job or they have been pensioned off earlier than usual. That's not forgotten. They talk about how life was in the GDR and that leaves an imprint on the younger generation even if they are not expressly interested in history.'

Outside the home they are just Germans.

'Yes, but what is a German? That's very much contested, and the East Germans are still a bit more nationalistic, they have more nationalist feelings or at least want to have – they want to attach a certain meaning to being a German whereas many Westerners don't care that much. Particularly in this respect there are still some differences.

'Each *Länder* has its own curriculum and there are not strong differences between those of East and West but the teachers are still different and they have an impact on how topics are dealt with in class. To a certain extent the perceptions of the students are also different. They live in different environments and the standards of living are different and they read different books. They watch more or less the same TV shows and so on, they're working on the Internet and there is no physical divide – that's all the same – but in the more personal surroundings there might be a remarkable difference.'

How long will it take?

'We know that history changes all the time. I was born in 1945 and therefore just in the Nazi era, but the Nazi experience of our parents had a strong impact on our political consciousness, and that might be the case for East Germans.'

One of the fascinating things is that nobody had ever faced this before.

'It was really a big historical experience.'

That's one of those impossible German ironies, the historians making history while they were actually teaching it.

Pieces from an old wall ...

Kerstin Paust-Loch went to Düsseldorf, so long denied, to visit her relatives. 'It may be strange to say this but I was a bit disappointed. I found it slightly ugly. They rebuilt it after the bombing like an American skyline.'

Welcome to freedom of travel – and expression.

The GDR produced textbooks portraying Britain to students, specifically *Britain: Aspects of Political and Social Life*, featuring a clutch of Eastern university lecturers (some with English-sounding names) in 1985, updated to *Britain in Focus* three years later. The books are sophisticated propaganda which resemble a hall of mirrors: some of it is accurately reflected, some horribly distorted, some omitted altogether and the whole *seems* comprehensive.

Some ripe examples: 'Taking measures to destabilise progressive anti-imperialist regimes in developing countries has become an important trend of neo-colonialism.'

'Britain is a capitalist state, a bourgeois democracy, its form of government a parliamentary monarchy. The imperialist state is the most decisive instrument of power of the monopoly bourgeoisie. It is the nucleus of the political system of monopoly dictatorship.'

'[The] electoral system is reinforced by the ideological influence of reformism, opportunism and anti-communism on the British working class, which has contributed to the maintenance of the Labour Party as the political "working class" alternative to the Conservatives.'

The final eleven pages of *Aspects* are devoted to the Communist Party of Great Britain and imply that it was in the vanguard of a peoples' struggle, rather than a small, irrelevant group constantly rejected at the ballot box (no voting figures are given for its performance in local or general elections).

By 1985, when *Aspects* appeared, the Party was moving inexorably towards complete oblivion and dissolution. Willie Thompson in his history *The Good Old Cause* writes: 'The nadir was reached at the Bermondsey by-election of 1982, when the CP ... ended up with fewer votes than the Official Monster Raving Loony candidate.'

No hint of this permeates *Aspects*, of course.

Instead, obsessions run throughout the book: the crisis of capitalism ... imperialism ... class struggle ... contradictions between the working and capitalist classes ... the imperialism of NATO ... instability of the imperialist system and so on.

By 1988, when *Focus* appeared, the GDR was itself moving inexorably towards complete oblivion and dissolution. No hint of that permeates *Focus*, of course, either.

If you didn't know Britain, had never been able to visit, never read British newspapers, never asked British people about the country, both *Aspects* and *Focus* were plausible portraits. They deployed statistics, adopted a scholarly tone and did describe the mechanisms of how the country functioned. Monarchy, parliament, general elections, education, political parties and so on – they are all there. The GDR student would be convinced, no doubt, and this is how he got his or her information about *everything*, not just Britain.

Small wonder that, when The Wall came down and they – successive generations who'd passed through this 'information' system – found themselves standing confronted by an onrush of all the information they'd been denied, it became another piece of *The Wall in the Head*.

Nor did the release from the hall of mirrors usher these virgins of history towards a single mirror which reflected everything truly. Ute Frevert, writing a chapter 'How to Become a Good European Citizen' in *The Making of Citizens in Europe*, says that

recent years have seen a growing disposition in many European countries to pay more attention to the shadowy aspects of their own history rather than indulging in tales of national greatness, victimhood and heroism. When it comes to the crucial experience of the Second World War, France, Belgium, and the Netherlands have become more and more aware of the legacy of active and wilful collaboration with German occupation forces. In Italy, the history of fascism is deeply contested. (Former West) Germany has witnessed painful fits of self-investigation and has gained a reputation for relentlessly unearthing the nation's criminal record. Austria has stopped talking about itself as Hitler's first victim. And Poland, for whom innocent victimhood seemed a birthright, has been confronted by its own history of anti-Semitism and mass murder.

This development has led some observers to declare 'Holocaust recognition' to be the 'contemporary European entry ticket' (Judt 2005: 803 Assmann and Novick, 2007). … 'Gulag recognition' increasingly figures side by side with the Holocaust, due to the intervention of those new EU member states that experienced traumatic periods of Soviet repression. No one knows, however, how durable this consensus will be. Domestic policies might soon call it into question or put an end to it. Moreover, such stances require constant reaffirmation by a critical public – but, again, public discourse may shift in focus or position.

It may be that the young people who grew up in the certainties of the GDR and emerged, at whatever age, into all this found themselves, instead, standing in another hall of mirrors.

Notes

1. www.howtogermany.com/pages/germanschools.html.
2. www.kmk.org/dOssir/organisation.pdf.
3. *Education in Germany since Unification.*
4. Which became seven: Humboldt-University zu Berlin; Technische University Dresden; Ernst-Moritz-Arndt-University Greifswald; Friedrich-Schiller-University Jena; Martin-Luther-University Halle-Wittenberg; Karl-Marx-University Leipzig; Wilhelm-Pieck-University Rostock.
5. *Education in Germany since Unification.*
6. Herbert Henning at www.didaktik.mathematik.uni-wuerzburg.de/history/meg/mathedb3.html.
7. *Education in Germany since Unification.*
8. Ibid.
9. *Divided by Unity? Rebuilding Culture and Society after 1989: The Case of the Universities* (Eine Konferenz der Heinrich Böll Stiftung in Kooperation mit dem Canadian Centre for German and European Studies) at York University, Toronto, 19 November 1999.
10. Secret in the sense that for a GDR citizen to have a Western address was not a good idea.
11. GDR citizens could apply for permission to travel to the FRG if a relative there had a special birthday, a wedding or serious illness. This gave rise to a certain creative approach from some of the families in the West: aunts posed as mothers and so on. In at least one instance someone died but the family maintained a pretence that she was still alive so the Easterner could get permission (and did). Couples couldn't go, on the theory that if one had to stay behind the other would return. A woman recounted how her husband had secured permission to go to France, where a relative had a vineyard, but she was refused and the immigration officer asked her in all seriousness 'why would you want to go?'
12. Wilfried Hanisch, *In der Tradition von Müntzer, Scharnhorst, Engels und Thälmann?* Quoted in *Requiem for an Army.*
13. Of the many bizarre belief groups – the end-of-the-world doom merchants, the Flat Earth Society, the religious fundamentalists who insist the world was made in six days and a wooden boat was built which held at least 10,000,000 animals, the Aliens-abducted-me-ers, the Bermuda Trianglers and the bores who have found Atlantis, the full range of New Age claimants, the alternative medicine disciples, the clairvoyants, the faith healers, the levitators and telepathy communicators – the Holocaust deniers are unique. All these others (even the ones who insist we are ruled by lizards) seek to persuade us something existed, exists or will exist. The deniers seek to persuade us that something did not exist, namely the death of millions of Jews, many in gas chambers.

In one sense they give a perfect example of how German history invites outrageous manipulation in a way few other histories do. In another sense they show how dangerous and agonising German history can be half a century on: the deniers deny regardless of the fact that the Holocaust is confirmed by a wide variety of primary sources – human, physical, documentary – which all interlock to form their terrible picture, and in doing so the deniers hurt, and where they can humiliate, survivors.

That the best the deniers can do is try to find small discrepancies in the mountain of evidence reveals the paucity of their position. That none of the deniers has ever advanced a convincing counter-explanation of what happened to all those Jews reveals the impossibility of their position.

I am afraid we are going to meet another branch of this particular group at Dresden in Chapter Ten.

14. *Rewriting the German Past.*

15. The Pact, sometimes known by the names of the respective foreign ministers, Molotov and Ribbentrop, was officially called the Treaty of Non-aggression between Germany and the Union of Soviet Socialist Republics. It was signed in Moscow on 24 August 1939 (but dated 23 August). It carved up Poland between the two countries and, among other things, passed the Baltic states into the Soviet sphere of influence. The pact had two effects: it convulsed the world Communist movement which was dedicated to fighting fascism (and had been in the Spanish Civil War) but was now being told the fascists were friends after all; and it removed the danger of Hitler having to fight on two fronts. The East was safe and he could attack the West.

No history of Germany could conceivably make sense without full coverage of the pact.

16. www.unesco.org/courier/2001_11/uk/education2.htm.

7

AS IF THERE WASN'T A BORDER

The consequences of the GDR's only free parliamentary elections on 18 March 1990 – where, of the 400 seats contested, a pro-unification coalition called Alliance for Germany won 192 – would have a direct impact on every aspect of life, as we have seen, but particularly on the police and armed forces. There was an obvious imperative to put them and their Western counterparts together: stable countries function within a single legal framework and their survival is ultimately guaranteed by a single army.

When the parliament had voted by 299 to 80 for unification under the FRG's Basic Law – in real politics to become part of the FRG – it carried direct implications for both services but sidestepped (forgive me) a sequence of minefields strewn in all directions as far as the eye could see. From this moment on the FRG's constitution took precedence over everything in the East and the FRG could justify this by saying *the GDR voted for it so this is what they want. We are simply giving them that.*

The initial minefield centred round the nature of the GDR, where every aspect of life had a political value and a political function (don't forget weather forecasts were regarded as state secrets), and everyone above a certain level was politically active or politically sanctioned. This was particularly true of the People's Police and the National People's Army (NVA) because of their vital roles: maintaining civil peace and defending the very existence of the state.

How do you assimilate such policemen into a Western force which was resolutely non-political and, moreover, had what has been described as a value system of 'citizen friendly' police?

If anyone had said to a GDR policeman *you are the guardian of our socialism* he'd have understood.

If you'd said to a FRG policeman *you are the guardian of democracy and capitalism* he wouldn't have understood or, if he had, he'd have been offended, perhaps very offended.

The answer to the big question was that with very few exceptions senior personnel from the East – police and military – were regarded as fatally tainted and dismissed.

Bernd Finger is sitting in his office in the Criminal Investigation Department opposite Tempelhof airport and, by coincidence, it's the day the last flights will come and go before the old airport is finally closed. That might be particularly poignant for him. 'Because of the nature of my job I had to take aeroplanes when I wanted to leave West Berlin: it was too dangerous to go through the GDR. They might have arrested me.'

Detective Police Commander Finger – then chief of criminal investigations in the borough of Charlottenburg and leader of the education department for the criminal branch of the West Berlin police – was a central figure in unification.

Was it inevitable the West would take over?

'The East German population had been asked in a referendum how they wanted the integration process to be and they all decided for the Basic Law.'

When they voted 'this is what we want' it meant the West would come.

'They wanted the D-mark and of course they wanted to travel. They wanted a Mercedes like everybody else. It was a democratic procedure but there had been thinking in the Citizens' Movement[1] about how you could take things from the GDR and incorporate them into a new Germany – that the new must not necessarily be a mirror of the old West Germany. It wasn't possible in view of the speed world history was travelling at in 1989. We didn't have years to think about it, we had weeks. I was part of the negotiations of the reunification treaty and we only had a little time to decide whether it would be a federal state' – as in the Federal Republic of Germany – 'or an association of states. The answer was federal.'

Finger's life story condenses important facets of two Germanys.

'My father was a Social Democrat and a police officer after the war, 1945. He had been in the resistance against the Nazi system and he was one of the first democratic policemen here in Berlin. From this time he was under scrutiny from the communists *because* he was a democrat. The communists tried to make everybody in the People's Police the same politically. In the West, the police are not political and not ideological at all. My father fled to the West in 1948.'

Finger was born a year later. 'My wife, too, was born in West Berlin so we lived all the time in the inner circle of The Wall, so to say.'

Before The Wall came down, suppose I come from a city in the FRG – say Duisburg – and I rob a bank in West Berlin. I could go to Checkpoint Charlie, cross into the East and you couldn't follow me there.

'There was a number we could telephone but it didn't have any ringing-out tone on it. We could give information but we wouldn't get a response. We'd say "criminal X or Y is on your territory – he crossed at Checkpoint Charlie". There was a voice at the other end; someone was listening. They'd say "I have taken notice of this" – that was all, no further communication. What they did with the information and what they did with the criminal if they caught him we didn't know. They never returned anybody and they never even said "we have found him". Nothing. No feedback.'

What would happen if they had a problem? The man from Duisburg commits a crime over there and flees here …

'We were not informed by the East about such things.'

Alexanderplatz was another world and you didn't know it.

'That is correct, and they didn't know our world.'

It began to change, of course, when The Wall came down.

'It was improvisation from minute to minute. I live in Charlottenburg and The Wall went through the district. The Brandenburg Gate was in it. On the night of 9 November we saw on television and we heard it on the radio what was happening. We all went voluntarily from our homes to our offices because we had a feeling this was going to be a world-altering event.

'In the days after, we tried to make contact with the GDR police officials but it was very difficult the first time because they were very "separated" and reserved. In November and December 1989 there was an attempt by both sides to find out what we had in common in order to be able to talk to each other, to discuss, to build the initial bridges. It was also to take the first steps towards being able to rely on each other.

'We saw The Wall was breaking down[2] and that was the time when the people – like a great *floating* – were going back and forth. We realised we really had to talk to the other side to enforce law and order. Potsdamer Platz was open. People could steal things and run home with them – suddenly in West Berlin you had a huge increase in shoplifting. A lot of people [from the East] didn't have enough money. They came to the Western shops, they saw all the things – the glittering world – and they wanted to have them. Naturally, you can understand this and very quickly the West Berlin Senate introduced the welcome money, which enabled those people to satisfy their first desires.

'It was a very human reaction for the police to look for the things we had in common, and look immediately.'

In *Divided in Unity*, Andreas Glaeser writes that high-ranking People's Police officers suddenly had the freedom to think about reforms. 'For them, as for many people in the civil rights movement, it was a chance to participate in the writing of history. It was also a time in which many of them sought contact with Western officers in an attempt to collect models that might be worth emulating. Many Western officers who had informal contacts with

People's Police officers randomly visiting Western police stations in search of police laws, regulations, and a chat, describe this time as one of friendly exchanges and relative openness on both sides.' This changed in mid-1990 when the West Berlin Police 'advised all its officers that these unofficial contacts were no longer tolerable'. By then the West understood that it would ingest the People's Police. 'High-ranking People's Police officers in particular remember this change in attitude quite vividly as a shift from waiting partnership to open rejection.'

Finger explains that 'then at the beginning of 1990 I went to the GDR. I was sent to see how the security authorities could cooperate with us – police, fire brigade, ambulance services, civil defence, bus services, handling of foreigners – almost everything. There was also the question of the *Stasi* but not how to cooperate with them, how it could be dissolved. The *Stasi* was a special thing.

'I had a *Stasi* file and I looked at it. The file was very thick and the first document was my birth certificate. I mention this because my parents fled and almost exactly forty years later I went back helping to unite both Germanys. Anyway, in the file was my school, my *Abitur* and that I had studied law before I became a policeman in the investigation branch. Every police station of my career was documented and even my exam marks. They knew that I had had relatively quick promotions because I have always been a good student. The reason they collected the information was that if I got higher in my career, a top position, they might be able to use it.

'They were able to find it all because they had spies in the Western bureaucracy. They could in a sense follow me here because we know about 3,000 *Stasi* agents lived in West Berlin. They observed us and many other people. It was a general observation of the West, especially the security forces and the armed forces, because we were the class enemies.

'They had whole halls full of useless information but they believed they could recognise the world better, and especially what happened in West Berlin. It was mostly an illusion because life is so varied and moves so fast.'

Is it also fair to say that in the back of their minds they thought 'one day we will take West Berlin and we will know all the important people there'.

'That was the plan. They had lists, and these lists had all the names of those they thought would cooperate, thousands of others they knew they would have to remove from office and those they planned to arrest. The top levels of administration and especially the security services were to be arrested. I would have been arrested. My father would have been arrested and perhaps my mother, and that was especially worrying. When I saw it I felt great anxiety because I thought of what could have happened to me. Thanks to God it didn't come to that. I also want to mention that there were plans for internment camps.'

I wonder if this made you a little more sympathetic to people in the East, because what you were frightened of – being taken over by the other side – happened to them.

'Yes, but there weren't these plans and preparations in the West. They didn't know that but we explained it to them very quickly. It had become very clear that the Eastern bloc, the GDR, the NVA and the police were highly prepared for confrontation. The GDR maintained the notion of East–West confrontation.

'Putting two police forces together was a lot of work,' Finger says.

This was because the two systems were built on separate ideas of what a judicial system should be. The GDR system aimed at the 'fostering of harmony, the pedagogic [teaching] ambitions of GDR law, the preference of collective over private solutions' and placing 'public order above individual rights'.[3]

In *Divided in Unity*, Glaeser writes:

> In order to guarantee that the (Western) law would be effectively enforced in the East, it was ... decided to transpose complete Western leadership into all Eastern precincts, backed up by a core of experienced Western officers. This transfer of leadership was comprehensive: it ranged from the head of a precinct all the way down to the leaders of the patrol car shifts and their deputies.

Finger explains that 'there was very strong resentment, yes, at the leadership level in the East because they felt the class enemy had defeated them, but the ordinary policemen who dealt with crime on the street were happy. On the one hand, they could now travel with their families and on the other hand they had a freedom in a bigger sense, the freedom to say what they wanted. They were also happy the leadership had been replaced because these were the ones they only knew as political officers. The lower levels were really glad to get rid of the political dimension and be able to concentrate on the real police tasks. The challenges were so big they just didn't want to have the other stuff.

'Retraining? There was a six-week course – that was the immediate adaptation course, a crash course. That was for the first months after The Wall came down and then there was a one-year course but we were not able to send everybody because nobody would have been on the beat! Because the GDR police didn't necessarily know the law they were working under, we mixed them: we'd try and have one West policeman with one East, so it was training on the job. They could be in the East or the West. It applied to both, and a policeman from the East could find his new working area was in the West.'

Where are we now?

'You don't know the differences any more because all of us are together: one police force and there is no differentiation between *Ossi* and *Wessi*.'

On the day of unification 10,775 employees of the People's Police (9,467 police, 1,308 civil servants) joined the West German force. Five years later only 5,115 remained.[4]

If the Western police knew nothing of Alexanderplatz, the Eastern police knew nothing of the Kurfürstendamm, the famed and fabled shopping avenue in the West.

Raymond is not his real name, and that needs explaining. Anonymity is unappealing in any book, it raises suspicions about authenticity and it liberates interviewees to say whatever they want without worrying about the consequences. Raymond was quite happy to give his real name and at no stage insisted on anonymity. I have given it to him because I worried about the consequences. What he said might well cost him his job without him perhaps realising it.

He had been a border guard before joining the People's Police at Potsdam. Like so many others he was at home watching television the night The Wall fell, and like them remembers Günter Schabowski's fateful words.

'I saw the Press Conference and I thought well, I can go over and have a look. I had seen the West as a border guard and I had always thought life was quite normal over there. It looked different but it didn't look evil or anything. I saw there was a difference between what I saw on television and what I could see myself! When I was in the watchtower I could see people and I could see buildings but not shops. When The Wall opened I went to exactly the spots I had seen – I absolutely wanted to see them – and they looked the same.

'Of course I had wanted to go to the West before the fall to have a look and then come home again, but I knew it was not possible so I lived with it. I wasn't allowed to cross at first [as a policeman] – I think it was perhaps a week before I could. The first time I went I was with my parents and grandmother to get the welcome money. I bought long playing records. I can't remember what they were! I had never been to the West until that day.'

His life story touches hard on many aspects of life in the GDR, and unconsciously reflects how far away it was from the world he could see all the time from the watchtower.

He was born in a small town in Brandenburg near the end of the 1960s.

'I learnt to be a mechanic and I wanted to study engineering but I had to do my National Service before I could start. It was normal to go for a year and a half but if I said that they could keep me waiting for a long time. If you agreed to do three years you could go immediately so I said "yes, I'll go for the three". It wasn't clear where I would be sent, could have been anywhere, but I didn't want to be far from home. I was put in the border guards. I had no doubts about joining them, not at all. It was nothing unpleasant to me. I had responsibility – I became a border guard officer responsible for about twenty people'

But you might have had to shoot somebody trying to escape.

'It was possible. You might have to use your weapon. Looking back I say thank God it didn't happen but at the time I would have done it, yes. I never did shoot at anybody.'

It's very difficult to judge history if you take it out of context, and to understand the shoot-to-kill you have to have the full context.

'Yes. Actually, it was very boring.'

It was also riven by mistrust. As Raymond says, 'you had two people in the watchtower and you were not meant to know the other one very well, although you would of course know them. This was to prevent guards arranging things.'

He left the border guards after the three years, at the end of 1988. 'I'd given up the idea of studying engineering because it wouldn't have meant much money. I would not have earned more than anybody working in a factory. You could earn quite good money in the police, a little bit more than 1,000 marks a month. I had always been interested in it and I wanted to be a criminal policeman. The police came to the border guards on a recruiting drive and asked if we'd join afterwards.'

Presumably to be a border guard you had to have Stasi clearance.

'Yes, and it could have been a very good way to get into the police. While you were a border guard you were checked all the time for your behaviour and your family relationships, like with your children. When you were a border guard you could be deployed in an area where you were responsible for yourself so it was necessary to have reliable people.'

Presumably the police was a very pleasant change from the border guards?

'Yes, I thought so.'

And then The Wall came down.

'I was a policeman in Potsdam.'

The GDR police was taken over by the West.

'Maybe more intensely in Berlin because it was two parts of a city, but with us we had a lot of the officers who just stayed. We had to learn a new law and that, I should say, lasted at least three or four years. The police from the West came and prepared some retraining and further education. No, it wasn't difficult because, for example, the penal codes of the GDR and the FRG were quite similar, and a murder is a murder. The criminal technique methods were similar, looking for clues and everything. What changed a lot was the whole administration – it was more bureaucratic.'

It seems surprising that you were allowed to remain in the police after unification because you had been a border guard. They checked for Stasi files.

'It was a difficult time for me because when I was with the border guards I was an informer. It was difficult for me because I knew they knew and they would "touch me", so to say. I was asked to watch everything that happened and I had to report. They wanted me to remain an informer when I joined the police but I said "no, I don't want this any more".'

The People's Police were required to fill in questionnaires which covered their personal as well as professional lives, in order to reveal how closely involved with the political system they had been.[5]

'After the *Wende* they checked us all and they said "everybody has to leave who had anything to do with the *Stasi*". I really had to ask myself the question *what do I do? Do I tell them that I was with the* Stasi – *and what do I do then?* It was clear I would have to go. Or I could wait until they found out and then I would be discharged. We were asked the question, of course, and I said "no, I wasn't with them". I waited to see what would happen.'

Nothing happened.

'I didn't tell them for a very long time. After three years I said to myself *I have to come clean* – I was having stomach problems worrying about it. I went to the person who was responsible for internal security and told him. They checked all the documents and they couldn't find anything so I continued although I had to change the place where I worked. I am still in the criminal police. I say that's where I work and people always ask "have you caught a murderer?" I haven't! We have had bank robberies with guns …'

To be an informer in the border guards is quite different to being an informer about your wife, your children, your uncle, because the border guards were protecting the country. In a sense you were doing your duty by making sure that all the other border guards were reliable.

'I told myself that. I only felt I was serving the service.'

Again, the context is very important.

'That's why when I left the border guards and joined the police I said "no more". If I hadn't, it would have become a general thing.'

Twenty years: when you look back and look at today what do you think?

'I spent my childhood and youth in the GDR and I can say that I didn't miss anything. I wasn't limited by anything. I had everything I needed.'

Was it difficult for policemen in the East to adjust after the Wende?

'No, I wouldn't say so. The laws were quite similar but the feelings of the people were different. When you were a policeman in the GDR people would look at you with respect. This has completely gone. No respect. You ask yourself *why do people behave like this? How have they become like this?*

'For my generation it was really the right time to stop one thing and begin another [the *Wende*] and the police are like the army, disciplined, so if somebody says "we are going to do this a different way" they just do it. I could accept that this was new, with new superiors. I could live with that. Actually, they only changed the flags. All the other things were more or less the same. Certain things were as if there hadn't been a border between them. In the German police they don't have American expressions like "10-4". I could speak on the radio and nobody could say if it was East or West. You can say how surprised I was by how similar everything seemed. It was funny that there were two very different systems and yet they were the same.'

Glaeser has written that the similarities were so pronounced that some Eastern officers 'actually compared the legal codes line by line, marking the differences, which they found to be minimal. Some claim that they even mixed up the paragraph numbers during the retraining programmes because the biggest difference between laws East and West was the sequencing of the articles.'[6]

I mention to Raymond: *You don't look as if you are a man who has regrets about anything very much.*

'No, I don't have. I can say I didn't miss anything in the past but I am open to new things. I think this change has enriched my life in a way which would not have been possible before. I'd have just lived on in the old system. Now you have to look to the right and to the left, see what's happening. You have to be more attentive to things.'

You are the first person we have met researching this book who seems completely happy. All the others drew a balance, plus-minus, plus-minus, but you didn't.

'I went to school and it was good. I could do my apprenticeship, everything was fine. I wonder what would have become of me if I had taken up the studies in engineering and sometimes when I go past the old factory – the Karl Marx Works – I notice that it's closed. It's not there any more.'

Frank Thomas, born in Thuringia in 1953 and now in a motorbike division, was another who had never been to the West. 'I grew up in the GDR. When I was eight my parents divorced. I lived for two years with my mother but then I left to live with my father. He went to Cottbus in the 1970s and I went with him. I started an apprenticeship as a metal worker and in 1973 or 1974, in something called Socialist Help, I was sent from the factory I was working in to Ludwigsfelde where they built the lorries, the W 50. I took a welding exam.

'When I was a metal worker I earned around 450 marks a month and I worked only day shifts. When I went to Ludwigsfelde I earned 800–900 marks and worked in shifts. It depended on how the health regulations were. For instance, the people who sprayed the lorries got 1,200 because that was a greater risk of illness.

'I reached the age when I had to do my National Service and at the time I had a friend who was pregnant, so when they asked me whether I'd do one and a half years or three I said "if I have the choice I want to do one and a half".'

They means the *Wehrkreiskommando*, which was a district recruiting office responsible for registering young men fit for military service and for covering the personnel needs of the National People's Army.

'They said "you have to wait" and I went back to work. I was twenty-four or twenty-five when I began my National Service. Then I met my now wife.

Finally I went into the army shortly after the birth of our two children –
twins, girls, very small, premature and in an incubator. They were fourteen
days old when I had to go. They have developed very well!

'I was in the riot police in Potsdam which was recognised as National
Service. It was a special branch that made sure law and order was maintained
in the cities. If a Russian soldier tried to desert, the riot police searched for
him and found him. If Russian soldiers had too much to drink, that was
taken care of by the Soviet authorities. We didn't have anything to do with
that.

'At the end of my year and a half somebody came and asked me if I'd like
to stay. I don't know where he was from – the riot police or the *Stasi*. I'd
really had enough so I went back to Friedrichsfelde as a welder. I got training as a trade union leader in one of the departments of the company and I
was responsible for around 500 people. I was replaced in 1984 because there
were some misunderstandings and problems that I had. They didn't like me! I
continued for another four months as a welder and then in 1985 I joined the
police in Potsdam.

'When I started they sent me to the police school for a year and I had to
learn law. At the time the laws were very strict, very regulated and very clear.
We had to learn the laws by heart and deal with the penal law. Of course, we
also did Marxist theory in order to be able to communicate with people and
settle arguments.'

(One of the reasons the Western police considered the People's Police so
poor was that they trained for a shorter time and spent between 30 per cent
and 40 per cent of the time on Marxism-Leninism.[7]

After police school, Thomas 'went to be a policeman on the beat – on
patrol – and newcomers from the training school would accompany me. I had
to show them everything.'

Was there a lot of crime?

'Not as far as I experienced. I was on the beat, then there was the traffic police and the criminal police. I became a sergeant. There wasn't much
drunkenness and fighting, so people could go out at night and nothing
would happen to them. There was a case of a drunk who had hit an old
man on the nose and his glasses broke. I had to hold him until my other
colleagues came. It was all very limited. It was easy to buy alcohol. It's true
that a lot of alcohol was consumed but it was not a problem because there
was a very close connection between people in the family and the social
surroundings, if I can put it like that. When we'd finished work we'd buy a
bottle of schnapps and sit together, talk, have a little schnapps and go home
– and, say, five or six young men who'd finished work on a Friday could go
and buy as much as they wanted.'

Then The Wall came down.

'We noticed in the time before that more and more people would gather in Babelsberg at the church and, as the numbers increased, people exchanged views, but when The Wall fell I was really frightened. I was at home, I saw the press conference on television, then The Wall opened and it was clear to me that everything was kaput. What I knew was that the people in the GDR who had a safe job would think *OK I can travel now*. Everyone had their work, their secure job: it was a duty to work and a right to work. If somebody had been in prison, when they came out they were provided with a flat of their own, sometimes even with furniture and everything, and they also got a job.'

The NVA people were not allowed to go across to have a look or for shopping or anything. Was that the same with the police?

'We were not allowed to either. We got a telex and it said that anyone wanting to cross had to have a special stamp. In our police department they opened an office where you could get this stamp. I got one, but only weeks later. We took a bus and crossed the Glienicke Bridge to go to West Berlin and get the welcome money. The West was nice and colourful and we bought our first colour television. In the GDR television sets were quite big and you could hardly get a colour set.

'After the *Wende* some people said maybe we should think about early retirement. On the one hand they suggested to the older policemen that they retire and it was in the form of an offer: you'd get compensation. On the other hand, it was also a little kind of a threat: "If you don't go now with the compensation, later you might just be given notice."'

Now you're going to have one police force but it was a takeover.

'Some of our higher ranks were either downgraded or sent elsewhere and people from the West came to take their places. It was a time when some of the old laws were still in force and some of the new laws were coming, so actually it was a time without a law. A free time! We tried to keep order according to the old law but we got an order to be quite relaxed with everything and not to interfere in a very hard way.'

The People's Police lost authority more or less in proportion to The Wall coming down and the GDR coming down with it. The mood of the force was drawn between uncertainty and paralysis.

'Many People's Police officers who actually had to do the police work remember this time with deep dismay. Without proper instructions from superiors, they felt lost; they felt that they no longer knew when, how or where to intervene, and they were afraid of the anger and perhaps even more of the scorn of the people.'[8]

Nor was this all: a central tenet of the People's Police was as a bulwark for the class mission – something else which had come down. Nor had ordinary people forgotten that the People's Police were not necessarily gentle during the November demonstrations.

The ingestion involved an accounting for the past, itself necessarily an uncomfortable process.

'There were questionnaires and checks about whether you had worked for the *Stasi*,' Thomas says. 'Those were discharged who, when they had to fill in the questionnaire, were afraid to tell the truth. If it was discovered they'd lied they were discharged. Some of the officers who hadn't lied were downgraded and became policemen.

'I know that when I was in Potsdam somebody lived in the apartments who was a *Stasi* officer. We got friendly with him and he visited us. He certainly created a file – because he was in our flat without us knowing. Somehow he got the key we had for my mother-in-law. We don't know how and I only learned that after The Wall came down. He shot himself.'

How long did it take until you became one police force again?

'A long time. After the *Wende* we had to go on courses where we were given questionnaires like an exam, and only after that were we able to go on probation [to see if they'd be accepted]. In the GDR there were Party meetings and what appeared in the newspapers was evaluated. That ceased completely. The courses we went on were to see our factual knowledge.

'I can't say the Western law was easier and there were different steps: for instance, you had to continue your work outside on the streets in addition to these courses. We had to do everything – traffic accidents, burglaries. The burglaries increased because people bought new furniture but put the old in their basements. The burglars knew this. These basements only had wooden doors and it was very easy to break in. We were trained about security aspects, how to stop a car and also exercise a certain control by making sure they carried their first-aid kits and warning triangles. Driving the more powerful Western cars was relatively OK – the power was nice, of course – but one of the big changes proved to be going from gears to automatic.'

Did you find that you were getting a new kind of crime, like drugs?

'Yes. It was completely new dealing with drugs. Once I saw a Russian injecting himself and I actually didn't know what he was doing: I had never seen this before. We had no drugs in the GDR, or none that I knew of.'

What about hippies and drop-outs who knew their rights?

'That was a transition and I had to glide to it!'

What do you think now about the police?

'I feel it's getting worse. There are fewer people for wider and wider areas of work. The traffic is getting heavier. You can't anticipate problems, only react to them. The police force is now one, although of course you have to add that there are different laws in every *Länder*. It's more a personnel question. Before, you had enough time to prepare things, but now you have to work very quickly.'

And if you had a magic wand to go back to 8 November 1989, what would you do with the magic wand?

'That's difficult to say. It would have to be a mixture of a reply. The social structures that we had – the care for children and so on – they were wonderful. We had hardly any unemployed people. The doctors were free of charge. The social background for the young people was better – we had the youth clubs – and that has all gone.'

Pieces from an old wall ...

The shoot-to-kill at The Wall produced very complex, nuanced court cases after the fall, involving principally Egon Krenz. A Berlin court ruled that although, of course, he did no shooting himself, he shaped the orders which led the border guards to. He was given six-and-a-half years for manslaughter. He took his case to the European Court of Human Rights in Strasbourg but in 2001 the judges there voted 14-3 to uphold the conviction.

Krenz and others complained loudly of 'victor's justice', although such accusations can never be avoided. That wasn't the complexity. Could Krenz be tried and found guilty by applying retrospective justice, especially if he acted within the laws of the GDR, a sovereign member of the United Nations?

The judges circumvented this by ruling that the GDR decision to maintain closed borders 'at all costs' should not have overridden a basic constitutional requirement: the protection of life. Senior GDR politicians 'evidently could not have been ignorant of [the] Constitution and legislation, or of its international obligations and the criticisms of its border policing regime that had been made internationally'.

So many aspects of unification involved what appeared from the East to be a settling of scores and from the West a settling of historical anomalies: the property maze and so on. To have left the matter of the deaths at the border untouched would, in the new climate, have been unthinkable in the eyes of virtually every German and the world.

Krenz emerged from prison in December 2003.

He had no reason to feel bitter. He didn't get a bullet in the back, fired from a watchtower.

Notes

1. The Citizens' Movement, a grassroots democratic movement which briefly wielded great power.
2. Strictly speaking, The Wall opened on 9 November 1989 but was only dismantled in its entirety by the end of 1990.

3. *Imperfect Justice: An East–West German Diary* by Inga Markovits, Clarendon Press, Oxford; reviewed by Georg Wiessala in www.timeshighereducation. co.uk/story.asp?storyCode=163469&sectioncode.

4. *Divided in Unity*, Glaeser.

5. Ibid.

6. Ibid.

7. Ibid.

8. Ibid.

8

BOOT ON THE OTHER FOOT

'The basis of socialist military education is to educate citizens towards socialist internationalism and socialist brotherhood-in-arms, towards socialist patriotism, love of the socialist fatherland, self-sacrifice on behalf of the achievements of socialism.' These words are from the GDR 1973 Military Handbook.

'Those in charge of socialist military education are not content with overcoming pacifism as an obstacle to defence-preparedness. What they find indispensable is *an image of the enemy* – not merely of a particular system, state, coalition or class, but of an enemy personified and even named. If the enemy is to be fought, he has to be hated, and hatred is something for which men must be trained.' These words are from Thomas M. Forster's authoritative study *The East German Army*, published in 1980.

The two paragraphs, both closely interwoven in their theme, set out the inherent problems in unifying an army, the GDR's NVA (*Nationale Volksarmee*), which had been taught the hatred, with the *Bundeswehr*, which had been founded on more benign principals, if you can say that about any army. Because the *Bundeswehr*, like the FRG, could not escape being the successor to the Nazi regime, it strove to banish the tradition of Prussian militarism[1] and make its service personnel ordinary members of society. Their rights would only be 'abridged'[2] enough to meet the demands of being a serviceman or woman.

The discipline and codes of conduct verged on the brutal in the NVA, with unquestioning obedience the basis and no questioning of anything permitted. The orders came from above and were to be obeyed. Nor did the concept of individual human rights exist. Dale R. Herspring, in his penetrating study *Requiem for an Army*, recounts a story of how two officers came upon someone wearing an NVA coat clearing snow. They assumed he was absent without leave and gave him a beating. In fact, he wasn't even in the NVA. If they had done that in the *Bundeswehr*, whether the man was a serving soldier or not, they would have been dismissed instantly (and subject to prosecution under the criminal law).

The NVA was more than just an army. It was intended to be an indispensable part of the Warsaw Pact, locking the GDR into the Soviet Union, because one of the GDR's fears throughout its existence was that the Soviet Union would strike a deal with the FRG and abandon it. The more indispensable the NVA, the less danger of that happening. In terms of budget, the NVA was given enough to create an ultra-modern, massively armed fighting force – 2,000 tanks, 1,600 artillery pieces, 400 combat aircraft. It had 1,070 facilities in 532 different places.[3]

To bring it even closer to the Soviet Union the NVA modelled itself obsessively on the Red Army. It was also politicised: political officers, ideological courses, indoctrination and one estimate suggests that by 1962 more than 98 per cent of all officers were Party members. The NVA was, however, a secretive, remote, isolated organisation which did not fraternise with the populace (soldiers wore uniforms at all times so there was no mistaking them).

Dr Rüdiger Wenzke, the Eastern military historian we met in Chapter 6, gives an intriguing anecdote about the 1968 Prague Spring, when the Czechoslovak government tried to liberalise and fellow Warsaw Pact countries invaded.

'GDR did not march into Czechoslovakia. The troops stayed on the border and within the GDR. They were involved in the preparations for the operation but at the last minute they were ordered to stop. They were, however, ready to go.'

The symbolism of German soldiers re-entering Czechoslovakia – the Sudetenland – is too much to contemplate when the images of Germans doing that in October 1938 remain so fresh as a decisive step towards Hitler's war.

'It would not have been so difficult for the GDR. They would have said "if it has reached this point we go". They wouldn't have had a problem with the symbolism.'

This is a very strong and revealing point, implying that the preservation of Warsaw Pact countries for communism took precedence over all other considerations, including whatever the people in those countries wanted for themselves, international outrage and an implicit admission that the Pact could only be held together by naked force. If the Warsaw Pact, rigidly controlled by the Soviet Union, was prepared to act like this – as it had during East Berlin riots in 1953[4] and the 1956 Hungarian uprising – the notion that, within a couple of decades, it would wither away *and* the Red Army would leave the GDR perfectly peacefully *and* NVA soldiers would be in NATO was fantastical. No wonder nobody planned for it. They had better things to do with their time.

These events did not, of course, pass unremarked on in the GDR. The dissident (but then Party member) Rudolf Bahro has said:

At first there was absolutely no public discussion about Czechoslovakia. Because of the Soviet military presence in the GDR, the man in the street saw little possibility that anything similar would happen there. Those, like me, who were critical of the regime had far greater hopes, but the average citizen, despite some sympathy for what was happening, was sceptical about its prospects. In the weeks before the invasion, people began to hear of GDR troop movements near the Czech border and grew increasingly afraid that war would break out. On the day of the invasion, there was an atmosphere of apprehension in the trains and buses, as people talked about the danger of war and the part their own soldiers were playing. I sat down in a corner, wrote my letter of resignation from the Party ...[5]

The two blocs were easily the most powerful military forces on the planet, but a geographical curiosity meant they only faced each other on the ground in Germany and a portion of the Czechoslovakian border (plus the top of Norway).[6] By definition a conventional war would almost certainly have broken out in Germany, wherever it spread to after that. By definition, too, Germans would have been trying to kill Germans, perhaps within minutes rather than hours.

Dr Wenzke says that 'the ratio of ground forces was 2:1 in favour of the Warsaw Pact.'

Because of this ratio, the West was never going to invade the East.

'But in the East they had a different point of view. They felt there was an aggression in the West and at some point they would invade.'

You must have known that was not true.

'It's a difficult question. Some people say the political leadership in the NVA knew that it was like that and others were really convinced the West would invade. It was disputed territory. The propaganda on both sides was different because each side blamed the other. There were reasons to say the Warsaw Pact was aggressive and NATO was aggressive.'

Timeline: 9 November 1989. The Wall opens.
'That night I was at home watching television in Potsdam,' Dr Wenzke says. 'I noticed that something strange was going on. I woke my wife up and said: "Have a look. You won't believe what is happening. I don't know what will come of it" – because I had dealt with the military and the security service I knew what might happen. "This could be dangerous." I really had a bad feeling in my stomach because I didn't know how the government would react, and the Red Army had huge military might here.

'The first time I went to the West was that November. I crossed at the Glienicke Bridge. I had not been to the West before. My idea was to go and have a look. I was impressed that the cars were so silent and didn't smell. On the other hand we had Western television so we knew what it was like, and I had relatives in the West. My first impression was not that the GDR was finished. I didn't see it that way. For me in 1989 everything was still open: nobody knew what would emerge from it and many people said "this is a chance to improve things in the GDR". I didn't think the GDR was at stake.'

You can argue with Hagen Koch over The Wall, respect the religious communities, understand the artists, appreciate the strengths and weaknesses of two health systems, wonder how the teachers coped with two histories, admire the pragmatism of two police forces. None of these groups had anything but the most minimal effect on each other during the long separation and no hatred was necessarily involved. They co-existed and coalesced more easily afterwards because of that.

The possibility of killing made the military aspect quite unlike any of these. German international radio station *Deutsche Welle*[7] compressed it into a couple of simple sentences. 'The two armies had different traditions, different mentalities and different leadership styles. The NVA soldiers would have to go through a more difficult transition than the majority of East Germans.'

Timeline: November 1989. The NVA carries out a reform of itself.
Coalescing seemed, certainly moving into 1990, very difficult in practical terms. Leaving aside the human conditioning, the *Bundeswehr* would inherit an immense quantity of armaments, including 2,222 tanks, 2,378 personnel carriers and 163,039 assault rifles[8], all of course made to Warsaw Pact specifications.

Timeline: 30 January 1990. Hans Modrow, new GDR premier, visits Moscow for talks, and Gorbachev says that ultimate German unification 'has never been doubted'.

Timeline: 18 March 1990. Free GDR elections, the Christian Democratic Union taking 40.8 per cent and paving the way for unification.

Timeline: May 1990. 2 + 4 talks (the Germanys, Britain, France, USA, Soviet Union) in Bonn on unification.

In July[9], the *New York Times* wrote a comprehensive review of the practicalities, pointing out that a new German army would be created, 370,000 strong, absorbing some of the 170,000 GDR force, although officers and career enlisted personnel wouldn't be among them. Like the police, the political tainting would prove fatal to many careers and the higher the officer the more certain the political involvement – not to mention the *Stasi*, who naturally busied themselves with such matters and such people. Some estimates put the number of NVA officers who were members of the Communist Party at 95 per cent and NCOs at 50 per cent.[10] As Dr Wenzke says: 'political officers were not taken over. None of them.'

Again like the police, the fact that the GDR had voted to join the FRG meant the FRG could dispense with niceties and ride hard through the problems: no question of two armies standing side by side, or the NVA having its own department within the *Bundeswehr*.[11]

Timeline: 6 July 1990. Negotiations begin on political unification of the Germanys.

Timeline: 15–16 July 1990. FRG Chancellor Kohl meets Gorbachev in the Caucasus and they agree on a Red Army withdrawal from the GDR. They also agree that no foreign troops would be stationed in the area of the GDR and no nuclear weapons installed there.

Dr Wenzke says that 'in the beginning there wasn't a task like trying to put the two armies together. It was to democratise the NVA and that's why in November 1989 there had been the military reform. Only afterwards did it become clear that there would be the unification, and this military reform got lost in the sand, so to say. The defence minister and the leadership in the NVA thought there would be a putting together.

'We thought it would be very difficult to do and the idea, rather, was one state, two armies, because the mentalities were so different; they would grow together. That was the Eastern view. The Western view from the beginning was to disband the NVA, abolish it. However, it was not as if the West crushed everything because there were efforts to put things together. In October 1990 tens of thousands of soldiers had been taken over. They were not just sent home.'

How did that work because here they are a hostile army?

'That was a very difficult process. It started at least in summer 1990 between the leadership of the *Bundeswehr* and the NVA and was long. They began thinking how they could do it.'

The GDR forces had sworn a new oath to preserve peace and defend the GDR, a radical departure from the paragraph at the beginning of this chapter. Admiral Theodor Hoffmann, the NVA's chief, said the new oath – which some 60,000 career soldiers swore – ought to make them acceptable to NATO. However, units stationed in what had been the GDR would not be fully incorporated into NATO until 1994, when the Soviet troops were to have left.

At unification the combined armies would number 600,000 but, because they no longer needed to prepare to fight each other, the number would be cut to 370,000 with 50,000 coming from the East (half professional soldiers, half recruits).

Timeline: 3 October 1990. The GDR becomes part of the FRG.
Jörg Schönbohm – then in charge of the *Bundeswehr*'s Eastern Command – explained that the GDR soldiers 'went into their barracks in NVA uniforms and on the next morning they came out in olive green NATO colours. The GDR flag was lowered, the flag of the Federal Republic raised. The mood was subdued, marked by waiting, and by mistrust.'[12]

Timeline: 3 October 1990. The Bundeswehr's Eastern Command takes over the NVA.

There were immediate differences. 'The command-giving tactic had to be replaced by the assignment-giving tactic. This was something that most NVA officers learned with great effort,' Gunnar Digutsch, a military expert from the University of Hannover, said, but pointed out that there were immediate benefits too. Recruits from East and West met so 'the *Bundeswehr* was a kind of contact point for young people'.[13]

Dr Wenzke points to a further difference. 'I believe that before 1989 the *Bundeswehr* really was an efficient army ready to fight although the NVA said the *Bundeswehr* was much more civil. Soldiers could go home at the weekends whereas in the NVA, 85 per cent of staff was always on duty and always on alert.' This needs stressing. The 85 per cent readiness applied equally to weekends and at least one lieutenant colonel said that when he was in his garrison he was given twenty minutes from an alarm sounding to be at action stations. Some two-thirds of equipment was kept loaded and a captain recounted how after an alert, six battalions of motorised rifles were out of their garrison and en route, with ammunition for eight days and provisions for twelve.[14]

It leads to a hard question.

How would an ordinary GDR soldier accept orders from a West German officer?

'Many of the soldiers didn't have a choice,' Dr Wenzke explains, 'but a lot had already retired – some involuntarily, some because they wanted to. Some said "I will not serve in an army that's not mine" and others said "I'd like to try" but were forced to retire because of their age or rank.'

Nor was all the traffic one way.

'When you talk to GDR service personnel today there are several things they say were superior. For instance, discipline – there was a different perception of discipline. There were cases where they thought their techniques were better too.'

It seems that when the unification happened the West decided that nothing in the East was of value so they would replace it all.

'Maybe to a large percentage but it wasn't like that 100 per cent. Some of the material was used or sold, for instance the MiG 29 jets. They were used in the *Bundeswehr*.'

What about the ships?

'Sold or given away. They went to Indonesia.'

Presumably most of the equipment couldn't be used because it wasn't compatible?

'That's true and it's why they thought of getting rid of it, a question of spare parts and so on. This involved several hundred thousand tons of munitions – tanks, armoured cars, jeeps, weapons, ammunition.'

Presumably some NVA personnel had a lot of very sensitive information about the Soviet nuclear systems, how it worked in a nuclear alert and so on.

'There were very few who knew about it and they were high ranking. The Soviet Union wouldn't let others look at their hand of cards, and the few who did know are silent today. They wouldn't however know the nuclear codes and the NVA didn't have atomic weapons.'

The border guards numbered around 40,000 in the 1980s and were quickly disbanded. 'They were simply not needed – there were no borders. It was difficult for them to get jobs because people looked at their record and said "no thanks". Some of the border guards went to the customs or guarding things like factories. Very good security!'

There was also the question of NATO accepting people who had, after all, been trained to kill NATO soldiers just months before. Dr Gregory Pedlow, Chief of the Historical Office, Command Group, says: 'I was here in post as the head of the SHAPE[15] Historical Office and SHAPE Historian during the period, as was my British deputy (the Assistant SHAPE Historian). We followed events very closely (I have a particular interest in Germany because my PhD is in modern German history and my wife is German) and we participated in the weekly meetings of the senior leadership of SHAPE discussing all current issues.

'I also had close personal contacts with many of the senior German officers on the staff due to my fluency in German. Neither my deputy nor I can recall a single instance when the integration of NVA personnel was a topic of discussion here at SHAPE (and thus even less so at NATO Headquarters). The integration of the NVA personnel was always viewed as strictly a national issue for the Germans to handle themselves.

'As a senior strategic level headquarters, most of our military staff consist of experienced staff officers in the rank of lieutenant colonel and above, and I do not believe that the *Bundeswehr* took on very many, if any, officers from the NVA at that level (with the exception of some military historians to work on the history of the NVA at the Military History Research Office (MGFA), which soon moved to Potsdam from Freiburg). So none of the German staff officers serving at SHAPE after German unification would have come from the former NVA.

'This was always a matter for the Germans to settle for themselves, and rightly so. You must recall that we are an alliance of sovereign nations, and they determine who serves in their armed forces and who fills international posts such as in NATO.'

Dr Wenzke gives an example of the fate of senior NVA officers. 'A general would be politically very much involved. Something about the generals is very interesting. There had been the thinking in the *Bundeswehr* leadership in summer 1992 to take over some of the NVA generals – very carefully selected and younger – but in the end not a single one was, because, and I think it's very plausible, you couldn't take a general who had been very involved in the system but discharge people of lesser ranks. That would have been difficult to explain. Some of the generals were made civilian counsellors for the military and one became a military doctor. However, he was discharged very quickly because there was proof he'd had contacts with the *Stasi*. Contacts was not the same as just having a *Stasi* file, contacts was more than having a file. Every professional NVA soldier was checked for a *Stasi* file.

'Some 38,000 NVA soldiers were doing National Service and they went into the *Bundeswehr*. The time that they had served in the NVA was calculated quite normally and recognised in the new army' – so if you'd been in the NVA doing a year and a half and you'd already done a year of it you'd be out in six months. 'They were not checked politically because they were the normal National Service intake.

'The highest rank taken over was some first lieutenants and maybe a few colonels but it depended on their age. The greater part were those who were not above the rank of major. Of all the professional soldiers 550 officers and 1,000 junior officers were discharged immediately because they had a *Stasi* past and cheated in the application procedure.'

Summing up generally, Dr Wenzke says 'the old life was taken away and you have to say the people were given a new life, but the transition was very, very quick and very painful for many of them. It will last a long time – until we have the same standard of living – and that is true as far as the army is concerned. It's only this year [2008] that they created the same level of salaries for the former East Germans.'

Where are we now twenty years later?

'It is a united army I think.' He adds a further, general reflection. 'For my daughter, who is thirty-two, these things don't play a role in her life any more.'

Pieces from an old wall ...

Dr Wenzke, an affable man who gave the interview in a heavy military building – actually a villa dating from 1825 – in Potsdam, revealed quite naturally that he has been checked for security 'five times, the last time this year. And it's not over. There may be another one.'

Just for a moment, it chilled the room – as if nothing had changed.

One question – intriguing in a theoretical way, terrifying if theory had become reality – is whether Germans really would have shot at Germans.

'This is very speculative, although from the beginning of the 1970s there was sociological research in the NVA asking exactly that question: would you? The answer from two-thirds of the officers and soldiers was "yes". This percentage decreased during the 1980s.'

But those questions are notoriously unreliable because it's one thing to say yes and quite another to actually do it.

'The idea was to let the GDR soldiers fight against the British or the Americans and not fight the other Germans, but we don't have a written document, and also, if there had been a war it would not have been feasible. Supposedly, if events had moved that far – an imminent war – the Soviet planners would have had to think about it, but ... if there had been the order, I think a large number of soldiers and officers would have followed it. There is even more speculation that if there had been the order to shoot the demonstrators in 1989 in Leipzig some officers said they would not have done it in Leipzig – they would have refused – and others say "I would have followed the order".'

The border guards are a special problem because Germans did shoot at Germans.

'It was like that.'

The situation in the FRG was no clearer. One survey in the early 1980s claimed astonishingly that while 71 per cent of Americans and 62 per cent of Britons would defend their country, only a third of the FRG's citizens would. Leaving aside the curious notion that 29 per cent of the Americans and 38 per cent of the Britons would simply watch their countries being invaded, the FRG's total – whether accurate or not – does surely reflect the deep, profound and unmoving desire that Germans never shoot at anybody anywhere ever again.[16]

So the real answer to the question – would Germans shoot Germans? – is that nobody knows, and mercifully nobody will now.

There was another question. The NVA, having sworn to defend the socialist fatherland, watched it break up without intervening. That answered the question would East Germans shoot East Germans. There are conflicting reports over how close this came, notably in Leipzig as the street demonstrations became more and more powerful in October 1989, and East Berlin. At those moments the structure of the NVA, and its obedience to its political masters, became crucial. The political masters had no idea what to do and the NVA couldn't possibly envisage trying to impose what would have been martial law of its own volition. Nobody had any idea what to do.

To try and hold back the tide running through Eastern Europe into the GDR in the autumn and winter of 1989 by armed intervention, tanks on street corners and, inevitably, bloodshed, would have been insanity.

You can trawl the enormous archive material and you find a lot of GDR people in a lot of desperately difficult situations in just those moments, but none, as far as I can ascertain, recommended anything insane.

All this is in wonderful contrast to a parliamentary report[17] on the state of the 3,500 German soldiers in Afghanistan. It pointed out that in 2007 they drank 1,660,750 pints of beer and 90,720 bottles of wine, while in the first half of 2008 they drank 896,000 pints. A *Bundeswehr* report revealed that 40 per cent of the soldiers between the ages of eighteen and twenty-nine were overweight, an unfavourable comparison (35 per cent) with comparable civilians. They were, in sum, too fat to fight.

Everything *had* changed.

The NVA would never have stood for any of it.

Notes

1. Prussia, in Germany's far east, was the area traditionally associated with militarism. After the war, Prussia was divided between the Soviet Union and Poland.

2. *From Confrontation To Cooperation*, Zilian.

3. *Requiem for an Army*, Herspring.

4. The riots in the summer of 1953 were about the GDR government threatening to cut workers' pay if they didn't meet their work norms while at the same time increasing those norms. The workers struck and their protest grew until they were making political demands. The People's Police and Soviet personnel quelled it by using force although nobody is sure how many people died. A reliable estimate seems to be fifty-five, including four women. The event haunted the GDR leadership and in 1989, as dissidence grew, Honecker demanded 'is this 1953 again?'

5. *From Red To Green*, Rudolf Bahro.

6. Of the Warsaw Pact countries, Poland was of course to the east of the GDR, while most of Czechoslovakia and Hungary faced Austria, which was studiously neutral.

7. *Deutsche Welle* German radio, 3 October 2005.

8. Zilian, op. cit.

9. Craig R. Witney, *New York Times*, 23 July 1990.

10. Zilian, op. cit.

11. *Deutsche Welle*, 3 October 2005.

12. Ibid.
13. Ibid.
14. Zilian, op. cit.
15. SHAPE, Supreme Headquarters Allied Powers Europe.
16. Figures quoted in *Rewriting the German Past*.
17. *The Times*, 3 December 2008.

THE PROCESS OF APPROACHING ONE ANOTHER

To reach the little office where Marion Drögsler dispenses maternal wisdom you cross familiar East Berlin terrain: the broad, straight roads; the tall apartment blocks standing shoulder-to-shoulder; the web of tram lines. You have the familiar feeling that it was all put together to be utilitarian rather than anything else. It feels somehow ragged at the edges.

Drögsler's office is in one of the apartment blocks, a curved building at a crossroads. The office is utilitarian too. It's called the *Arbeitslosenverband Deutschland* e.V, an umbrella organisation for the unemployed, and Drögsler is chairwoman of the whole organisation and the Berlin branch.

Part of her work involves debt counselling, 'mostly people from the East. There are several reasons they are in debt but first of all they have lost their jobs without warning. Unemployment throughout the world is the main cause of people getting into debt. They lose their apartment.

'It was hardly possible to get into debt in the GDR. We didn't have these huge "catalogue houses" where you order things and they send them to you. We didn't have so many kinds of credit and if you took one out you only got part of it. You had to be able to pay the rest yourself. We had banks with cash cards – but not American Express! – and cheques we could pay with.'

If a table cost 100 Marks and you didn't have the money?

'Then you wouldn't buy the table. You saved up until you could.'

And if you wanted to buy a Trabant?

'You had to save up for a lot of years and you had to wait more than fifteen years for delivery.'

The point I am trying to make is that the GDR's citizens were confronted by a society that was geared to spending money.

'Suddenly this came to the East and people didn't cope very well. Today it is still the same. Before The Wall fell you could find ways of obtaining West

Marks to buy things, but after The Wall it was just too much. People were not able to decide what they really needed.'

You can go into a grocery shop and have all the fruits of the world in December and January but you have to be able to choose and you have to be able to pay. I wonder if it was most difficult for the housewife with two children who went to the shop at the corner and everything had changed.

'Of course people went there and they bought a lot. Only then did they notice that they really hadn't the money. I lived in East Berlin from 1983 and I was a teacher. I taught history and citizenship, so I had studied capitalism and I knew about it before I even experienced it. I wasn't shocked when it arrived.'

Others clearly were, and from both sides: the Easterners shocked by how much was in the West, the West shocked by how little there was in the East. And more shocks were coming.

The *Treuhandanstalt* – *Treuhand* for short – was created by the GDR parliament in March 1990 to take over running the centrally planned economy. Initially it was staffed by GDR personnel and the first West German didn't arrive until that June, when unification loomed. The *Treuhand* became an instrument of privatisation – disposing of public property, which meant the companies and factories which had been owned by the state and therefore by all the people – under the Finance Ministry in Bonn, although it was independent. It was to privatise the Kombinates and other firms according to market economy principles – making them capital companies. It also became the most controversial aspect of unification, its Berlin offices firebombed and one of its presidents assassinated.[1]

The emotional impact on the GDR is hard to evaluate because, whatever the GDR had or had not been, its workforce built the factories, ran them and drew their livelihoods from them. They were common property, however remote a concept that might have been to an ordinary worker. The scale was breathtaking: a total of 10,500 companies with 4 million workers spread across 45,000 locations. At one stage it was the world's largest industrial enterprise and its last president, Birgit Breuel, was described as the most powerful woman in Germany.

A senior manager, Dr Christoph Reimnitz, was quoted as saying: 'Of course there were no textbook examples and there were no studies made in advance. It just happened by learning as we went along.'

Breuel said variously 'we are cleaning up forty years' and 'privatisation is the best restructuring'. She faced an extraordinary task: trying to persuade Western companies – and not just companies in the FRG but as far apart as New York and Saudi Arabia – to take on the dilapidated, uncompetitive factories which had been run with little or no regard for the environment; to eliminate the jobs of a vast number of workers and, as someone noted, make the people of the GDR start to think in terms of markets rather than central planning. It was brutal but deemed preferable to a long, lingering death. Breuel was in physical terms dismantling a whole country.

By 1994, when the *Treuhandanstalt* was dissolved, it had raised approximately 60 billion Marks, but spent 300 billion.

It is easy to miss the view from the West.

The five *Länder* in the East represented a third of German territory, had a fifth of the total population but in 1992 contributed less than 8 per cent of the country's economic output. There had been 10 million in work in the GDR but this shrank to 6 million. Eastern growth rates were sustained by vast improvements to the infrastructure but from 1997 the gap widened again.[2]

In May 1998 unemployment in the East touched 18.1 per cent, almost twice that of the West. In 2007 unemployment in the East was 16.5 per cent compared to the national average of 9.8 per cent and 'tens of thousands of locals are still leaving for the West and some cities and towns, where the jobless rate is above 50 per cent, are virtually defunct'.[3]

Professor Dr Norbert Walter is Chief Economist at the Deutsche Bank Group and a former American Institute for Contemporary German Studies Research Fellow. He has written[4] that 'discussions in informed circles considered setting lengthy transition periods to allow the "two states" to converge and to integrate step by step, after securing gradual adjustment of social and economic conditions. By early 1990, all these ideas – however professionally prepared and well meant by their authors – had been scrapped. In my view for a very convincing reason. In practice, such plans would have required a new wall to be built' – by the West to keep the GDR citizens out.

Instead, 'all rules, institutions, taxes, benefits, and the currency were the same for all Germans ... This meant that the 15 million East Germans had to accept a complicated bureaucratic system with which they were not familiar and for which they did not have the necessary advisers (tax accountants and lawyers are just two examples).

'It meant at the same time, however, that a considerable tax and social-contribution burden, plus an enlarged government deficit had to be shouldered by the better-off West German citizens. Since 1990 almost 5 per cent of all West German income has been devoted to financing unification. [To which Ms Kubisch writes: 'hold on – we have all been paying for it since 1991!'] Never in history did such an enormous transfer of resources take place anywhere. It has mainly gone into East German pensions, health expenditures, unemployment benefits, as well as support for ailing businesses, substantial tax subsidies, and the building of infrastructure. ... From 1990 to 2002 some USD 800 billion went east. This is 8.6 times Malaysia's 2002 GDP ... and Malaysia is a country with 24.4 million inhabitants.'

The *Treuhandanstalt* 'helped to privatise more than 10,000 state-owned enterprises in only five years. In the rush, not everything worked out in the most ethical and humane way. Mistakes were made. But the high speed and determination attracted more fresh equity, more much-needed management know-how, and created more international networks (almost overnight) than any other strategy would have achieved.'

However …

'Something very basic went wrong with German unification. Instead of offering helping hands, an open mind and a sympathetic heart, West Germans opened their cheque books. While the money helped materially, it did no good at the human level. In the West, taxpayers developed a condescending attitude. In the East, the status of "poor relation", of permanently receiving help, damaged self-confidence. Some people developed a habit of not even trying to help themselves. The situation encouraged dependence.'

Marion Drögsler says that 'when The Wall came down I became unemployed immediately. I was forbidden from working as a teacher again. Why? Because I was too red! I was a member of the Communist Party.'

Was it the fact that you were a member of the Communist Party?

'Yes, it was all the citizenship teachers – they were all unemployed.'

Did anybody consider whether you were a good teacher?

'No. It was an occupation and this is what victorious people act like.'

Now you know what it's like to be occupied by the Germans.

'Yes, and it's not so good.'

Suddenly you don't have a job. How did you cope with that?

'In the beginning I didn't cope at all. I broke down. I couldn't even go shopping. I withdrew completely. Suddenly you didn't feel you were worth anything. I met a neighbour and we talked a lot and he helped a lot. I can cope with it now because I'm helping people who can't.'

Is it better for you that you have experienced this so when people come in and say 'what do you know about my problems?' you say 'I have experienced them too'?

'Yes, I think so.'

Now twenty years later what are the problems?

'Long-term unemployment, high debts, and still people who psychologically cannot cope with it today. There are people who have not worked for these twenty years and will never work again. They do look for jobs but it seems senseless to them and that's why they are so depressed. First it's psychological, then it becomes physical. What we try to do is help people with the authorities, show them how to fill in applications, where to go, how to write and challenge things. We explain how to do that but we also try to encourage people by talking to them and listening to them. It is painful sometimes. In the beginning it was worse for me because I'd take these people's problems home with me and for whole nights I couldn't sleep. Then I reached a point where I said to myself *I can't go on like this any more, I cannot help them if I keep taking it home*, so I managed to switch off in the evenings. It was very difficult.'

What happens next?

'In the next twenty years it is going to get worse, much worse. The government doesn't take care of the human beings in the country and especially not of the unemployed. We will have a big problem of old age poverty. We will have problems with young people unemployed until their old age. The next generation, which doesn't remember East and West, will have the problems of a capitalist society but they won't have the memory of the time when it at least tried to cope with these problems. If a family lives in the East they will always stay East Germans because the problems are specific.'

In the West people were taught to be problem-solvers, be self-confident. Easterners seemed submissive.

'I must say that we were very self-confident in the GDR and we were very proud of being East Germans. It wasn't that you were forbidden to say things or that the *Stasi* were everywhere. We did our work and we lived quite self-confidently. I was standing in front of my pupils just doing my work. That was okay. And the pupils today still know me; they come and talk to me. When there was a teacher's day I always had huge bouquets of flowers.'

However ...

'An East German would find it difficult to sell himself like a Westerner because before he hadn't had to.'

Her conclusion: 'My impression is that for forty years the West tried to get back this part of Germany but they didn't take it seriously. They said it but they didn't really want it. Then when suddenly they finally did get this GDR they couldn't say "we don't want it".'

The *Sozialwerk des dfb*, part of the *Undine Wohnprojekt*, is another face of East Berlin, a house on one of those many, many terraced streets which spread from the centre as inner suburbs. The house looks entirely unexceptional, just one among the terracing, and that's entirely fitting because it is intended to be normality.

Angelika Engel, team leader of the housing project and a professional social worker with a diploma from West Berlin, explains that 'we take care of people who are special emergencies'. This will involve counselling and accommodation. 'The social welfare office pays for it. If somebody is threatened with homelessness he or she is entitled to support from the social welfare office. You either go there or you come here directly. These are people who have lost their apartments or are threatened with losing them because of debts or alcohol addiction – all the social difficulties, including unemployment.'

People who grew up in the GDR would have no knowledge of a problem like eviction and homelessness.

'I come from the FRG and the problems have been there for a long time. I know these problems. It is a multi-faced problem so you have to look at it from a very individual point of view. Why should it be a bigger problem for people in the East than people in the West who have been facing it all the time?'

Because in the West that's the way it always was.

She concedes that 'life is really difficult if you are not capable of pushing yourself through all the completely new systems to find somewhere to live. You weren't born into the system.'

Did that start to make people drink?

'Yes, certainly. Another problem was the debts you could run up. Suddenly you could buy and buy and buy.'

Did it make it worse that the shops were so full and you're out of a job and you haven't any money?

'That's also a problem in the West. Once you have difficulty coping with society and the system, and you're not one of those people who can find their way through, you will end up like this' – at the *Sozialwerk des dfb*. 'When people come here they get an apartment and that gives them their dignity back so you can begin to become a human being again.

'Society as a whole has changed in the last twenty years, and that includes the West. The gap between rich and poor has been widening and this is a problem that affects people in the West as well as in the East – the whole of society. The shop windows are full, of course, but more and more people cannot afford what is in the shop windows. That makes it worse but it is also a characteristic of the whole of society.'

Birgit Hartigs, of the *Undine Wohnprojekt*, explains that the people who come to the housing project 'have the unemployment benefit and they don't have to work. The money for taking care of them is given to the housing project (by the social welfare office). They are registered with the unemployment office. We have a lot of volunteers. The women in the laundry downstairs work for free; the ironing is done for free. The food in the dining area is a labour office project but the residents also have little kitchens in their apartments. They can eat together when they want. Once a month we have a three-course menu at the weekend and ten or twelve people go to that.'

Loneliness can be the hardest part.

'Yes. It's often said the unemployed lose the everyday structure of their lives, but we have found it is also difficult for them to withstand conflicts and to work in a team, so sometimes it's very difficult for us to not have misunderstandings all the time. We look at each person and try to work with them. They get the apartment, they settle down and we start trying to find a perspective for them. We try to concentrate on these problems – like alcoholism and debt – and we have success in that a lot of people are eventually able to leave. The woman who does the cleaning is a volunteer who comes every day to work. That gives her something to live for, something to be appreciated for, but this is also a success for us.

'Young people learn a job or a profession – they do vocational training. The ones in their mid-twenties have very specific problems because the older people can say "we have reached a certain age, we have reached certain things in life" but the younger people haven't reached anything. The first thing they have done is be unemployed.'

Two case studies from the housing project. In both the interviewee requested anonymity.

Regina S. is an East Berliner, born in 1949.
'Before The Wall came down I worked in electronic data processing. I'd studied that and organisation. I only learned The Wall was open the morning after. I went over that first week to visit some relatives in West Berlin and I did not foresee what would happen to the GDR, not at all.'

As a mother and as a housewife what was it like adjusting to shopping?

'In the newspapers at the time there were a lot of reports about people who had gone and bought things – furniture, for example – and got deep into debt. We in the GDR had furniture; we didn't live with orange boxes, so why buy everything new?'

Very quickly you had all the foods you had never seen before.

'First of all, I tried to buy things I knew like the Eastern face cream, but you couldn't get it everywhere anymore, you had to look for it. At the Metro I got a staff discount and I began to buy things there. Also a new face cream! I cannot remember the weekly shopping [being] a very dramatic change. I wasn't one of the ones who bought everything because it was new, and living in Berlin was always different to living in other places. We had certain things other areas didn't have. We knew what a banana was. I do remember wholegrain bread which I ate because I thought it was healthy, but then I got stomach problems. I went to the doctor, after that I started eating normally again.'

Of all the things that you could buy, which did you like most?

'Oh my God, that's a huge question. Actually, a car. A Citroën, a little car. It was good.'

Regina 'continued to work until 1991 in the same company – it was a trading company making machinery. I was in the organising department. We wrote computer programmes and introduced them into the different departments to be used, for example, in book keeping. Then it became clear the company would be dissolved.

'The company sold part of the ground it stood on to a big West German wholesale company, Metro, who sell a range of products to the trade. We were given the opportunity to apply to work for them so I applied: their data processing unit. They said the department was in Düsseldorf. The man handling it told me to apply for a job as a shop assistant with them in Berlin. I had angst. I said "I won't be able to do this" but he was a good man who understood people. He said "You will. Just try." He was a *Wessi*. So I started, specialising in all the electronic equipment which meant the work was in the same vein as my profession. I was happy.'

Her happiness was having enough time to advise customers and discuss solutions with them in depth. In 1997, however, she applied to a different company because it was nearer home. She found she didn't like the work there 'and when you get to fifty you belong to the old iron, as we say in Germany. It means you're too old. They found a reason to get rid of me. I was now unemployed.

'That was in 1999. I had never been unemployed before and for most of my life never imagined being unemployed. It wasn't bad immediately because the work had been very stressful – ten hours a day and not even in shifts – so in a way I was quite glad. I was also hopeful of getting another job in my field.'

Relatively quickly she got on a retraining scheme for a year – Project Management in Technology – and she was happy again. For a short period she did web design but 'they wouldn't pay me'. She did more retraining – learning different programming languages – and websites for other people. That didn't pay much. 'At least it was work and it was some money.'

Under the Hartz reform[5], where unemployment benefits were changed to help the unemployed, she got work at the housing project. 'Looking back, I know that I had a lot of help from my family. I'm not married anymore but my children support me. For many years I have sung in a choir and they also gave me strong support. The choir helped me to strengthen my self-confidence and I found something to do there: treasurer, as well as doing the website for them.

'I now have a real job with a salary. I take care of other people who work here.'

Friedrich E. from Sachsen-Anhalt, born in 1954.

'[I was] already a mature man when The Wall came down. I was living on the outskirts of East Berlin working in a security company. I went to the West a week after. I had never been there before. It was strange to see all the people going from East to West and I remember the Easterners looking everywhere. It was 100 per cent clear that this was irreversible.

'I started with the security company responsible for the S-Bahn[6] around this time. I was a guard. Now I could get to know stations in the West that I'd only known by their names, like the Zoo and Westkreuz. I had never imagined unemployment. It wasn't in your mind. You couldn't deal with it in your mind.

'I worked in this business until 2000 but for different companies, and also as a security guard in museums. Then I had an operation in October 2000 – groin – and it went a little bit wrong. I needed another operation. I went on sick leave because during the second operation they cut through two nerves and I had a lot of pain. The doctor said he would put me on sick leave. Since then I have still had the pain and my groin cannot be operated on any more. I live on pain-killers. Then the sick payment was stopped and I had to go to the social welfare to get benefits. Then came the Hartz reform and I got unemployment benefit type 2. It is enough to live on if you really work hard at it. It's not easy but I'm on my own and I can do it. You have to keep calculating all the time.

'I knew many guards who had lost their jobs because a lot of the security companies went bust. It was not a profitable business. I don't know what happened to them. I don't have contact with them anymore because I was ill. I only know they also lost their jobs because the companies weren't there any more.

'Before the *Wende* I had two jobs. I was also a train driver and I learnt to be a cook. It's true that there was a lot of talent in the GDR. All my friends from when I was a youngster had at least one kind of talent and some were very talented. The fact that the West came and closed factories was not the fault of the people who had talent but the fault of the people who didn't want the talent.'

If the GDR had survived and the same things had happened to you – two operations, can't work – would you have been better off?

'Yes, financially. It was a different social system. Of course they would have checked whether I was able to work but, when they found out I couldn't, I'd have had a pension I could live on. My mother and grandmother had pensions they could live on, so the social system did give financial security. I have had to come here [to the housing project] but partly it is my fault.

'In 1996 I separated from my partner and my children although I don't want to dwell on the reasons. I couldn't cope with this separation. I came to Berlin; I had lost my courage and my motivation. I was without a home and I lived with people I knew. Then I got a flat from the social welfare office. I was glad to have it but when I was there I was completely on my own and I couldn't cope with that. I didn't do all the things that I would have to have done to keep the flat. I really let loose. I got into debt. I didn't pay the rent. So I was thrown out and went back to friends. That was also very bad.'

Now we're approaching twenty years what do you think?

'It may be a strange answer but I give it very spontaneously: how fast these twenty years have gone. We had forty years of the GDR and I try to measure against that the twenty years of unification. Half of the lifetime of the GDR! Somehow you can't grasp it.'

Is it one Germany or two?

'I don't believe that there will be one in our lifetime. Differences remain, and I notice it with some friends I have in Saxony because they are still getting used to things.'

If you had a magic wand and could go back to 8 November 1989 would you change anything that was to happen?

'I would have to think of all the other people, not myself, because at the time I knew that millions of people wanted it – the *Wende*. Some of the people who wanted it may have found what they were looking for but a lot only got that for a short period. Afterwards [they] might have been asking themselves "was this really what I wanted or were there things I would like to have kept?"'

To balance these bleak studies, please meet again Richard Piesk, as much GDR as Regina S. and Friedrich E., but with a rare ability to reinvent himself whenever necessary. We met him briefly in Chapter Three watching Germany play Russia. He has done a lot more than watch television.

'I was born in Leipzig on 16 January 1941. I had three brothers and a sister who died shortly after the war. My father was a soldier and he fell near Leningrad in the battle for the city so I have no memory of him. There was a huge air attack on Leipzig in 1944 and my mother received severe injuries from an incendiary bomb. She was paralysed. I grew up in Leipzig and life was very hard. I was in many orphanages because my mother died in 1950.

'My brothers and I were separated when we went into the orphanages so I grew up alone. In summer three of us would be together before we'd be separated again. Later on we tried to get together again but the youngest – Manfred – was with an uncle.

'In terms of education in the GDR it didn't matter that your parents were dead or you had no money. I was in an orphanage at the time and I went to school quite normally. When you reached eighteen you had to leave the orphanage and I took a room. First of all I learnt piano-making and I started studying at evening school at the same time. Piano-making in the GDR wasn't that strange a thing to be doing because in the Eastern part of Germany there had been a number of piano-making companies with long histories.'

The GDR needed so many things that pianos would surely be a low priority.

'Some were exported, depending on which company. I worked for a private company, Blüthner, and in 1970 part of it was state-owned. I learnt my craft in 1959 and I worked there until 1970 doing my *Abitur* in the evenings. I am musical and I can play the piano a little!

'It took four years to learn the making of the pianos and I always felt it was a great honour to be able to work with this company. Afterwards I studied electrical engineering for four years, until 1974. In the GDR you could leave a job and study for four years if you had an *Abitur*. Studying was free because the government regarded it as an investment and this was how you could raise the educational level of the population, by letting everyone study.

'Afterwards, you wouldn't look for a job yourself, you'd be given one. I was thirty-three, relatively old to be starting a new career and I was the oldest student in my year. On average they were ten years younger than me.'

What about the girls?

'Good! This was the Karl Marx University in Leipzig [*Ökonomische Kybernetik* – economic cybernetics]. It was okay with people ten years younger and we did a lot of things together. I would have liked to study something which had to do with piano-making, but to study it you needed to study music, and I couldn't play an instrument well enough.'

He chose electronics and began work in an electrical plant (*Institut für Elektroanlagen* – Institute for Electronic Systems) 'responsible for conceptional planning, especially micro-electronics. We had no professional relations with the West. Of course we had a lot of literature which the company bought because in the West micro-electronics was very big business. I also had colleagues who were allowed to go there but they would be members of the Party. I was not a member.'

The government was prepared to invest enough to give you four years education. Why did they not invest in you going to the West to see all the research and learn from that?

'That was a question of whether you were a member of the Party or not. They wouldn't let people out to see. They tried several times to convince me to become a member. If I had gone to conferences and research centres I would have brought valuable knowledge back but I wasn't considered a secure person. They thought I would stay in the West.'

Would you?

'I tried when I was a piano-maker. There used to be a big piano-maker in West Berlin – Bechstein – and I applied. Everything was settled and I was about to start there. That was in 1961, in August. I went with a group of climbers to the Tatra Mountains in Czechoslovakia, we came back on 28 August and The Wall was up. I couldn't do anything.'

The GDR government must have understood it was in competition with the West for micro-technology.

'Yes, they trained a lot of people.'

But they still wouldn't let you go.

'I see it above all because they couldn't be sure I would come back. The second reason, of course, was the money. In the West they knew that the people in the East were trained well and if you'd gone they would have tried to keep you. Some of the colleagues who went didn't come back and naturally that made it more difficult for people like me. The first time I went was after The Wall came down.'

Did you feel that the gap between the East and the West, in terms of micro-technology, was getting wider?

'Yes. I must say that at first the GDR really neglected the field of micro-electronics. They only realised it was so important when they saw that the West was making big progress through micro-electronics. The GDR slept through this development and they didn't realise what you could do with it. My colleagues all saw that it would be very important.'

You were in a privileged position before The Wall came down because you could see what other people couldn't see – that the gap was getting wider.

'It's true. There were people in a lot of other professions who could see that but micro-electronics turned out to be decisive in the whole economy. The GDR realised it ten years too late and it was not possible to catch up. In the West they were going faster and faster, and not only faster but they also had completely different prerequisites. Our economy was one of shortages and the West had an economy of surplus. They could use whatever they wanted; they had all the potential to develop something because they had everything they needed. I remember when Honecker presented the first micro-chip to the public and we really laughed about it. In public it was said to be a big success but those people working in that field just laughed.'[7]

I've heard somewhere that it would have been more efficient to buy Western micro-chips − to go to the West and simply buy them − than make them yourselves here.

'It would have been cheaper but it would have been a loss for our economy. We wanted to produce it ourselves. We had a lot to do with the Russians, especially as far as micro-electronic problems were concerned and we thought that the economic organisation (COMECON, Council for Mutual Economic Assistance), to which all the socialist countries belonged, could succeed. That was Poland, Czechoslovakia, Bulgaria, Hungary, Romania and the USSR. We exchanged information and machinery. In this group the GDR was one of the leading countries and thought that the problem could be solved within it.

'The night The Wall fell I was one of the first to cross at Bornholmer Strasse.[8] I was watching television. I saw the Schabowski press conference and when he spoke the words about travel I got into my car and went to Bornholmer Strasse. There were two or three young guys − I didn't know them − and I gave them a lift. There were already thousands waiting. Then the checkpoint simply opened. I left the car in the East and we walked to the Kurfürstendamm. Everybody was going there and you just had to follow them. One of the young guys had some Deutschmarks and we drank a Guinness. Then we walked back.'

Did you think the GDR was finished?

'Yes. That night. It was clear to me once they opened The Wall.'

Did you have angst for your future because now you are going to have to compete with all the people in the West?

'I had angst. It was also clear to me that under Western conditions professionally I wouldn't have any chance. I stayed another two years. The institute I worked for was part of the big Kombinat − KAB − and the whole system broke down. There was a big restructuring so the Kombinat, which consisted of fourteen big companies all over the GDR, was privatised and all these companies would become independent. The Kombinat ceased to exist in its original form. All the people in the Kombinat who worked at the conceptual level weren't needed anymore and I was one of them.

'Those people were to form project groups cooperating with West German companies. There was a company in Heilbronn where I went very often and we tried to develop something together, but they already had plans to cooperate with a company in Leipzig so nothing came of it.'

Would it have been possible to save the GDR micro-electronic industry with help from the West?

'They kind of put the East and West German micro-electronics together in a form of cooperation but on a very low level. The West was interested in the land and the buildings but not in the people who had worked there. They didn't need the people. They already had their own people.

'My contract was changed to what was called short labour, which meant zero hours, so actually you had a contract but you wouldn't work. That was a very common way of doing it – not throwing the people out immediately but changing their contracts to zero hours. This was the moment when I told myself I had to look for something else. I went to a further education course in East Berlin but this time I wasn't the oldest! Many people like me had to go to further education, had to find something new.

'It was 1992 and I was fifty-three. I studied tax. Yes, completely different: piano – micro-electronics – taxation. I found the change exciting but the real thought I had was *taxes will always be there, they will always have to be paid* so I wouldn't be unemployed. Since I didn't have a clue what taxation involved – apart from paying them – I did the further education to find out. I worked for a company in West Berlin and it was different. I had a boss who came from Bavaria and when The Wall came down he had already started to cooperate with firms in the East in terms of preparing takeovers, preparing guidelines because they had seen the possibilities of making businesses. The whole of East Berlin was like a blank canvas. It was not only a question of taxes but accounting, book-keeping, everything.

'Of course we had book-keeping in the East but the Western system had completely different main criteria. We were a private company and we had to make money to survive. I had colleagues in the Kombinat who just didn't understand and waited for somebody to approach them to tell them what to do. They had the mentality that somebody would come and give them a new job.'

What do you think now, looking back: three lives, two countries, one world war?

'I think I have been quite flexible.' [Long laughter]

Do you feel German?

'Yes, yes, one can say so.'

East German?

'German. Not an East German.'

Do you think Germany has become a normal country?

'What do you mean by a normal country?'

A country which is united, in which everybody has the same rights, no walls in the middle – like France or Holland or Denmark.

'Speaking of it in these terms – how you formulated the question – there is only one Germany, but within Germany there are huge differences.'

How long will it take?

[Long silence] 'A lot of things have changed, a lot of things have improved since The Wall fell, so the process of approaching one another is continuing but it is going to take more time.'

But this is twenty years on.

'It's half of the GDR's life but people in the GDR had a completely different development. That's why it is taking so long.'

Pieces from an old wall ...

The GDR had, of course, a full diplomatic service with embassies far and wide. They would go – and for the familiar reason. An FRG official said, 'with the best will in the world, they only know how to represent the old Communist system and they won't be very useful to us.'

Birgit Kubisch's father was an ambassador in Conakry (Guinea) from 1986 to 1990 and he also dealt with Sierra Leone.

As a young man he did his *Abitur* combined with a vocational training as carpenter and cabinet maker, then studied industrial construction, then International Politics and International Law, then did his doctorate in sociology in developing countries. When the GDR broke down he had spent eleven years of his life abroad working in development aid, trade and foreign policy, mostly in Africa, but he had also travelled to Iraq, Kuwait and Iran.

I think I remember him saying that the West German and the East German diplomats down there were on quite good terms, and that there were inventory lists for everything – and everything had to be given over to the West German embassy, of course.

Afterwards he found himself a job as a construction engineer and worked mainly in developing building projects.

He bought, as a souvenir, one of the paintings on the embassy wall but never made a big thing of it, although he did say 'I still have the receipt and it's in a safe place'. That was in case any zealous observer claimed he hadn't paid for it.

Notes

1. For a scathing view of the economic, political and social developments, see *German Unification: The Destruction of an Economy* (published 1995). It is edited by Hanna Behrend who taught English literature and women's studies at the GDR's prestigious Humboldt University, and has contributions from seven

others. The book is an unremitting and myopic lament, a sort of endless accusation, but valuable because it does set out – clearly – alternative views about what happened.

2. 'Warning in East Germany's Dependent Status' by Brandon Mitchener, *International Herald Tribune*, 30 June 1995.

3. By David Gow, *Guardian Unlimited*, 4 April 2007.

4. *American Institute for Contemporary German Affairs*, Commentary Archive, undated.

5. Named for Peter Hartz who headed a 2002 commission on reforming the German labour market. It was enacted in four parts. Hartz I and Hartz II (introduced in 2003) were intended to ease the creation of new types of jobs.

6. The S-Bahn is the overground Berlin railway system, closely linked to the U-Bahn (underground) but runs separately. The Allies decided after the war that it would remain under the control of the Reichsbahn, now being run by the East.

7. Honecker was evidently extremely proud of the GDR's progress in making micro-chips, without understanding that the West was already making a new generation of them with a great deal more capacity and cheaper to buy. This was taken as an example of how out of touch Honecker was.

8. The Bornholmer Strasse checkpoint (see map for its location) provided some of the most dramatic television images of 9 November as thousands waited, hoping to cross, then suddenly crossing in a great, jubilant torrent. For the story of the opening see *The Wall: The People's Story*, Sutton Publishing, by Hilton.

10

THE WORD IN STONE

The columns of footsloggers are being moved around at a consistent, insistent pace from landmark to landmark. At each, they gather round their tour guides and listen, quite passively, as its particular history is explained. More than any other place you've ever been, in Dresden you need tour guides and explanations for what you are seeing, why you are seeing it and, of supreme importance, what you are not seeing.

This is not the geography and geometry of Leuschnerdamm, this is something else altogether.

Imagine the broad River Elbe flowing in a curve like the crook of an arm and, along the south bank, a great rebuilt panorama of stone terracing, porticos and pillars, cupolas and spires, roofs guarded by statues placed like sentries, battlements and towers. Imagine impossibly ornate churches, their stone blocks a strange, unsettling, piebald mosaic; some blocks dark, some clean and new and sandy coloured. Even from a distance the stonework looks mottled. Imagine a precious few narrow, cobbled streets, the buildings tall and painted pastel shades.

Dresden is not black and white, literally or figuratively; Dresden is many shades.

Imagine, just beyond this tightly packed cluster of streets and churches and squares and museums, another great panorama stretching into the distance, but this one standing in absolute contrast to all the stonework: straight, broad boulevards in the east European socialist style with rank after rank of tall, cliff-face workers' apartment blocks placed like different sentries. Because there are no buildings in between the two panoramas to moderate the contrast, it is immediate, strange and unsettling. The best of the distant past and the worst of the modern gaze at each other, and you wonder what the footsloggers make of that if the guides even bother to point it out. Workers' apartment blocks

don't, by definition, usually count as landmarks on anybody's tour. They count
here. In historical terms they are as evocative and instructive as any of the
rebuilt buildings.

Dresden is not one city but several, not one history but many.

And still the columns of footsloggers tramp to the next landmark, the next
commentary, the next explanation. The commentaries reflect the nationalities
of those who have come. What are they not seeing? One of the most beautiful
cities on earth, once of such delicate, fragile, doll's house memory. Hitler once
said: 'When peoples experience inwardly periods of greatness, they represent
these periods through external forms. Their word thus expressed is more convincing than the spoken word: it is the word in stone.'

Dresden was the word in stone and is again.

Between 13 and 15 February 1945 it was destroyed by bombing and fire.
There is a reason why some of the stone blocks are dark. The fire burnished
them. Some of the rebuilding is genuinely beautiful to behold, genuinely awe-
some in the way it has been accomplished, but the Dresden of 12 February
1945 is gone forever. No doubt the Japanese footsloggers have their own
thoughts about fire storms from the sky.

As long as the past is remembered, Dresden will represent a maze of moral
questions in the present. The answers are always difficult, for historians and
everybody else. Dresden remains a symbol of the mechanised power of
modern war in all its brutality and, although others were too, Dresden stood
apart. Its immortally beautiful city centre, famous throughout the world, was
pulverised to the point where essentially it ceased to exist.

This is what the columns of footsloggers do not see. The hollow teeth and
the rubble are gone forever just as the city of 12 February is gone forever,
although some burnished stone blocks remain visible, retrieved from the ruins
and used in the reconstruction. The clean new stones positioned around them
make them darker still.

You can glimpse what the city was in old photographs, of course, and when
the footsloggers reach the Zwinger Palace, as they will, if they pay 7 Euros
for the art gallery there they can see the Canaletto paintings of the eighteenth century. These depict the old market, the new market, the view from
the other bank and the *Frauenkirche*, the church which is perhaps the most
emotive name of all. The paintings are rich in architectural detail (as well
as people) and the fact that they were painted in the 1700s becomes itself
a haunting thing because they could just as easily have been painted in the
1830s or 1930s, or even 12 February 1945, but never after 15 February.

The *Frauenkirche*, the church of our lady, is almost too heavy in overt symbolism. Its history goes back into the mists but was built anew from 1726 to
1734 with a mighty main dome weighing 12,000 tonnes. It was so robust
that during the Seven Years' War the Prussian army fired cannonballs at it and

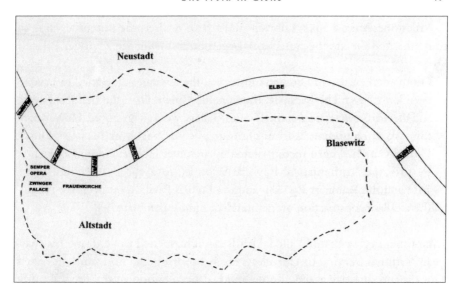

Map 7. The simplest way of understanding the scale of what happened at Dresden. Everything within the broken line – approximately five miles (8.0km) wide – was built-up area and bombed with, at its centre and towards the river, almost 100 per cent destruction.

they bounced off. Legend insists the residents drew the conclusion that it was indestructible, a feeling which seemed to have been confirmed during the great bombing raid as 300 people took refuge in the crypt and the bombs bounced off the dome again. They did blow the windows out and start a fire in the woodwork, including the pews. One report talks of temperatures of 1,000 degrees celsius, weakening the sandstone.

At about 10 on the morning of 15 February, anyone in the square around it heard a slight cracking sound and then a terrible roaring as eight interior pillars supporting the dome gave way. The outer walls also gave way and the dome came down with such force that it smashed through the church's floor. Two stumps remained, pointing upwards like burned hands with an immense mound of rubble between them.

The GDR government left it like that. There are reports they wanted to make the area a car park but the residents protested. The remains assumed a symbolism of what war meant, which suited the GDR government, and a symbolism of what the Allies did (and, by definition, the Red Army did not do), which suited the GDR government even better.

Ulbricht, himself a Saxon, envisaged a socialist Dresden. As a lifelong communist of the dourest kind he was unlikely to concern himself with the restoration of churches or fine houses. He wanted the wide boulevards and the workers' apartment blocks, and he got them under what has been called the doctrines of socialist ideology. Like Berlin, thousands of volunteers cleared the rubble away and in the 1950s the rebuilding began.

Milestone, August 1945: Ulbricht must have realised the potential value of museums and theatres because work began on restoring the Zwinger Palace.[1]

> On the darkest day in Dresden's history ... the Zwinger ... seemed to have been lost forever. The Rampart Pavilion, the Crown Gate, the Bell Pavilion and the northern section of the Picture Gallery were all destroyed. However, the task of rebuilding ... from photographs was begun in 1945–46. The Crown Gate had been reconstructed by architect Hubert Georg Ermisch by 1951, the Mathematical-Physical Salon by 1952, the Bell Pavilion by 1953 and the Rampart Pavilion and the French Pavilion by 1954. By 1963 the whole reconstruction programme was almost complete.[2]

Milestone, 1953: a Briton called Alan Russell happened to be doing his two-year National Service in Germany. He made friends with a student called Günter and one day asked about the Nazi persecution of the Jews. Günter accepted the criminal nature of that but posed a question of his own: *what about Dresden?* The answer, in time, would have profound consequences for Russell's life and the *Frauenkirche*.

Russell would come to know that Dresden 'was called by Hitler the Pearl of the Reich, which was why when he went down there he had the Theaterplatz renamed the Adolf-Hitler-Platz, which they changed back again rather quickly afterwards'. Russell came to understand, among many other things, that 'whereas West German cities like Frankfurt had been rebuilt – and to a considerable extent not very well rebuilt – quickly after the war, in Dresden everything went much slower because they were in the GDR and they didn't have the money. They did the essentials like providing flats and other things had to wait.'

Dresden and Coventry were linked by the bombing: Coventry had been pulverised by 515 bombers in November 1940 in an attempt to blast it, and its industries, out of the war. Incendiaries were extensively used and St Michael's Cathedral gutted.

Milestone, 1959: The two cities, in an attempt at international reconciliation, twinned – an astonishing thing for anywhere within the closed GDR to do.

Russell is interesting about that. The reason for the twinning he points out is that it would give the GDR some sort of recognition de facto. 'They were very keen to achieve recognition. The GDR had quite left-wing trade union people as friends in Coventry and they – the GDR – were very keen to use that as a wedge in the door to eventually get the door open and help make the GDR a legitimate state. There's no doubt about that.

'Dresden is linked with a lot of places, of course, including St Petersburg. Its link with Coventry was a rather natural one in the sense that these were two cities, both seriously damaged, and cathedral cities. They'd had this common

dreadful experience so it was quite understandable they should seek a twinning partner, but the GDR did have these other political motives.'

*How difficult was it for people from Coventry to go [to Dresden]? Twinning means
you go and stay and then they come and stay.*

'It was quite difficult, actually. People from Coventry did go but very often
the difficulties to be overcome were about visas and permissions, which could
take a long, long time to surmount. The GDR had delegations, but these were
all committed people. You could be sure they were carefully selected.'

Russell, working in Brussels in 1979, visited the GDR on leave. 'I went to
Jena and I wanted to go to Dresden but I didn't have enough time. I did see
a chunk of the GDR, not just Jena but other cities too, and I also visited the
terrible camp, Buchenwald.'

What did you make of the GDR?

'They were relatively successful economically at that time. My impression
was surprisingly of a country which was to a considerable extent at peace
with itself. The police were very polite; the Soviet soldiers were very well
turned out. The young people I met all knew what they were going to do
in life – engineers, this, that and the other. They believed in the future of the
system, as far as I could judge on a short visit. It was a sort of 1930s existence
and people remember that in Dresden today when they look at the crime
rates. They compare it unfavourably with what happened in the GDR time.

'It had a very strong political underpinning too. I remember talking to a guy
who spoke fluent English – my German then wasn't too great – and he had been
a prisoner of war in Britain for quite a few years. He said, "Why don't you let
Northern Ireland become free and get rid of this artificial barrier there between
the north and the south?" I said, "I don't think it's as artificial as the Iron Curtain
between Eastern and Western Germany." He said, "You don't understand." I'd
like to meet him again and have another discussion with him ...'

Milestone, 1985: in Dresden more important buildings, including the
Semper Opera House[3], were brought back to life but the priority was indus-
trial construction. Nine colleges, including the Technical College, kept
Dresden as an educational and scientific centre.

The *Frauenkirche* remained rubble.

Professor Norman Blackburn from Manchester was drawn to Dresden, and
the story of his visit[4] is so evocative of life in the GDR, its own rhythms and
frustrations, that I quote it extensively. I am grateful for his permission. Note
that his words encompass a whole attitude to life in the GDR and demonstrate how ordinary people would have to change to survive after 1989 – a
mere two years on from his visit.

[Dresden] was an uncomfortable city to visit, with the eternal queues for
restaurants, even when one could see unoccupied tables as one waited, its

Byzantine system of money – my wife was once unable to buy a 50 Pfg stamp with GDR currency even though she had just changed DM 70 into GDR Marks at the same counter – and its disorganised state, in which the information that one needed was simply impossible to obtain.

I arrived there with my wife by train from Berlin in 1987, and as we arrived at lunchtime we took a table in the station restaurant. No one served us until 1.45, and then the waitress came to say that service of lunch had ended at that time. We went out to take a taxi to the hotel, the Bellevue, a necessity for me on account of my lameness, but we had to stand in a queue for 45 minutes. It only made it even more annoying when we later found that the number 4 tram went directly from the station to the hotel. In the hotel we were able to have lunch despite the hour, but there only Western currency was accepted.

We were unwilling to go on paying the high prices of the hotel restaurant, and in any case we wanted to live like everyone else in the city, so we sought and found a restaurant on Strasse der Befreiung (Albertstrasse) in the Neustadt. We did eat there, and much more cheaply, but not once without queuing – not good for my lameness. Seeking something better we saw a *Weinhaus*, so one evening we tried to eat there. The attendants at the door hesitated to admit us, but finally we were allowed in: we had good food there and, incidentally, we discovered how good Saxon wine can be. We were even allowed to pay in East German currency, but when we tried to reserve a table there for the following evening we were told that this could only be done through the hotel. We had thought that we had escaped from the system, but … we had been recognised as from another land: we had been admitted on that account.

We wanted to visit Pillnitz [an eastern suburb], and we found information on how to go there at the tram stop. But the information about trams, in guides, maps and signs, simply did not correspond to what actually happened, and at our first attempt we did not get there at all. The confusion was not because we were strangers: on one occasion the locals were asking us if we knew the way! The next day we tried again and this time were able to unravel the system. It was close to lunchtime when we arrived, and as we approached the ticket office for the *Bergpalais* [the chateau], it closed. We were able to have lunch at a self-service place and we had a walk in the gardens. So we had succeeded in our aim, but so inefficiently: nothing seemed to be done with the intention of pleasing. On the return we again had troubles with the trams, and rickety old things they were. But they did take us through the Villa area of Blasewitz, a side of Dresden of which I had previously been unaware.

There was no advertisement of times of opening of the famous museums: you had to take your luck. It was thus that we did not visit the *Grünes*

Gewölbe [Green Vault, full of old treasures]: we tried on our last day there
and it was closed. These constant frustrations made us look forward to the
return to the West, but as we took a tram ride that evening my wife spotted
a plaque outside the *Marcolinipalais* saying that Wagner had lived there. I had
seen it only fleetingly, but the following year I spent two days in Dresden
and I returned to look at it then. On a bus tour of the city that year we
drove down Fetscherstrasse and the guide pointed out that the buildings on
one side were old and on the other new, because that had been the boundary of the firestorm.

By then I was beginning to feel familiar with the city as it was in the
GDR. As I waited for the tram at Postplatz I saw the sign: *Dresden grüsst seine
Gäste* – 'Dresden welcomes its guests'. It is still there. Well, it was not exactly
a welcoming city, but after what we British had done to it I felt lucky to be
there at all. I was able to make another short visit the following year, and
I saw *Moritzburg* and the *Sächsische Schweiz*, but that was 1989, and a few
weeks later the GDR all but collapsed.

It did collapse.

When it did, efforts within Dresden itself – forming *Call From Dresden* –
and abroad were concentrated on raising funds to restore the *Frauenkirche*.

Milestone, 1993: Alan Russell co-founded The Dresden Trust to answer
that call. He was initially moved to do something about reconciliation when
the Queen didn't apologise during her 1992 visit to Germany and, coinci-
dentally, a statue was being erected to Arthur Harris – who had headed RAF
Bomber Command – in London. It was highly controversial.

'We have always been very careful as a trust to present a balanced view,'
he says. 'Many of us think it was a strategic mistake, not just a human one, to
bomb Dresden in that way at that time, but this is in no way to criticise the
RAF people involved.' He saw what he was doing as a recognition of the
civilian suffering and an atonement while never forgetting that 55,000 Allied
airmen died too in the war.

Russell does not accept that the bombing campaign, designed to end the
war as quickly as possible, can be equated with the actions of the Nazi regime
or that the bombing of Dresden was the equivalent of Auschwitz. Nor does
he question the sincerity of Harris and Churchill in believing that bombing
would end the war quickly.

However, he has said: 'Nations must be able to look critically at what has
been done in their names in order to have the right to examine what other
countries have done.'[5]

Milestone, 1994: Russell first went to Dresden. He had been 'fully in favour
of unification but I think it would have been better not to change everything
quite so rapidly in the GDR'.

Here was a chance nobody thought they'd ever have and Chancellor Kohl thought 'we must seize it now and worry about the consequences later'?

'I think that's right, and remember when Helmut Kohl went to Dresden he was received with great joy. They were shouting "Helmut, Helmut". The GDR was bankrupt at that time. It couldn't go on, because all these social programmes effectively couldn't be paid for.'

How did that impact on Dresden, because suddenly here's rich Uncle Hans with lots and lots of money?

'They didn't like it. There was a lot of resentment about it. A lot. That definitely lingered on into my time in 1994. It's still there, I would say, to some extent. The activities of the body set up to take over the state corporations – the *Treuhand* – were very much resented, closing down and selling off the real estate values, all this kind of thing.'

In the city itself, did the impetus come from East or West Germans to rebuild the Frauenkirche*?*

'That's a very good question. The Dresdeners complain, and I think they are right to complain, that a number of the people who have had offices of influence over the last decade have been *Wessis*. It's been a patchy picture but regarding the rebuilding of the *Frauenkirche* the impetus has come from East Germans – although again not from all of them. There are architects there who wanted to rebuild Dresden in the modern way because they said "that's what you should do, you shouldn't be building Disneyland"[6] and so on. There has always been a lot of tension between the modernists and the people who wanted to rebuild it as it was. If you take the *Schloss*, which is now nearing completion, a good man called Dr Adler – who came back from the *Wehrmacht* to his totally destroyed city – was one of the people who fought tooth and nail to see that the ruins were kept and not swept away. The East Germans planted roses on the rubble at the *Frauenkirche*, and roses were a protected plant so that made it more difficult to move the rubble: the actual relics would still be there for people who wanted, right through the GDR, to get it rebuilt. They were coming together even before The Wall came down, so a lot of the impulse came from the East.'

There was, inevitably, the problem of property ownership. Dorothea Wiktorin of Cologne University made a special study of the land and property problems which Dresden posed some ten years after reunification.[7]

'Although the legislation and substantial funding packages came from national and regional governments, the key executors of all the legal requirements were local authorities. They saw themselves confronted with the ghost of German history, emerging within a few months after the reunification in the form of 2.2 million applications for restitution of dispossessed land property. In some inner cities like in Dresden and Leipzig claims covered nearly 80 per cent of the urban land.'

She points out that soon after the fall of The Wall, Dresden 'with 465,000 inhabitants was expected to be a main centre of economic growth. The city, especially the city centre, therefore, got under extreme investment pressure. But the desire to invest soon was confronted by a problematic urban structure. Not only the total annihilation by Allied air raids on 13 February 1945, but also the post-war reconstruction under socialist urban planning left deep scars in the townscape.

'Right beside the historical sights like Zwinger and Semper Opera one can find empty sites of enormous size, residential areas and old buildings falling into ruins. On the one hand, structural investments in the repeatedly destroyed city centre were urgently and quickly needed to restore the central functions, especially the retail business. On the other hand urban planners and local architects – supported by the public opinion – felt obliged to restore the significant townscape with a great deal of sensitivity for the cultural history. Such a task needs time and money – which were both lacking.

'… This basic conflict was made even more aggravating by the enormous extent of unsolved property claims in the inner city. Nearly 20 per cent of a total of 40,000 property claims in Dresden were located in the inner city.'

It was the same as Berlin, where more than one claim might be made on the same piece of land and sometimes involving the Jewish Claims Conference. It was made more complicated because 'land and property registers largely ceased to exist after about 1952 in the GDR since the state did not anticipate returning property to former owners in the future. So it was very difficult to identify former real estate boundaries exactly.'

Unravelling this took a long time but the ten years after the fall some 92 per cent of claims had been processed.

'So it can be said that the transformation of property rights has resulted in a rather small real estate market since many claims are still not clarified [and] any use or development of the covered sites like selling, raising a mortgage or even renovating an old building were prohibited and still are. As a consequence of very limited land supply, real estate prices exploded. In 1991 they reached West German levels. In top locations, for example Prager Str. or Altmarkt, a square metre of land changed hands for up to 9,000 Marks.

'Development of the central empty sites is several years behind schedule. None of the ambitious great building projects in the inner city have been completed [Wiktorin was writing in 2001). The utter desertion and emptiness of the old socialistic city centre has not yet been overcome – with a couple of exceptions, however.

'To make matters even worse, the decay of building in the old inner city continues, although the local authorities are responsible for the maintenance of property that has not been returned to their former owners yet. But since the old owners are not legally required to pay for work carried out after unification without their consent, most local authorities – also in Dresden – cannot afford to spend their limited resources on reclaimed housing. At the same time, prospective new owners cannot invest until their claims are legally established.'

She noted that 'private professional developers are those who profit from the transformation process mostly: for example, real estate agents, property companies, investment funds, joint-stock, retail and office companies and so on. Admittedly it is a heterogeneous group, but most of these new owners have something in common: their main interest is a commercial one, namely to maximise the exchange value of the land. In general, business corporations from West Germany predominate, and also the private persons who invest in real estate are mostly not habitants of Dresden. The traditional landowner, type owner-occupier, who uses his property as a reliable asset and whose interests are not only commercial but determined by consciousness of tradition is – at least in city centres – a dying out species.

'Though it was wished, the historical parcel layout in the inner city of Dresden – especially on the huge empty sites – could not be restored, because a) the claims of the former owners were not entitled, a fact that is not only true for Dresden but for all cities in East Germany. The data till 1998 shows that on average only a quarter of all claims lead to a restitution of property in kind (tab. 2). In most cases the former owners had been lawfully dispossessed and had gotten a financial compensation. The statistic for Dresden shows that only 17 per cent of all property claims in the inner city were entitled.'

The Dresden synagogue, torched in the orgy of violence on Jews in 1938 on the Night of Broken Glass – Kristallnacht – was rebuilt. The original Star of David, saved by a local fireman who concealed it until the end of the war, was set above the new entrance.

This is impossibly sensitive.

'There were maybe 5,000 Jews there before the war. Half escaped and I'm afraid the other half went the other way,' Dr Russell says. 'Dresden wasn't a particularly Jew-free city. It persecuted its Jews as did other places. Dresden also became not just a beautiful, beautiful city but a holiday place for SS and Wehrmacht officers. Having been a Red city it went Nazi. You don't read much of that in the GDR history books. I can show you a GDR film made in the 1980s talking about how they were rebuilding a socialist city and so on, and how the Allies had only bombed the highly populated cities and not the industries. They were prepared to make capital out of it.

'The property claimants felt they should get financial compensation and so they should.'

Dresden must have been particularly intractable because so much had been bombed flat.

'It had gone.'

And people had rebuilt on top of it. How are you going to unscramble that?

'You can't: they simply have to have compensation. You can't pull down a whole block of flats in order to give it to someone who lived there in 1933. One or two people have, to my regret, shown twinges of an old anti-Semitic view – "well of course he wasn't German, he was Jewish". It makes me turn over.'

To illustrate the complexities and the undercurrents, Dr Russell says: 'It is interesting that they are just now completing the refurbishment of the *Altmarkt* which is where all the bodies were burnt, thousands of them – terrible – and they have put an underground garage there. We have tried to get a statue erected, together with a born Dresdener and wonderful, wonderful lady called Karin Churchill – of all things! – who came over to Britain after the war and married a Captain Churchill. She was in Dresden in 1945 and only just failed to get her mother out of the hole she was trying to crawl from before the building collapsed. Her mother died.

'Captain Churchill, who was on the Normandy beaches, is 100 per cent with her and that's absolutely as it should be. She is a sculptress and she wanted, with us and some Dresden friends, to put the new statue up where the statue of Germania has stood in the *Altmarkt*. Germania was put up in 1871 as a celebration of the Prussian victory over the French, although the statue in itself wasn't in any way vainglorious or warlike. A lot of us felt, because the *Altmarkt* was the scene of this gruesome burning of so many people, that there should be something there in the middle of the square.

'We never managed to persuade the city council and the idea has never come to fruition – whether it will, who knows? People said they didn't want it a) because it was where Germania had been and might be taken as depicting Prussian victory and b) because "we have two memorials to what happened here". One is the *Frauenkirche* in which hangs the old cross, battered and bent but now rebuilt, and the other is the moving remembrance area just outside Dresden. It's where the British Embassy and the trust lay their wreaths every year as thousands of Dresdeners remember. It's a very dignified thing with memorials which mark Coventry, Stalingrad as well as Dresden. The ceremonies which are held there are in no sense an attempt to justify or to glorify the dead; it is just a remembrance place. So they said "we have these, we don't need another one".

'We do feel that something should be put there. Until they started to recreate the *Altmarkt* area, the only memorial that they had was in the cobblestones: little individual letters on steel pegs saying that this was where all these people were cremated. The cars rolled over it and the people walked over it without realising.'

Rüdiger Patzschke, a Berlin architect, helped found the Association for the Historic Dresden Newmarket (*Gesellschaft Historischer Neumarkt Dresden*) to rebuild the area as near as possible to exactly how it had been. Gabriele Tagliaventi – a leading figure in European urban renewal – and his students at the University of Ferrara began work on a plan for all of the Newmarket.

'A lot of people don't realise that parts of the city were not blown down,' Dr Russell says. 'If you go out into the suburbs where the hills and all those great villas and the three castles are, there is a lot of beauty which survived. Of the city centre only a limited amount will be rebuilt in the old style. The river front, which has largely been rebuilt, is the main part of it. They can't rebuild the old residential town because the houses have all gone. There were medieval houses all along one of the streets behind the *Altmarkt* where some of the Bach family lived. None of that can be recreated. It's just gone.'

You couldn't do it from paintings, old photographs?

'You'd have to knock all the buildings down which stand there now, so that is not feasible. I think the reason why a lot of people have been so fierce about the *Neumarkt*, particularly the society for rebuilding it, is because it is the one place where you can rebuild. There was huge resistance to the proposal which came out when they had a competition to build a new kind of arts centre there, which was hyper modern. A lot of people, including me, thought it was very ugly indeed. Anyway, it's been put on one side.

'You can't rebuild the city as it was then because the inhabitants were mainly ordinary poor people. The land now is so valuable you couldn't do it.'

The city council laid down guidelines that rebuilding must be accurate. The streets should be where they were originally and the building material authentic. There was talk of as many as eighty old town houses and hotels.

The majority of the GDR apartment blocks which run full to the city centre won't be coming down any time soon. They are, Dr Russell concedes, 'not very pretty, but in some cases they [are] a lot better than the living had been before the war where people lived in little houses in the middle of Dresden where the light didn't come, which were rat infested and so on. It's not bad housing apart from the fact they don't have lifts so the old people have to walk up four and five flights of stairs. The actual flats are very decent. They have been modernised and made prettier since The Wall came down. People now have to pay a lot more rent but they have far better flats. Some blocks have been pulled down already on the banks of the Elbe. One has gone completely; the other is now a hotel.'

The rebuilding of the *Frauenkirche* would work at different levels but even making a start proved problematical.

'The Evangelical church was at first very opposed to the rebuilding and I know some of the people who made very distinguished contributions to the rebuilding effort had a lot of doubts about it,' Dr Russell says. 'They thought it should perhaps even stay as it was to remind people what had happened and what they and their fellow citizens had been responsible for. The rebuilding of the *Frauenkirche* was seen partly as a religious matter but primarily as the symbol of the city, a great symbol, which had to be rebuilt to enable the city to rediscover its historic soul.'

That represented two levels, religious and civic. A third was improving British-German understanding by removing stereotypes, something which would happen quite naturally as people came to know each other, and a fourth that Dresden, with the *Frauenkirche* once again watching over it, would become a symbol against all war and all crimes against humanity. Not everybody living in a quiet street in the genteel south-coast English town of Chichester thinks like this, but Alan Russell did.

The Trust raised some £1 million from several thousand individuals and more than a hundred companies. 'We had money from pilots who were on the raid and pilots who were not on the raid. Also from one of the RAF stations in Lincolnshire where some of the bombers flew from.' This enabled it to present the church with an exact replica Orb and Cross to go on top of its dome. A technical committee did some in-depth research and commissioned a London silversmith to make the replica – 26ft high and made of gold. A son of one of the airmen on the bombing raid worked on it ...

Meanwhile, construction, using 3D techniques, the inevitable computers and every original stone block they could get their hands on, proceeded.

The construction of the reconciliation was working too.

'Sometimes,' the magazine *For a Change* wrote, 'there were profound personal stories behind these gifts. For example, Richard Murray from Horsham in the south of England had been much angered by German wartime bombing. In 1957 he had found freedom from his hatred and had "apologised in tears" to some Germans for his bitterness. Now, in 1997, he gave half of a legacy he had inherited. ... [H]e believes that, according to the canons of war existing in 1939, the Dresden raid was morally wrong and had something criminal about it.'[8]

The German stonemasons found themselves working alongside Britons, Frenchmen and Spaniards.

Milestone, 1999: Dr Herbert Wagner, Dresden's mayor, made an official visit to Coventry. Councillor Nick Nolan, the chair of Economic Regeneration, had visited Dresden four years earlier for the 50th anniversary of the bombing. Before Dr Wagner came he said: 'Coventry and Dresden set the tone for peace and reconciliation at civilisation's darkest hour. Our future role now must be to set a standard in joint economic cooperation and development links with other European cities. I am looking forward to meeting my old friend Dr Wagner again.'

There was to be a special service at Coventry Cathedral with, as its centrepiece, the Cross and Orb for the *Frauenkirche*.

Milestone, 2004: the Cross and Orb were placed on the *Frauenkirche*, in front of 60,000 people.

Milestone, 2004: Queen Elizabeth made a second official visit to Germany and acted as host to a concert in Berlin to raise money for the *Frauenkirche*. There was speculation that she might apologise for the bombing. She did not, even in coded words.

At least the footsloggers, moving from landmark to landmark, are spared all such dilemmas. They get the commentaries and the verbal picture postcards instead.

Milestone, 2005: the *Frauenkirche* was consecrated with all appropriate pomp and ceremony, and a full cast of German dignitaries. The Duke of Kent, patron of the Dresden Trust and the British-German Association, attended. He said: 'To be able to share in the pain of others, and in a small way work with them in building reconciliation into friendship and cooperation, is at once healing and fulfilling.'

Milestone, 14 February 2005: the sixtieth anniversary. The Reuters news agency reported that some 10,000 residents wore white roses to symbolise reconciliation and many lit candles. Representatives of the four Allied powers attended a wreath-laying ceremony at a mass grave.

The anniversary also attracted the neo-Nazis, the revisionists, the people who wanted to exonerate Germany and those trying to rehabilitate Hitler. An estimated 5,000 came in what was described as one of the largest such gatherings since the war. The National Democratic Party (NPD), a hard-right group, was instrumental in the organising. They had already made their contribution to historical debate a month before at another anniversary, the liberation of Auschwitz. As the Saxony parliament commemorated it, they walked out. Their leader had been quoted in the German newspaper *Die Welt* as saying: 'Only great leaders can commit great crimes.'

By his own definition, that would have bestowed greatness on Churchill for the bombing raid, although whether the leader was capable of such extrapolation, or indeed any form of extrapolation, is unclear.

The police were mustered in large numbers, deploying water cannons to extinguish a new burning problem. The far right wore their new uniforms, heavy boots and bomber jackets; they waved their new flags – black – and they marched to their traditional music, Wagner. They had balloons with the legend *Allied bomb terror – then as now. Hiroshima, Nagasaki, Dresden and today Baghdad. No forgiveness, no forgetting.* And, of course, no mention of Guernica, Rotterdam, Coventry or Warsaw.

Some seventy arrests were made.

The German Chancellor, Gerhard Schröder, had already indicated it would be unacceptable for the far-right to try and hijack the anniversary. He decried the attempt to 'reinterpret history'. The premier of Saxony, Georg Milbradt, spoke of democracy, of remembering and of how there was no wish for 'others' to do any hijacking.[9]

The elusive part is normality, a word which has run like a theme throughout this book. Two Dresden residents kindly tried to find it.

Christoph Münch says that 'the "ordinary Dresdener" doesn't exist. Everybody who experienced the bombing personally – and there are still quite a lot of people alive who saw at least the fires or the ruins as children – will never forget these memories. Therefore, their attachment to the bombing of Dresden is very close and personal, even if it is also human that people don't want to be reminded always. However, many use the commemoration day on 13 February to do that.

'For the younger generation, the bombing of Dresden is part of common history. They usually don't feel more concerned than young people in Frankfurt, Cologne, Hamburg, London, Coventry or Tokyo, just to mention some cities which were damaged partially or heavily in World War Two.

'The commemorations on 13 February are more political than personal: left and centre against war everywhere, extreme right against democratic systems and for revenge.'

Cornelia Triems-Thiel was born in the city in 1963 and lives near the airport. She is a bank clerk. 'It has become a normal tourist destination – (stronghold). There are almost no ruins left, and also much of socialism has gone: that is, buildings you would say were typically socialist, like our *Fresswürfel* (a restaurant complex nicknamed the "eating cube"). The tourism has already slowed a little. With the building of the *Frauenkirche* it was rounded off somehow.'

How conscious are ordinary Dresdeners of the bombing still? (Mythology says that to mark the first air-raid alarm, at about 9.45 p.m. on the first anniversary, two schoolboys climbed the steeple of the *Kreuzkirche* and chimed the bells. Since then, every year on that day at that time, all Dresden bells chime.)

'That is when we think about it. I can hear it where I live because we have so many churches here. It's all over town; it's like everything being paralysed. The bells don't actually chime for very long but, you know, long is only just a word. I have never looked at my watch – but you hear it and you notice it.'

Apart from that, through the year?

'Nothing. It is rather that one day when everybody notices it.'

Do the old people you know speak about it?

'Rather less. They don't want to know of it anymore. If I ask my parents-in-law how they have experienced it they don't really want to say. They were children at the time. There are stories of how they went to filch the coals out of trains and so on.

'I don't feel like somebody special. I would say it is a city like every other city, it is life like life everywhere.'

If you had a magic wand and could go back to 8 November 1989 would you change anything that was to happen?

'No, but I would change things so you would have more spare time again – more time for your family – like it was before. And the security: that your children could go to kindergarten and you could go to work. I would like to live for one month in the GDR again and do what I did then [laughs]. It was such a good time ... on the whole ... everything was always so easy, somehow. Actually, I felt that life was easier than it is now. We had more fun – but maybe you'd also have to ask a different generation because this was just my youth.'

You couldn't go to, say, Rome.

'But I didn't miss this. I went to the Baltic Sea or Berlin and that was enough for me. You don't miss what you don't know.'

The reconciliation went on.

British independent schools had been offering places for free or at a reduced cost for mostly senior students from Dresden and Saxony. They got to experience British life in all its guises, including sport. The Dresden Scholars' Scheme was created by David Woodhead of the Independent Schools Council and a member of the Dresden Trust.

The footsloggers are coming now. In terms of overnight stays: 6 million in 1999, rising from 7,791,661 in 2004; then as the *Frauenkirche* was re-consecrated the following year 8,712,957; then 10,321,037 in 2006, falling back in 2007 but still over 9 million. They come from all over the world: in 2006 from more than fifty countries. In 2007 some 63,159 Americans stayed overnight, Switzerland next on 52,661, then Austria 40,298, Britain 39,854 and Japan 38,587.

For comparison (and accepting that Coventry has many virtues but isn't exactly a tourist destination), here are the 2006–7 figures for overnight stays in York, population 137,500. Total: 4,182,000, of which 15 per cent (627,300) were from overseas (47 per cent from Europe, headed by Germany, Holland and Belgium – 294,831; 26 per cent from the USA – 163,098; 14 per cent from Australasia – 87,822; 6.55 per cent from the Far East – 40,700; 6.5 per cent from the rest of the world – 40,700).

There are obvious differences. York wasn't bombed and its Minster rebuilt. Dresden is much easier to reach. In modern parlance its catchment area – a day's drive in coach or car – takes in middle Europe, the *Frauenkirche* is an obvious attraction, as the Dresden statistics show, and it has a certain novelty still.

Even the footsloggers who know nothing of history cannot escape the conclusion that something truly dreadful happened here. Any picturesque panoramas from before 13 November 1945 – they're on the postcards the footsloggers can buy – spread a vision of how dreadful it was because so much does not exist anymore. What the footsloggers surely can't visualise is what the firestorm did to ordinary people's bodies, because the human mind has safety valves. In that sense, Dresden takes its place with Hamburg, and

Auschwitz, and Warsaw, and Hiroshima, and Nagasaki as beyond imagining, beyond experience, beyond the register of words.

By a grotesque irony, the bombing opens the way to reconciliation but, as we have seen at the sixtieth anniversary of it, can still be used as a tool for those with political agendas. Even with the latest developments in research and the body count, there is no reason to imagine they will stop using it.

A Royal Air Force memorandum in January 1945 said: 'Dresden, the seventh largest city in Germany and not much smaller than Manchester, is also far the largest unbombed built-up the enemy has got. In the midst of winter with refugees pouring westwards and troops to be rested, roofs are at a premium. The intentions of the attack are to hit the enemy where he will feel it most, behind an already partially collapsed front, to prevent the use of the city in the way of further advance, and incidentally to show the Russians when they arrive what Bomber Command can do.'

The arguments have long been explored, and exhaustively. To reprise them in summary:

You can construct a compelling argument that Dresden was an undefended international heritage site of limited military value bloated by refugees fleeing the Red Army, and equally that it had many industries feeding the German war effort;[10] that it was a pivotal railway junction for reinforcing the German front against the Red Army and, *because* it was unbombed and of such fragile beauty, pulverising it would deal Germany a profound psychological blow.

You can construct a compelling argument that, very soon, many millions of Soviet soldiers would be in the heart of Europe and wouldn't be going home, but millions of American soldiers would, opening the Continent to Stalin's appetite. Reducing Dresden to its foundations *had* to be a precise illustration of what, as the memorandum said, air power could do to him.

You can construct a compelling argument that strategic bombing might have been justified – but 1,300 heavy bombers dropped enough high explosive and incendiaries to make thirteen square miles of the city resemble hollow, blackened teeth in a static sea of rubble; or that, after Guernica, Rotterdam, Warsaw and Coventry, the Germans had it coming.

Neo-Nazis, revisionists in general, anyone who wants to exonerate Germany and those curious people working to rehabilitate Hitler – all can reach for the tool and try to use it. Their motives are invariably obvious and their methods shameless. One is equivalence: if the Nazis behaved badly by killing all those Jews, the Allies behaved badly by bombing all those civilians in cities up and down Germany, culminating in Dresden. *We are all equally guilty and consequently Hitler can't have been so bad after all.*

It seems fertile ground, not least because there was an inevitable measure of confusion after the bombing and subsequently, with Dresden isolated in the GDR, real investigative work with original documentation was virtually impossible. Nor could anyone know definitely how many refugees were in the city. This combination of circumstances allowed speculation, invention, manipulation and outright distortion to be applied to the number of dead.

I give you a blatant example from a website:

> More than 260,000 bodies and residues of bodies were counted. But those who perished in the centre of the city can't be traced. Approximately 500,000 children, women, the elderly, wounded soldiers and the animals of the zoo were slaughtered in one night.

And, further down:

> The death toll was staggering. The full extent of the Dresden Holocaust can be more readily grasped if one considers that well over 250,000 – possibly as many as a half a million – persons died within a 14-hour period, whereas estimates of those who died at Hiroshima range from 90,000 to 140,000.

The first point is that none of these claims are sourced, so you cannot check their provenance or, more importantly, if they have any provenance.[11] The second point is the use of the phrase 'Dresden Holocaust' – a clear attempt at equivalence. The third point is that, far away from these claims, a great deal of work was done by professional historians. Until October 2008 a figure of 35,000 dead represented their best estimate (for a full discussion see *Telling Lies About Hitler* by Richard J. Evans[12], judiciously balancing what was known, how it was known, what weight to place on it and, crucially, what was plainly wrong with the revisionist totals).

In October 2008 a special commission of leading German historians announced, after four years work, that the maximum number of deaths was 25,000 and the true figure probably lower. The man leading this, Rolf–Dieter Müller, said: 'In the course of its research the commission has so far identified around 18,000 victims of the air raids in Dresden.' The commission also said that the firestorm did not generate temperatures high enough to make human bodies disappear, something revisionists and neo-Nazis used in their conjuring.

After the commission, the conjuring will be harder but it won't be deterred. Nothing will do that and Dresden will have to live with it just as a reunified Germany will too.

Alan Russell has become a Dresden resident with his own flat in the Neustadt. 'Half of it was not destroyed and it remains much as it was when it was planned in 1685 and the years thereafter. There are beautiful houses there and fine restaurants and shops. When I first went there in 1994 it was in a state of total dilapidation. What are now fine houses had trees growing through their roofs. There was an attempt to obliterate all traces of bourgeois culture but I notice with some relief that something of the old Dresden has been preserved. A lot of people worked very hard, even in the GDR years, to make sure that that was so.'

Russell has ambivalent views about the GDR. 'Dresden was known as the Valley of the Clueless because they couldn't get Western TV and they knew that they couldn't,' he says. 'That said, I think that there was always a strong subterranean wish to be able to come out of this isolation which had been imposed on them.

'When I was going in the early years to bone up on German – before I did my A levels which I did when I was sixty-seven – I used to go and have lunch with old ladies in an old peoples' centre to practice talking and listening to them. This was in Dresden. Like a lot of women they had good memories of the GDR because in terms of the care of the elderly, in terms of education and job opportunities for women it had been relatively good and it did have good sides to it – but you have to remember this: I have a good friend, a vicar, and his sons could not go to higher education because they came from a bourgeois family.' Russell points out that he once visited the the prison cell of a man in his twenties serving a long sentence 'because he tried to leave the country [the offence was 'Republic-flight']. The GDR had a downside to it. Don't forget the *Stasi*. It was a very unhealthy political system.'

Do you see Dresden becoming a world centre of reconciliation?

'I do hope so, I really do hope so.'

I mean, beyond the bombing – I mean a symbol of human madness?

'Yes. During the rebuilding, or to help with the rebuilding, twenty-four or twenty-five friendship groups were set up, most of them in Germany. There was a big one in America which gave a lot of money, a smaller one in Paris and then our own, of course. After the completion of the *Frauenkirche* and its re-consecration, everybody in these groups – about 5,000 or 6,000 altogether – started to ask themselves "well, what do we do now?" They had been working under the umbrella of the Society for the Rebuilding of the *Frauenkirche*. Its successor has become the Society for the Promotion of the *Frauenkirche*.

'Some of the friendship groups dissolved themselves, for example Munich. They'd done a great, great deal to raise money and were one of the most successful but they kept a kind of friendship going. They are now talking about revising their group because there is a possibility to go into one of the houses near to the *Frauenkirche* and have a kind of parish meeting place. If this goes ahead I think our friends in Munich will want to come back and play a part in that. Some of the others have dissolved themselves and they won't.

'Of the remainder we all meet twice a year, once in Dresden and once in a city in another part of Germany to make sure that what the *Frauenkirche* means is spread round and the building is meaningful for people living outside Dresden. The people who effectively organise the meetings are very keen that the British shouldn't just disappear off the radar. The Americans, for all sorts of complex reasons, have largely dropped out and the British presence is valued, to my great surprise, very greatly.

'It is reconciliation but it is also what comes afterwards – there was a banner on the *Frauenkirche* "BUILD BRIDGES FOR RECONCILIATION DAY BY DAY". We created the Friendship Garden in the middle of England – at the National Memorial Arboretum, which is where the big new monument for British soldiers killed since 1945 stands. The Trust, together with the British-German Association, planted a simple garden which consists of two rings of trees and inside that a ring of stones taken from the *Frauenkirche* with, on the one side, the names of seven cities badly damaged in Britain, and on the other, seven from Germany, including Berlin and Dresden. We would like to get money to do a bit more there, and it reflects the desire that what this coming together has meant can be continued.'

Is that true of both Germanys as well?

'The remaining eighteen or twenty friendship groups exist in the West. They are not in the old GDR area. Well, one is. The big groups – in Munich, Cologne, Hamburg – were reaching out to Dresden because they heard the call: "We are going to rebuild the *Frauenkirche*. Please will you help us?" A lot of German cities including Cologne, which had suffered horrendously in its own bombing, rallied round.'

They were also reaching out to Dresden as, now, just another German city very much like Cologne: on a river, one dominated by a cathedral and the other to be dominated by one again. Becoming just another German city: how easy it is to write that, how easy to forget that to reach it from Cologne on 8 November 1989 you needed a visa and you had to cross the Iron Curtain – the wire, the watchtowers, the death strip, the tank traps, the guard dogs, the scatter guns activated by trip wires. You had to go through a chilled checkpoint where uniformed, armed officials never smiled. You had to navigate an autobahn from the 1930s on the other side; narrow, uneven, following the contours of the countryside. The speed limits were different, the road signs different and you were not allowed off it. The village rooftops and spires you could see were truly in another country. You might see convoys of the Red Army, the pug-faced lorries equidistant, as they slogged forward to wherever they were going. That wouldn't be, everyone thought they knew, going home.

It has all gone, gone as completely as parts of old Dresden.

There's a new autobahn now, just like the ones round Cologne. The speed limits are uniform and so are the road signs. The forbidden, glimpsed villages are just villages in the *Land* of Saxony, one of German's sixteen, and you can go if you want.

Dresden is there waiting for you, just like Cologne.

Notes

1. The Zwinger is a breathtaking baroque complex in the city centre consisting of ornate pavilions linked by galleries. It was built between 1710 and 1732.
2. www.germany-tourism.co.uk.
3. An opera house has stood on the site – next to the Zwinger – since 1678, although repeatedly burnt down. It was constructed in the High Renaissance style between 1871 and 1878 but destroyed by the bombing. It reopened in February 1985 with a performance of *Der Freischütz*, the last opera to have been played in it before the bombing.
4. *Why Dresden?* published by The Dresden Trust.
5. *For a Change* magazine, August 2006: 'Answering Dresden's Call' by Philip Boobbyer.
6. Disneyland in the sense of a fairytale, enchanted place – which Dresden was, and which the restored parts are again.
7. www.wlu.ca/viessmann/Onlinepapers/2001/no10_99wiktorin.pdf.
8. *For a Change*, op. cit.
9. Reuters: 'Neo-Nazis storm Dresden bombing tribute', 14 February 2005. Extremism is alive in Germany, of course, although this book is not about that because by definition extremists are minorities, and what effect unification had on them – certainly in the West – is by no means clear. There was certainly an ugly growth in right-wing extremism, with all that that entails, in the East.

The Federal Office for the Protection of the Constitution, which monitors such matters, said that in 2006 there were some 31,000 left-wing extremists and 6,000 were ready to use violence (*Spiegel Online International*, 15 May 2008).

The extreme right began its rise in the early 1990s. The number of 'propaganda offences' rose from 8,337 in 2004 to 10,881 a year later (*German Law Journal*, 1 February 2007).

The National Party of Germany, neo-Nazi in character, holds seats in East German regional parliaments.

As someone who has visited Germany regularly since the 1960s I detect no groundswell for any of these extremists, however much their actions generate headlines. My feeling is quite the opposite: the extremists show the Germans exactly what Germans never want again.

10. For a full examination of these industries see *Dresden* by Frederick Taylor, 2005, pp. 173–5.

11. I was curious to know about the sources and sent a message to the website explaining that I was writing a book about Germany today with a chapter on Dresden and could they give me the sources for these strong claims so I could check them myself. I wanted to know who counted the bodies and where the documentation was about totals. No reply came and I would have been amazed if it had. The silence is not only evocative but very, very revealing.

12. *Telling Lies About Hitler*, Evans.

AFTERWORD

Marzahn mirrors the past, the present and the future with disconcerting accuracy. Once upon a time it was a small, anonymous village in the countryside just east of Berlin with a history stretching to the mists of antiquity and likely beyond.

During Hitler's time it had a labour camp which was used to keep gypsies out of sight during the 1936 Olympic Games. Later they were deported to Auschwitz. In 1941 a machine tool factory was built and forced labourers were worked to death. Many are buried in a nearby cemetery.

In the 1970s, the GDR times, a vast new town was built around it to try and solve East Berlin's chronic housing shortage. That brought 150,000 residents to four miles of high-rise apartments with a web of roads veined between them, broad as rivers. The apartment blocks look as if a giant had set them down one at a time like toys in a vast playground. They lack any human scale, any suggestion of community or any notion that they are in fact in the countryside. Most European new towns look like this but are not so big or so stark. The place is almost brutally functional and even the decoration of Western shops can't soften that.

The original village, now called Old Marzahn, displays Germany as it was. Venerable, solid, slightly ornate houses and a windmill are grouped around a long green with a church, the *Dorfkirche*, in the middle of it. A church has stood here from the 1300s and one of the bells dates from 1660, but if you stand beside the door you can see the tower blocks looming beyond the trees. The contrast between past and present is so complete and so sudden that it is slightly shocking.

The people walking past the green this autumn Sunday are elderly and clearly Easterners. You can tell by their clothing, the slowness of their gait and their absence of body language. The clothing was bought for warmth and longevity, without any thought of making the wearer look good. They walk in a gentle, timeless rhythm, unhurried, perhaps because in the GDR which formed them there was nothing to hurry for. They haven't heard about dieting any more than they have heard about Western body language and its *look-at-me* imperatives. A couple in their late sixties hold hands quite naturally.

There's a little coffee shop on the other side of the church, chic in its way, with two Muslim girls in headscarves serving, but the Old Marzahners don't go there, they walk on by.

Birgit Kubisch watches all this carefully and we fall to talking about the past and the present because these Old Marzahners will be carrying their past, unchanged, into the future like a generation living outside time.

Many, she says, have lost everything they knew – the GDR lasted from 1949 to 1989 and enveloped almost everybody living within its distinctive framework. It has not been replaced by opportunity because it's too late for that. The old people, she concludes, have enough money to live but they are 'exiles in their own land'.

To compound that, Marzahn was absorbed by the Berlin borough of Lichtenberg in 1920. It became a borough in its own right in 1979 but in 2001 was joined by another borough, Hellersdorf, as well as three other vil-lages – Kaulsdorf, Mahlsdorf, Biesdorf – giving today's Marzahn-Hellersdorf, one of the twelve Berlin boroughs.

Kaulsdorf is a community of detached houses with neat gardens and an abundance of fruit trees. A grey Trabant has been parked in one of the streets and, among the VWs and Audis and Mercs, it looks like it's from a museum. This contrast between past and present is total too.

Woodland spreads to one side of the village, a railway line and station to the other. The restaurant on the corner is named for that, *Zur S-Bahn*, and it is themed: all manner of railway artefacts are ranged within it, station name plates, wooden seats from trains and more. There are framed U-Bahn and S-Bahn maps on the walls, charting the great division and its various phases. Sometimes on the Eastern maps various Western stations are included, sometimes fewer, sometimes hardly any, as if by cartography the West could be made to disappear. The maps make a curiously passive impression because they are so ordinary, just printed paper in the frames showing where the lines and the stations were – or weren't. This autumn it is very difficult to grasp that they chart places where any Easterner would be shot because they wished to go from one part of their own city to the other. The maps are un-evocative, and that's deeply satisfying. It's like looking at dinosaur bones in a natural history museum. They tell you something important but they don't change the way you live: too long ago.

There are framed photographs of Berlin's mainline stations in the old days, each solid brick and stone, holding images of a city the bombing raid destroyed forever.

No doubt the restaurant's owners trawled far and wide to find the arte-facts, gathering whatever could be found wherever they could. Patrons donate them too. Collectively, and unconsciously, the images represent a reaching back to when Germany was one, was divided and then one again. You can't tell this autumn Sunday whether the clientele is predominantly East or West. They're just diners exploiting the extensive menu. Kaulsdorf has a different feel to Marzahn, bourgeois, but here the diners are one again and – East or West – that's their own history up on the walls.

The *Zur S-Bahn* has an even more wonderful theme: normality. True unification doesn't come from great speeches in the Reichstag, grand regional plans or massive ministries occupying themselves with Very Important Matters, it comes from being at ease with the history up there on the walls, being at ease with whoever is sitting at the neighbouring table because they're just like you, and having a beer while you're waiting for the food to come. Everybody else in the *Zur S-Bahn* seems to be having one except some of the women, who take wine.

The two waiters flit under the gathering impetus of orders as the place fills. They're from the East and one of them says all this talk of unemployment is wrong; there's plenty of work if you're prepared to hustle for it. He's been, among other things, a truck driver and a taxi driver 'and now this'. He smiles. It's normality, and will continue to be from here on out.

The very literal past is in the borough of Friedrichsfelde as we drive back from Kaulsdorf. The *Zentralfriedhof* – Central Cemetery – has a special area called the *Gedenkstätte der Sozialisten* (the Memorial to the Socialists).

The parking area is broad but only three cars are there this autumn afternoon. The iron gate is open and unguarded. There's an alcove with photographs of who lies where, and what they were. There's a lawn with, at its lip, a small stone to the victims of Stalinism. This evidently has created controversy because Germany's socialist heroes are buried in the circle of matching tombstones just over there: Ulbricht, Wilhelm Pieck and Otto Grotewohl who were the GDR's founding fathers; Rosa Luxemburg and Karl Liebknecht, iconic communist figures – she a Polish-born Jew and Marxist theorist, he a lawyer and Marxist theorist also. They took part in a left-wing rising in 1919 and were murdered.

A red-brick wall curves round the circle and headstones of more socialist heroes are set into it. Honecker is buried in Chile and he's about the only one missing.

This is a shrine, of course, and a very silent place as befits that. It is also potentially a site to raise the strongest emotions either way, which makes the fact that it is unguarded surprising, and the fact that there is no graffiti more surprising still (although some seems to have been cleansed from the outside of the wall).

There are no flowers on any grave except Liebknecht and Luxembourg as if, in their idealism and their tragedy, they remain unsullied by actually trying to make it work. Whatever else martyrdom bestows, it bestows that. Every second Sunday in January socialists and communists gather there to commemorate them.

This autumn afternoon some old people come, respectful, talking in whispers. Perhaps their dreams lie here, never to be disinterred: a better world, a fairer society, no more poverty and hunger, no more wars fought for the capitalists and consequently no more wars – just *from each according to his ability, to each according to his need*, an end to history, the proletariat forever victorious and forever deploying the victory with benevolence, the agonies of human existence finally over. Perhaps these old people worked a lifetime for this and felt across the hard years that they were actually getting nearer. Every GDR statistic proclaimed it, and no statistic or statement ever suggested setbacks.

The more you put it in that register – triumphant socialism, new age man and the rest – the more you realise it was always doomed because at some point it would have had to change human nature, and you'd need a much bigger graveyard than Friedrichsfelde to accommodate all those who have tried that.

Whatever, it's over – here, anyway.

Normality is ordinary people preferring a beer at lunchtime in the *Zur S-Bahn* to world revolution, and that's the way it's going now. Apathy can be dangerous, but not in the *Zur S-Bahn* version of it among the station maps and wooden railway seats.

A strange thought, however. You cannot imagine a comparable right-wing cemetery with tombstones for Goering, Goebbels, Bormann (identified by his teeth long after the war), Eichmann, Speer and the rest, never mind unguarded and graffiti free. In fact, you cannot imagine a right-wing cemetery at all, even constructed like a fortress and permanently protected by dogs, riot police and razor wire.

I think there is a reason. The GDR did try for a better world and constructed aspects of that – despite the mistakes, despite the *Stasi*, despite the paranoia – before it imploded. The Nazis created a world beyond civilisation and half a century afterwards the barbarism of that world hasn't gone away. Perhaps it never will.

The FRG went another way, reserved, conscious of guilt for the sins of the fathers, content to make money and enjoy it. This made it an attractive destination for migrants from all over the world and, in the end, irresistible to the ordinary GDR citizen. After twenty-eight years of waiting he wanted his share and the moment The Wall opened he would not be denied it any longer.

When the opposition in the GDR was trying to promote what they called the third way between communism and capitalism, people shouted *no more experiments!* I have the strongest feeling that twenty years later – despite the reservations, despite the *Ossi-Wessi* tensions, despite the supposed right-wing resurgence – people feel just the same and that Germany is too far into the process of becoming a normal country again for it to be reversed by anybody or anything.

It's good news for the owners of the *Zur S-Bahn*.

There is a memorial to the site of the bunker where Hitler died but, like so much of central Berlin, the area has been developed intensively and no sense of what it was lingers. The bunker is buried deep under new buildings and the courtyard where his body was taken to be burnt has vanished completely. An information board stands beside the pavement on a small segment of grass. The tourists, including Germans, ebb here from Checkpoint Charlie ten minutes away to try and find something else which doesn't exist. They come in parties, gaze at the map and stand obediently while their guides recite the facts.

The Hitler legacy can no longer be digested physically because, apart from a few buildings, it has vanished as completely as the courtyard. Mentally it is still being done because he remains the man in your mind or, more accurately, the monster in your mind. How many generations will it take before he becomes a figure like Attila the Hun, dangerous by reputation but safely distant? Or like the terrifying dinosaurs: too far away?

Nobody knows.

The memorial to the victims of the Holocaust is within sight of the information board and the tourists ebb towards that. It is situated on what used to be the death strip not far from the Brandenburg Gate. The tourists are confronted by 2,711 unmarked concrete slabs arranged symmetrically, meaning each is freestanding and you can walk through them from north–south or east–west, corridor after corridor. Each slab slants slightly and is a different size, just as the victims were, and the middle of the area is lower so you are constantly descending or ascending.

The architect, Peter Eisenman, has been quoted as saying: 'I fought to keep names off the stones, because having names on them would turn it into a graveyard.' At the opening ceremony Chancellor Gerhard Schröder made all the right noises and insisted that Germany was now 'facing up to its own history'.

Inevitably the memorial has drawn to itself praise and criticism – it's too abstract, it was done too late (the idea only approved in 1999, opened in 2005), it does not commemorate all the others apart from Jews who died in the Holocaust.

The BBC reported:

> The stones have been treated with an anti-graffiti agent that authorities hope will ward off vandals and neo-Nazi sympathisers. Even the anti-graffiti agent provoked controversy: initially the architect felt graffiti could benefit the memorial; later it emerged that the company supplying the agent once manufactured poison gas for use in Nazi death camps.[1]

'Facing up to its own history' cannot be a trite politician's phrase, moulded to a specific occasion like the memorial. In Germany, and particularly in Berlin, it involves layers so deep, so complex and so poisoned that it cannot be a trite author's paragraph either, like the one I am now writing, but something about how human beings approach the basic profundity of what other human beings have done, and have had done to them. The stones don't answer such questions but – remorselessly, implacably, overwhelmingly – they pose them.

To children the memorial is a playground, the stones perfect for hide-and-seek, and they make full use of it. You can be prudish about not showing respect for the dead and so on, but in the midst of so much death they represent ever-renewing life in all its innocence, and after Auschwitz innocence is a very beautiful thing. Renewal through youth is too.

There's another way to face history, specifically by visiting the GDR Museum down beyond the Unter den Linden at the far end from the Brandenburg Gate. I asked a colleague and co-Berlin enthusiast John Woodcock to visit it with Axel, Birgit's boyfriend, and set down his thoughts. Here they are:

> More than a decade after the Wall came down, Peter Kenzelmann, an ethnologist and political scientist from Freiburg in south-western Germany, returned to Berlin to take his partner sightseeing. She had never been to the GDR, and he envisaged visiting a museum in its former capital that would help to explain everyday life in East Germany. Kenzelmann was flabbergasted to discover there was no such venue telling the story. Not in their reunited country anyway. Berlin's tourist information centre directed them to Amsterdam where there was a small arts-based exhibition on the subject.
>
> 'I quickly realized,' wrote Kenzelmann, 'that I could not be the only tourist in Berlin who had ever tried to find a historico-cultural GDR museum … It was obvious that Berlin needed one. After I had returned home, the thought kept lingering … I spoke to friends, relatives and colleagues about it, collected further information on the topic, and, as the months went by, the small idea developed into a big project.'
>
> The outcome is the DDR Museum which Kenzelmann and his team created in the basement of a new hotel and entertainment complex across the Spree from the Berliner Dom. The site was at the heart of the vanquished regime whose impact on its citizens over forty years is in part reflected through some of the 25,000 items many have donated to the museum as an expression of their lives under a totalitarian state (or, as Ms Kubisch says, 'simply because they find it a good place for their old things to be.')

In an introduction to a guide to the permanent exhibition, head of research Dr Stefan Wolle sets its aims in context: 'The historians have made up their minds, and their central points seem to be conclusive. The GDR was a satellite state at Moscow's mercy. The security apparatus was the iron fist that held everything together. The planned economy proved to be hopelessly inferior to the market economy. All the generous social benefits offered to the people were just too expensive in the long run and contributed to the economic collapse of the GDR. In 1989 the SED regime was brought down by a democratic mass movement. The vast majority of the people welcomed the reunification.

'This is where some might say the story ends. But there are still some points that cannot be easily explained. The GDR was more than just an artificial product of ideology and power – for millions of people it was their life. They grew up in this country, went through the educational system, served in the armed forces, went to work, founded a family, furnished a flat, and raised the children. It was possible to lead a happy life in the GDR. Sometimes it was quite easy to forget all about politics and ideology.

'But taking into account the general shortage of goods, life was far from idyllic. People were always hunting down scarce goods, but they learned to live with it. They bartered, worked after hours, or participated in illicit trading. Many withdrew into themselves. The dacha became a symbol of the way of life in the GDR.

'There was an inevitable gap between what people thought and what they said. They were afraid that they might attract attention to themselves or, even worse, come into contact with the *Stasi*. If it had not been for the humour, optimism and happiness, the situation would not have been bearable. This is why many people still smile when they think of the GDR, even though sometimes it is a bitter smile.'

Wolle quotes one of the party's slogans, the one that said *the human being is at the centre of attention*. 'Back then this was nothing but an empty phrase since the real focus of the SED laid on maintaining its own power. But looking back on it now, this old slogan has become reality. The GDR was, above all, defined by the people who lived in it.'

In attempting to convey this, the museum has attracted praise and criticism, as well as earning a nomination for the European Museum of the Year Award.

In one respect Kenzelmann's project is beyond dispute. Attendance figures have vindicated his belief that Berlin has almost a duty to present the implications for life under a socialist dictatorship which in population terms controlled a quarter of the German nation.

The museum opened on 15 July 2006, and by mid-October 2008 had had 548,891 visitors. A breakdown of the statistics is revealing. In its first two full years it attracted Germans from both sides of the Wall in almost equal numbers; 38.4 per cent of the total came from the former West Germany, and 37.4 per cent were former East Germans reliving aspects of their past.

Within a few days of the opening, the German broadcaster *Deutsche Welle* was reflecting differing and sometimes heated views on the project's emphasis and analysis, a debate which shows no sign of diminishing.

Heidrun Loeper, a 64-year-old literary scholar, and Ingrid Fischer, a former primary school teacher then aged 72, were pleased with the outcome. At times it made them smile. They glimpsed their personal lives in many of the exhibits: state-made stockings, Komet ice cream in powder form, Im Nu instant coffee substitute, Spee washing powder, Wodka Brillant …

The ladies felt that overall the museum presented East Germans in a more sympathetic light than previous judgements of history. It was important to them that perceptions were being challenged. 'We've been put down as Neanderthals and this shows that we lived like normal people,' Fischer told *Deutsche Welle*, adding that in her view many managed to avoid the worst aspects of repression.

Joseph Spadola, a 23-year-old philosophy student from New York City, agreed that the museum's focus on the mundane was a good thing. 'This is the part we never hear about,' he said – the 'ordinary', a snapshot of day-to-day life in which, by one means or another, individuals sought to detach themselves from the dreary dogma of their hypocritical rulers, and find an outlet for their inner self.

Others are dismayed by the exhibition. It's been accused of being too benign given the severe restrictions people were living under. One of those working to remind people of the dictatorial nature of the East German regime felt the museum had distorted reality. Gabriele Camphausen, who is in charge of educational programmes at the federal commission that administers files from the *Stasi* secret service, said she was stunned by the presentation.

'Visitors can leave the exhibition with the impression that this was a slightly bizarre state in the twentieth century,' she said. 'It doesn't become clear that this was a brutal dictatorship … Imagine if someone had done such a museum on daily life during the Nazi era. People would criticise it, and rightly so.'

Hubertus Knabe, director of the memorial at the former *Stasi* prison in Berlin Hohenschönhausen, claimed the museum's concept fell in line with recommendations by a government commission to concentrate less on places symbolising repression in the GDR.

At the time he was interviewed by *Deutsche Welle*, Knabe had not been to the museum, but his view was based on what it seeks to represent. 'I'm sceptical that depictions of everyday life can explain life in a dictatorship. It's not important how people ate and slept when describing a political system.'

The museum's curator, Robert Rückel, countered that the *Stasi*'s infiltration was clearly documented. He pointed to a section focussing on the secret police and where visitors can eavesdrop on conversations in another part of the exhibition. Rückel added that other museums in Berlin already highlighted The Wall and *Stasi* repression. 'Our goal is to focus on the daily lives of people,' he said. 'It's an experiment.'

For Thomas Ahbe, a sociologist who has written extensively on East German culture and identity, the DDR Museum works as far as it can. After all, it's attempting to describe, and in part reproduce, a hugely complex situation in a very small area, and on a commercial basis. At best 'it complements the picture,' Ahbe told an interviewer. 'The crimes that happened in East Germany have been documented extensively, but the scientific research on daily life has fallen by the wayside. I think it will take a long time before we can get to a balanced view of GDR history.'

A similar view is expressed by Birgit Kubisch. She feels that the DDR Museum is not a museum at all in the accepted sense but merely a collection of memorabilia – 'a funny collection of things. For me it doesn't work. I can see they've made an effort to present a lot of material, and in part it's amusing to revisit aspects of my past through some of the objects of the time. But it's not a serious attempt to explain the GDR and its history, and even some of the exhibits are stereotypes, as if they are trying to convince people that only ugly things – like ugly dresses and shoes – were available. It seems to be constantly making negative points, and reaching conclusions I don't recognise from my twenty years in that society.

'We need a proper museum; one that fully explores what happened and takes a didactic approach. Instead we have this place which, for all its limitations and distortions, is on a strategic site in Berlin and gives visitors the impression of being an official portrayal of the GDR. On the other hand I can't be too critical. The authorities have had enough time to create a serious museum, but nothing happened and it's not surprising that an outsider came along to fill the gap.'

Kubisch's boyfriend, Axel Hillebrand, is from Osnabrück in Western Germany, and even more dismissive of the exhibition. Perhaps because he didn't live in the GDR, but has made many friends among those who did, he is sympathetic towards aspects of what happened there and how individuals responded. That sympathy may also have clouded his judgement. Hillebrand emerged from the museum with a feeling that, instead of experiencing an objective attempt to describe another Germany from the one he knew, he'd been in a money-making enterprise of the kind he was all too familiar with. That's an observation its founder can hardly dispute. During an interview when it opened, Kenzelmann, then aged 36, said: 'I didn't want to become dependent on subsidies – we are a business.'

The museum receives no state aid or sponsorship and is self-financing, reliant solely on admission charges and retail sales. A drawback is its limited space, but there's no doubt that it crams a lot into it. There are interactive displays – a 'hands-on experience of history' as it describes its imagery of daily life in the GDR, supported by film and interviews from the era. Inevitably, there's a Trabant and with it the chance to take a simulated 'wild ride' through a concrete-slab housing estate of the kind which dominated urban landscapes in the East.

The museum's designers have developed the theme. Visitors step through the entrance area into what is meant to represent a housing estate whose blocks are used as partitions and display cabinets. Peeping into them and their private contents is encouraged. What they try to reveal is something of the irreconcilable conflicts and tensions between the all-embracing, all-seeing state, and the private lives which struggled for a personal identity within it.

You can enter an 'authentic' GDR apartment, with its basic home comforts, but with a bookcase devoid of works the regime would have considered inappropriate, or worse. As Axel Hillebrand points out, though, wouldn't the average living room in a Düsseldorf, Paris or Manchester high-rise have looked much like this (except for the political restraints) a generation ago? Don't products, packaging, fashions, and design become dated in any society? Doesn't every nation have its absurdities?

To an outsider, and a non-German, it can seem that the museum has a tendency, whether by accident or design, to mock a state which functioned under enormous external Cold War pressures. For all its cruelties, at another level it was well-meaning, and striving to improve living conditions for its people through a system which many considered to be fairer than capitalism.

Is it appropriate to present life in a country, whose vast majority was trapped behind a wall, as a form of entertainment aided by the creativity of the latest technology? It's probably no coincidence that in its first two years the museum has attracted younger age groups – 36 per cent of visitors were aged 17–29, whereas only 5.2 per cent were 60 or over. In other words, among those who were born just before the GDR came into existence, relatively few have felt the need to be reminded of the four decades some of them spent within it. Understandable. Who would want to pay an entrance fee to recall the queues for desirable items, the sixteen-year wait for a car with a body made from a mixture of cotton fleece and plastic, a speech by Erich Honecker, the Party Congress rejoicing over increased concrete production, or the fact that the *Stasi* had 173,000 informants?[2]

The dilemma for those of us who weren't there is balancing what the museum presents against the memories of East Germans who say their reality was rather different.

Nudism was popular in the GDR – 'politics without swimsuits' as the museum calls it. Its text claims that one in ten of the population, 1.6m, regularly peeled off in public, despite the pleadings of culture minister Johannes Becher to 'protect the eyes of the nation'.

If that's an exaggeration then so may be its conclusion that nakedness became a form of resistance 'to the eternal conformity of the GDR. Nudity was a sign of true classlessness. In the end those wearing swimsuits became the odd ones out.' There are similar sweeping statements in the exhibition's guidebook, which delves a little deeper into everything from education and youth movements, to housing, employment, the family, supposed sex equality that still left men in control, fashion, entertainment, holidays, and the media, in which 'the only real surprises were the weather forecasts and the football results'; 'despite thirty-nine newspapers, two television channels and four radio stations, there was only one opinion.'

We are told that East Germans devoured books, especially those outlawed by the state. 'Many a book had its own history. People told the story of how they had acquired them, and were just as proud of them as a hunter who had found his prey. It was almost as important to stay on good terms with the bookseller as it was to have good connections with a mechanic. There were inside tips about second-hand book dealers in remote and small towns, or other tips referring to the book sales within the National People's Army, which had on its shelves some literary gems without even knowing their true value.

'Those who liked intellectual nourishment formed an unofficial group whose members recognised each other by secret signs. They met in bookstores, libraries, theatre foyers, exhibitions and coffee shops … Many intellectuals withdrew into their own literary cosmos, just like other people withdrew into their dachas. Their literary castles in the air were just as illusory as the pseudo idyll the allotment garden owners had built themselves. Books, movies and the theatre portrayed the debates that were not to be openly held in real existing socialism. Readers and theatre-goers always hoped for critical allusions the censors had missed. "Brainworkers" owed their high status in the society to the simple-mindedness of the regime. In a way, the over-filled bookshelves in the living rooms of GDR intellectuals were a barrier against the triviality of the SED regime.'

Much of this may be true but it also exposes the museum to the risk of presenting the very clichés it invites its visitors to reconsider.

It was interesting to note that in October 2008, the overwhelming majority who gave the DDR Museum a positive review on a well-known website for travellers, came from the former West Germany, including Stuttgart, Hannover, Darmstadt, Heidelberg, Hamburg, and Cologne.

Maybe some of them had moved there from the old East. Or maybe they hadn't, and went away with their preconceptions and prejudices confirmed about that vanished other Germany.

That vanished 'other' Germany lingers in the woods near Wandlitz, north of Berlin, where the GDR leadership had its guarded compound: detached houses and a shopping complex on 413 acres, built after 1956 and first occupied in 1960. These days you can buy maps which show who lived where, Honecker, Mielke of the *Stasi*, Krenz and the rest. The houses are large but darkened because the trees around them are so tall, so sombre, somehow so forbidding. Their gardens are in no sense ornate but *petit bourgeois*: verandas with ordinary garden furniture, a bench or two, little lawns.

The Friedrichsfelde cemetery may or may not be a shrine but the compound just seems an emptiness.

The shopping complex – swimming pool, restaurant, sauna, medical facilities and shops with hard-currency goods – would have excited no emotion anywhere in Western Europe. The GDR was living in a different context. It was a society accustomed to austerity where the occasional appearance of bananas did excite emotion; and because it had built itself aggressively on egalitarian principles, the complex was shockingly opulent, a betrayal, when ordinary people got to see it.

At one point after the fall, Honecker took refuge with a clergyman and when he finally left, in a limousine, these same ordinary people beat their fists on its roof in rage.

In October 2007 a survey of 1,000 Germans showed that 19 per cent wanted The Wall back and 21 per cent felt *Ostalgie*. Did they really want it all back, the compound, the *Stasi*, rotund little Mielke (said to have compromising material on Honecker in a special safe) who drove from the compound to his Berlin headquarters in a medium-range French saloon so he wouldn't look too bourgeois, Krenz, 350,000 Soviet soldiers, a decade-long wait for a Trabant and the banana emotions? Or was it the kind of answer some people give to pollsters knowing they can safely give any answer?

And anyway, 75 per cent answered the other way, although 74 per cent of Easterners said they felt like second-class citizens.

A different survey in 2008[3] covered every aspect of German life in great and excruciating detail, revealing that the average German has sex 117 times a year, travels 24.5 miles a day, walks towards the right when entering a shop and so on (and on); their favourite dishes, unrefined by travel and globalisation, remained lentils, curry wurst (curry and ketchup on sausage) and Spätzle (Swabian pasta).

Kate Connolly wrote in London's *Observer*: 'The study concludes that "after turbulent centuries and catastrophic decades we have arrived in a state of a moderate, average democracy", in which being "lost in the crowd" and "public order" are in fact what citizens most desire.'

Yes, good news for the owners of the *Zur S-Bahn*.

Alan Russell is sitting in carpet slippers in his house in Chichester. He is a benign, softly spoken man and although impelled by religious motives he doesn't push that at all. I suspect he feels that if you want it you should have it and if you don't, you don't. This winter's day he is still recovering from a nasty fall some months before, so he moves slowly and there is a gentility in that. The fall has not dulled his sense of humour, nor his ability to make a very English lunch for us: his own cottage pie. If you want to know what it was like, we both had seconds. Somehow in Chichester you feel you are as far away from the bombing of Dresden as you can get, but in his presence you feel very close.

There's a word that keeps coming back and that word is normal. It's as if Germany has moved from an abnormal situation – Hitler, then the bombing, then the division – and now are they achieving normality? I wonder what you think about that word being applied to Dresden.

'First of all I'd apply it to Germany, which wasn't normal for some years after the war, was it? When was the FRG set up? 1949. And the GDR, same year. I don't think there's any country in Europe whose boundaries have changed so often as those of Germany, which means that the country has always consisted of some rather odd elements. If you go back far enough, it was a province revolting against the Romans. We are not subsequently talking about a normal nation state in the way that France or Britain were.

'Even now there are special things about the constitution. They almost never send soldiers outside the country – it was a very special thing to send them to Afghanistan but even there they are not on military duties [in the sense of combat rather than logistics]. I don't want to see Germany become a military power ever again.

'What I feel is that it was *not* an aggressive military power for a lot of history. It has been one of the seriously cultivated countries in Europe – the musical tradition, the scientific and medical traditions, the way they interpreted culture to bring in handiwork and artisans and so on. It's quite difficult to be German these days because of the terrible things which people did who lived only fifty years ago, but today's Germans can and should be proud of the cultural traditions of which they are heirs.

'That is Germany's role: to be a stable cultural central anchor in Europe.

'Germany is on the way to becoming, almost for the first time, a normal nation state but with certain things which angle its history in certain directions. Whether Dresden is a normal part of this normal Germany I'm not sure, but I think I'd say yes. It is becoming the Silicone Valley of Germany and there are a lot of industries. I get the impression the city is very well aware of the need to live on its wits, which means largely on science.'

A Berlin evening in Zur Rippe, a traditional German restaurant on the corner of Poststrasse, one of the little streets in the restored quarter near the Alexanderplatz (and beautifully restored, in GDR times). You can't help feeling a specific sadness because it's so stolid, so welcoming, so timeless – which of course is an awful contradiction in a restoration. The sadness is that Berlin had a thousand such before Hitler brought the bomber raids. The menu and beers are traditional.[4] The lone waiter is portly and jolly in a wonderfully welcome-to-the-world way, as all waiters in such places ought to be. He looks the part too: black trousers, white shirt, black waistcoat and a dark-green apron. I wonder if he is originally from the East or the West. 'Doesn't matter now!' he says, and laughs a great gale of a laugh, blowing the question away.

Next day, Bernd Finger, the senior policeman, recounts a story about the area in the south of the city where The Wall ran down streets with houses on either side and consequently the death strip was exactly the width of the streets. The Soviet authorities protested that someone in the West had shot and wounded a border guard – from an upper window a marksman would have had the border guard directly below him, in a patrol jeep or going to the watchtower there. The British and Americans became involved and an international incident threatened. Finger investigated and discovered that in one of the Western apartments a woman kept a tremendous number of pigeons. They were *everywhere* and they made so much noise they drove the man in the apartment above to distraction. He got himself a gun. As the pigeons flew out from the window below he opened fire. He didn't hit a single one but he did hit the border guard.

Doesn't matter now.

The first part of Adolf Hitler's war ended with the single shot one April afternoon in 1945, and the days before that have been captured in the film *Downfall*. It makes horror films look feeble. Here, as the actor Bruno Ganz brings Hitler's mysterious madness to life again – the trembling hand behind the back, the eyes which could cut diamonds, the sweeping philosophy of rebuilding Berlin in his own image, the old-fashioned courtesy to women, the saying that civilians' safety must no longer be considered – is the logical conclusion of entrusting absolute power to such a man. Here is Berlin, of the beautiful boulevards and beautiful people, bombed into the Stone Age and now being raked and ravaged, street after street, by the Red Army. Here are flames, confusion, terrible fear, children in uniform facing Soviet tanks, field hospital operations without anaesthetic – one man's screaming will stay with you for years – as what remained of the Reich descended into Dante's inferno.

I don't think ordinary Germans will be wanting that back, any more than they'll be wanting The Wall, Honecker, the great Socialist experiment or, as I said in a footnote to Chapter Ten, extremists of right or left.

However you viewed it, The Wall made the city not just unique but completely abnormal. The euphoria at its fall was a natural and inevitable reaction but dangerous because it unleashed desires which demanded immediate satisfaction but didn't allow time for due consideration, or any consideration. Nobody knew how much the forty years had moulded East and West in separate ways, or even whether there was still a common German identity – as we saw in the Foreword – but they went for it all the same and at full speed. The imbalance between populations (three *Wessis* to every *Ossi*) and economies (the D-mark so strong it could float the whole of the GDR), arched over by a sense of Western triumphalism (we won), meant that the forty-year moulding and separation could only be heightened.

In the early 1990s the fall of The Wall made the city not just unique but completely abnormal in a way it had not been before. Technically and legally it was one again for the first time since 1945 but it found itself living through a tremendous confusion of trends and currents, identities lost and found, contradictions and uncertainties wherever you looked, Mercedes trying to miss Trabants, Easterners feeling orphaned and stateless but eating bananas, Westerners beginning to think *we're paying for this, and paying, and paying.* The hippies and drop-outs and counter-culturalists seemed even more irrelevant than they had before. Quietly in the background, hesitantly, carrying inescapable prejudices and preconceptions, the citizens of the two Germanys reached towards each other. Far from immediate satisfaction for

the unleashed desires, ordinary people began to speak of it lasting generations.

Into the 2000s and moving towards the twentieth anniversary of the fall,
Berlin has settled. Long before, the Bundestag voted 337 to 320 in 1991 to
make it the German capital again, a major physical and psychological step
towards normalising both Germanys. Bonn, charming and provincial, was
never that and nor was truncated East Berlin, however hard it tried. These
days Berlin *feels* like a capital, open to global influences, important, bustling,
international, a place of government and embassies. Tourists have invaded the
city in astonishing numbers. They walk the streets the Red Army raked and
ravaged, and if you listen you can hear the hum of a dozen languages: Berlin,
just another destination on the trail to London and Paris, Amsterdam and
Madrid, Rome and Vienna – or trekking in Asia, backpacking in Australia,
shopping in New York; but there were watchtowers here not very long ago,
and scatter guns activated by trip wires, and shoot-to-kill, and not in any of
those other places.

The tourists who gather at the bunker site beside the information board
seem to feel it's a curiosity now and disappointingly empty of any reference
points. Actually, it's a peaceful corner and ordinary – just like Leuschnerdamm,
and the lake and the people sipping their white wine.

You sense that the Germans are now more at ease with themselves, that
the passage of time is doing some moulding of its own. You can argue that
time is deceptive in a German context because the forty-year GDR experiment ought to have produced an enduring Socialist normality rather than,
in 1989, a stampede away from it – but that, surely, was because the GDR
had always been an artificial creation, a bastard son of Hitler's first war, and
its government never once between 1949 and 1989 dared ask its citizens to
give it legitimacy in open, free elections. This in turn allowed the government
to function without the compromises and concessions which mark every
Western democracy. There were no checks and balances against extremism in
the GDR.[5] The government could reasonably count on longevity supersed-
ing legitimacy: coming generations would only have known totalitarianism,
however it was dressed up, and would not dream of questioning it. They had
no knowledge of anything else.

When the government finally did ask, in 1990, the people voted the whole
thing out of existence.

You sense that, whatever aspects of GDR life are still missed, ordinary
Easterners have accepted that these aspects won't be coming back and the
compensations are not too bad, thank you. You sense that many feel impo-
tent but express that passively. You sense that the under-twenties don't know
anything much about all this and care even less. They are very normal and the
future beckons, not the past.

In a moving study, *The Wall in My Backyard* (1994), two American authors interviewed twenty-six GDR women about their experiences before, during and after the *Wende*. One of the twenty-six, named only as Eva P. – she'd been a secretary with the Protestant church – said: 'Everything is getting better. Now after a hard day I can afford to buy something nice for myself, even if it's only a chocolate bar. Before, that wasn't possible. Before, if I got a chocolate bar I saved it for my grandchildren.'

If this is recounted to the grandchildren one of these days so long afterwards they'll think it bemusing that even in a capital city you couldn't just buy chocolate whenever you wanted: *strange and spooky*, they'll say, *what kind of a place was that?*

Anyway, an old lady finally enjoying some chocolate is about as normal as it gets after the Second World War, the Holocaust, the Cold War, the division of Germany, The Wall and the East–West nuclear standoff, although – you know how it is – some might prefer to celebrate normality with a beer or two.

I know just the place in Kaulsdorf, just beside the railway station.

Notes

1. BBC News Channel, 10 May 2005.
2. The *Stasi* have not been given their own chapter because, although they have loomed throughout the book as a sort of spectral presence, unification brought them to an end. Detective Police Commander Bernd Finger, the West Berlin policeman so involved in unifying the two police forces and dealing with the *Stasi*, explains that the decision to open the files the *Stasi* kept on millions of citizens was political, not one taken by the police. 'It was a good thing to do, a necessary thing to do, a realistic thing to do and it cleared the air. It also helped security. I know which people were working against us.'

The opening of the files proved deeply traumatic for many people who discovered that family, friends and workplace colleagues had been informing on them. Some 300,000 quickly asked to see their files.

The *Stasi* may have had a total of 600,000 informers (mostly men) during its history although, as befits an organisation living entirely through the medium of secrecy, you can read all sorts of totals. I am settling for a full-time staff which grew like this: 8,800 in 1952, approximately 20,000 in 1961, more than 45,000 in 1971, approximately 81,500 in 1982 and 91,015 at 31 October 1989. (www.bstu.bund.de/cln_030/nn_712450/DE/MfS-DDR-Geschichte/ Grundwissen/grundwissen node.html nnn=true.)

There's an interesting comparison with the 91,015 for a population of 16.4 million: Soviet Union (1990), approximately 480,000 for a population of 285.7 million; Czechoslovakia (1989), 18,000 for 15.6 million; Romania

(1989), between 15,000 and 40,000 for 23.3 million; Poland (1989), 24,390 for 38.4 million. (www.bstu.bund.de/cln_030/nn_712828/DE/MfS-DDR-Geschichte/Grundwissen/mfs hauptamtliche mitarbeiter.html nnn=true.)

3. In *Der Speigel*.

4. I had *Kohlroulade und Salzkartoffeln* (minced meat wrapped in cabbage, potatoes), Ms Kubisch had *Kasselerrippchen mit Sauerkraut und Salzkartoffeln* (cured pork ribs with Sauerkraut and potatoes), her boyfriend Axel had *Blutwurst mit Sauerkraut und Kartoffelbrei* (cooked sausage made from 20–40 per cent spiced blood – mostly from pork – 60–80 per cent rind and fat or bacon, and other ingredients like meat, giblets, onion, milk or cream, marjoram and thyme, Sauerkraut and mashed potatoes). That's traditional German food all right.

5. Extremism (by a state rather than fringe groups) is a highly relative term and clearly the GDR was nothing like Stalin's Soviet Union in the 1930s, Mao's disastrous Great Leap Forward or the ultimate madness of Pol Pot in Cambodia, never mind Hitler's institutionalised chamber of horrors. It did not set out to kill large numbers of people or indeed kill anyone, although it did give succour, comfort and support to terrorist factions in the 1970s and 1980s. The *Stasi* were unsavoury and the shoot-to-kill order an example of how an extreme measure could be imposed, but most of the population lived quite normally, without the feeling they were in a vast concentration camp. They went to work, drank beer, drove Trabis, visited relatives and friends, gossiped, laughed, complained, cried, attended births and funerals, and watched Western TV just like everybody else. It's tempting to represent totalitarian regimes as monoliths when they are, of course, full of human beings just like you and I. For a fascinating portrait of exactly this see Mary Fulbrook's masterly *The People's State*.

The point about extremism I am trying to make is a subtly different one. The GDR was able to act without reference to its own citizens; and the government – lacking a proper mandate from the ballot box – took for itself powers which no peacetime Western government would ever dare have contemplated: nationalising all industry, forbidding travel to all but a few approved countries, using all forms of knowledge to create the desired society, warping history and so on. As I have said, even the weather forecasts were regarded as state secrets. You are looking at paranoia writ large and consequently at a form of extremism.

In these circumstances it was entirely logical that when the *Ossis* did see the alternative – and at first glance it came to them as not only affluent, functional and efficient, but middle-of-the-road – they abandoned the extremism at the first opportunity. They didn't know how far to the right of the middle of the road they would have to travel, or how complete that would be, or how painful. They found out.

BIBLIOGRAPHY

Alter, Reinhard and Monteath, Peter (eds), *Rewriting the German Past*, Humanities Press International Inc., New Jersey, 1997

Annan, Noel, *Changing Enemies*, HarperCollins, London, 1995

Bahro, Rudolf, *From Red To Green*, Verso, London, 1984

Behrend, Hanna (ed.), *German Unification*, Pluto Press, London, 1995

Borneman, John, *After The Wall*, Basic Books, 1991

Childs, David, *The GDR: Moscow's German Ally*, Unwin Hyman, London, 1988

Clayton, Anthony and Russell, Alan, *Dresden: A City Reborn*, Berg, Oxford, 1999

Dodds, Dinah and Allen-Thompson, Pam, *The Wall in My Backyard*, University of Massachusetts Press, Amherst, 1994

Forster, Thomas M., *The East Germany Army*, George Allen & Unwin, London, 1980

Fulbrook, Mary, *The People's State*, Yale University Press, London, 2005

Fuller, Linda, *Where was the Working Class?* University of Illinois Press, Chicago, 1999

Georgi, Viola B. (ed.), *The Making of Citizens in Europe: New Perspectives on Citizenship Education*, Bundeszentrale für politische Bildung, Bonn, 2008

German Bundestag, Public Relations section, *Basic Law for the Federal Republic of Germany*, Ebner & Spiegel, Ulm, 2003

Glaeser, Andreas, *Divided in Unity*, The University of Chicago Press, 2000

Hearnden, Arthur, *Education in the Two Germanys*, Basil Blackwell, Oxford, 1974

Herf, Jeffrey, *Divided Memory*, Harvard University Press, Cambridge, Massachusetts, 1997

Hertle, Hans-Hermann, *Chronik des Mauerfalls*, Ch. Links Verlag, Berlin, 1999

—— *Die Berliner Mauer, Monument Des Kalten Krieges*, Bundeszentrale für politische Bildung

Hertspring, Dale R., *Requiem for an Army*, Rowman & Littlefield, Lanham, Maryland, 1998

Hobsbawn, Eric, *Interesting Times*, Abacus, London, 2002

Judt, Matthias (ed.), *DDR-Geschichte in Dokumenten* (GDR history in documents), Bundeszentrale für politische Bildung, Bonn, 1998

Kerl, Dr Dieter (ed.), *Britain in Focus*, Zentralen Fachkommission Englisch beim Ministerium für Hoch-und Fachschulwesen erarbeitet, 1988

Klausmeier, Axel and Schmidt, Leo, *Wall Remnants – Wall Traces*, Westkreuz-Verlag, Berlin/Bonn, 2004

Koehler, John O., *Stasi*, Westview Press, Boulder, Colorado, 1999

Kootz, Wolfgang, *Dresden, Saxony's Royal Residence*, B&V Verlag, Dresden, undated

Ladd, Brian, *The Ghosts of Berlin*, The University of Chicago Press, 1997

Laufer, Peter, *Iron Curtain Rising*, Mercury House Inc., San Francisco, 1991

McAdams, A. James, *Judging the Past in Unified Germany*, Cambridge University Press, Cambridge, 2001

Möbius, Peter and Trotnow, Helmut, *Mauern sind nicht für ewig gebaut*, Verlag Ullstein GmbH, Frankfurt am Main, 1990

Nagel, Jürgen, *Parole Zukunft*, BasisDruck Verlag GmbH, Berlin, 1992

Najman, Maurice (ed.), *L'Oeil de Berlin*, Éditions Balland, Paris, 1992

Nothnagle, Alan Lloyd (trans.), *The Dresden Frauenkirche*, Evangelische Verlagsanstalt, Leipzig, 2005

Phillips, David (ed), *Education in Germany since Unification*, Symposium Books, Oxford, 2000

Pierce, Brigitte and Russell, Alan (eds), *Why Dresden?* The Dresden Trust, 2006

Schäuble, Wolfgang, *Der Vertrag: Wie ich über die deutsche Einheit verhandelte*, Deutsche Verlags-Anstalt, Stuttgart, 1991

Schneider, Peter, *The German Comedy*, I.B. Tauris & Co. Ltd, London, 1991

Siegmund-Schultze, Dorothea (ed.), *Britain: Aspects of Political and Social Life*, VEB Verlag Enzyklopädie, Leipzig, 1985

Taylor, Fredrick, *Dresden Tuesday 13 February 1945*, Bloomsbury, London 2005

Thompson, Willie, *The Good Old Cause*, Pluto Press, London, 1992

Wolle, Stefan, *Die heile Welt der Diktatur – Alltag und Herrschaft in der DDR 1971–1989*, Bundeszentrale für politische Bildung, Bonn, 1999.

Woods, Roger, *Opposition in the GDR under Honecker 1971–85*, The Macmillan Press, London, 1986

Yoder, Jennifer A., *From East Germans to Germans?* Duke University Press, Durham, 1999

Zilian, Frederick Jr, *From Confrontation to Cooperation*, Praeger, Westport, Connecticut, 1999

INDEX

Note: because the book is about German reunification and is centred on Berlin there are no individual entries for East Germany (the GDR), West Germany (the FRG) or East and West Berlin. They would be overwhelming in number and self-defeating. For the general topics of putting the two Germanys together, see entry German reunification.

n = in a footnote   c = in a caption